Workshop Manual

PORSCHE 911 2.0-2.2-2.4 Litre 1964-1973

A Floyd CLYMER Publication by:
www.VelocePress.com
Copyright 2019 Veloce Enterprises

INTRODUCTION

Welcome to the world of digital publishing ~ the book you now hold in your hand, was printed using the latest state of the art digital technology. The advent of print-on-demand has forever changed the publishing process, never has information been so accessible and it is our hope that this book serves your informational needs for years to come. If this is your first exposure to digital publishing, we hope that you are pleased with the results. Many more titles of interest to the classic automobile and motorcycle enthusiast, collector and restorer are available via our website at www.VelocePress.com. We hope that you find this title as interesting as we do.

NOTE FROM THE PUBLISHER

The information presented is true and complete to the best of our knowledge. All recommendations are made without any guarantees on the part of the author or the publisher, who also disclaim all liability incurred with the use of this information.

TRADEMARKS

We recognize that some words, model names and designations, for example, mentioned herein are the property of the trademark holder. We use them for identification purposes only. This is not an official publication.

INFORMATION ON THE USE OF THIS PUBLICATION

This manual is an invaluable resource for those interested in performing their own maintenance. However, in today's information age we are constantly subject to changes in common practice, new technology, availability of improved materials and increased awareness of chemical toxicity. As such, it is advised that the user consult with an experienced professional prior to undertaking any procedure described herein. While every care has been taken to ensure correctness of information, it is obviously not possible to guarantee complete freedom from errors or omissions or to accept liability arising from such errors or omissions. Therefore, any individual that uses the information contained within, or elects to perform or participate in do-it-yourself repairs or modifications acknowledges that there is a risk factor involved and that the publisher or its associates cannot be held responsible for personal injury or property damage resulting from the use of the information or the outcome of such procedures.

WARNING!

One final word of advice, this publication is intended to be used as a reference guide, and when in doubt the reader should consult with a qualified technician.

TABLE OF CONTENTS

Chapter 1 - Engine (page 4)

1. Description
2. Routine maintenance
3. Engine removal and refitting
4. Removing and refitting cylinder heads
5. Servicing cylinder heads
6. Overhauling rocker gear and camshafts
7. Overhauling chain tensioner
8. Valve timing
9. Servicing lubricating system
10. The flywheel and clutch
11. Removing and servicing cylinders and pistons
12. Splitting crankcase, removing and refitting crankshaft
13. Servicing crankshaft and connecting rods
14. Servicing intermediate shaft
15. Reassembling stripped engine
16. Torque converter oil pump
17. Testing after overhaul
18. Fault diagnosis

Chapter 2 - Fuel System (page 35)

1. Description of system
2. Routine maintenance
3. Checking fuel system
4. Servicing mechanical fuel pumps
5. Servicing electric fuel pumps
6. The Solex carburetter
7. Servicing Solex carburetter
8. The Weber carburetter
9. Servicing Weber carburetter
10. The fuel tank
11. Fuel injection
12. Fault diagnosis

Chapter 3 - Ignition System (page 55)

1. General description
2. Routine maintenance
3. Ignition problems
4. Removing and refitting distributor
5. Ignition timing
6. Servicing distributor
7. Sparking plugs
8. Capacitive Discharge (CDS) ignition system
9. Fault diagnosis

Chapter 4 - Cooling, Heating & Exhaust Emission Control (page 61)

1. Description of cooling system
2. Routine maintenance of cooling system
3. Removing and refitting blower
4. Removing and refitting covers and deflectors
5. Silencer and heat exchangers
6. Heating system and controls
7. Exhaust emission control system
8. Fault diagnosis

Chapter 5 - Clutch (page 67)

1. General description
2. Routine maintenance
3. Removing and refitting clutch cable
4. Removing and dismantling clutch
5. Clutch driven plate
6. Refitting clutch
7. Servicing release bearing and fork
8. Fault diagnosis

Chapter 6 - Transmission (page 74)

MANUAL TRANSMISSION (page 81)
1. General description
2. Routine maintenance
3. Transmission removal
4. Dismantling transmission
5. Servicing input shaft
6. Servicing intermediate plate
7. Servicing pinion shaft
8. Overhauling and setting differential
9. Adjusting pinion shaft setting and backlash
10. Servicing front cover
11. Reassembling transmission
12. Gearshift mechanism
13. Servicing ZF differential
14. The four-speed transmission

SPORTOMATIC TRANSMISSION (page 93)
15. General description
16. Routine maintenance
17. Driving hints
18. Removal and installation
19. Separating and refitting transmission
20. Servicing control valve and sensors
21. Servicing gearlever and microswitch
22. Servicing torque converter and clutch
23. Servicing clutch controls
24. Overhauling gearbox

FAULT DIAGNOSIS & TRANSMISSION CHARTS (page 100)
25. Fault diagnosis (manual gearbox)
26. Fault diagnosis (Sportomatic)

Chapter 7 - Rear Suspension & Drive Axles (page 111)

1. General description
2. Damper maintenance
3. Servicing axle halfshafts
4. Removing control arm
5. Servicing and refitting control arm
6. Removing and refitting torsion bar
7. Adjusting torsion bar
8. Modified radius arms
9. Stabilizer (anti-roll) bar
10. Rear wheel alignment
11. Height adjustment
12. Fault diagnosis

TABLE OF CONTENTS

Chapter 8 - Front Suspension (pg 117)

1. General description
2. Routine maintenance
3. Servicing damper strut
4. Servicing and adjusting hub bearings
5. Servicing control arms (1st type)
6. Servicing crossmember (1st type)
7. Removing torsion bar (1st type)
8. The stabilizer bar
9. Modifications on 1968 models
10. Height adjustment
11. Wheel alignment
12. Fault diagnosis

Chapter 9 - Steering (page 127)

1. General description
2. Routine maintenance
3. Removing and refitting steering wheel
4. Servicing switch and steering shafts
5. The intermediate shaft and universal joints
6. The steering coupling
7. Servicing the steering gearbox
8. Adjusting toe-in
9. Steering and wheel alignment
10. Fault diagnosis

Chapter 10 - Brakes (page 137)

1. General description
2. Routine maintenance
3. Renewing brake pads
4. Servicing front brakes
5. Servicing rear brakes
6. Handbrake carrier plate
7. Servicing brake discs
8. Servicing single master cylinder
9. Servicing dual master cylinder
10. Bleeding the brake system
11. Servicing the handbrake
12. Fault diagnosis

Chapter 11 - Electrical (page 149)

1. General description
2. Routine maintenance
3. Battery maintenance
4. Servicing Bosch alternator
5. Servicing Motorola alternator
6. Servicing starter motor
7. The voltage regulator and relay switches
8. Servicing the lights
9. Fuses
10. Steering column
11. Flasher unit
12. Wiper and washer units
13. Reversing light switch
14. Safety belt warning system
15. Fault diagnosis
16. Wiring diagrams

Chapter 12 - Body (page 179)

1. Paintwork
2. Servicing doors
3. Luggage compartment lid
4. The rear lid
5. Fitting bumpers
6. Fitting front wings
7. Fitting side panel windows
8. Paint codes
9. Door hardware interchange

Chapter 13 - Technical Data (page 189)

1. Torque wrench settings
2. Technical specifications 2.0 Litre vehicles
3. Technical specifications 2.2 and 2.4 Litre vehicles
4. Lubrication chart

INTRODUCTION TO CHAPTER 1 - ENGINES & MODELS

Evolution of the 1964-1973 PORSCHE 911 (With acknowledgement to the official Porsche website)

As the successor to the Porsche 356, the 911 won the hearts of sports car enthusiasts from the outset. The prototype was first unveiled at the Frankfurt IAA Motor Show in 1963 as the 901, and was renamed the 911 for its market launch in 1964. Its air-cooled six-cylinder flat engine with two-litre displacement delivered 130HP, giving it an impressive top speed of 210 km per hour. If you wanted to take things a little slower, you could also opt for the four-cylinder Porsche 912 from 1965. In 1966, Porsche presented the 160HP 911 S, which was the first to feature forged alloy wheels from Fuchs. The 911 Targa, with its distinctive stainless steel roll-over bar, made its debut in late 1966 as the world's first ever safety cabriolet. The semi-automatic Sportomatic four-speed transmission joined the line-up in 1967. And with the 911 T, and the later E and S variants, Porsche became the first German manufacturer to comply with strict US exhaust emission control regulations. The Porsche 911 became more and more powerful as displacement increased, initially to 2.2 litres (1969) and later to 2.4 (1971).

1964–1969 2.0 litre air-cooled boxer flat-six

1969–1971 2.2 litre air-cooled boxer flat-six

1971–1973 2.4 litre air-cooled boxer flat-six

In September 1963, Porsche presented the Porsche 901 at the IAA in Frankfurt as a successor to the Porsche 356. One year later, as of model year 1965, series production of the model began and it was renamed the 911 shortly thereafter.

Originally built only as a Coupé, the 911 had an integral body-frame and was powered by a new 2.0-litre flat-six engine, which initially delivered 130HP.

As of model year 1967, the 911 was also available as a "safety cabriolet" (Targa) with permanently mounted roll-over bar and removable soft top. As of model year 1969, the wheelbase was lengthened by 57 mm, resulting in increased driving comfort and simultaneously more stable driving dynamics.

The 911 S, the first engine derivative of the 911, was also launched on the market. In the years that followed, models bearing the additional designations T, L and E were launched.

911 Targa (1967-1973)
Porsche introduced the Targa model in response to increased safety requirements for open-top vehicles in the USA. Thanks to the fixed bar, the occupants were protected from injury in the event of the vehicle overturning.

911S   (1967-73)
Due to various engine modifications, the sports version of the 911 initially had a power output of 160HP, ultimately increasing to 190HP. In addition to superior equipment, the S model was the first 911 to be given "Fuchs" rims with their distinctive 5-spoke design.

911T   (1968-73)
The "Touring" version became the new entry-level model in the 911 family, initially developing 110HP and later 130HP. Its equipment matched that of the four-cylinder 912 model. One of the ways in which it could be distinguished from more powerful models was the fact that it had a silver rather than a gold logo.

911L   (1968)
With the introduction of the T version as the new standard model, with a less powerful engine and 4-speed manual transmission, the previous 911 was renamed the 911 L. The engine remained unchanged.

911E   (1969-73)
The existing 2.0-litre engines entered their final year of construction in 1969 and were replaced by new 2.2-litre engines. The L version was renamed the 911 E following the introduction of the new generation of engines and delivered power outputs of between 140HP and 165HP.

1964 - 1973 ENGINE TYPE NUMBER - YEAR - & MODEL DESCRIPTION CHART

Type Number	Year	Description
911	1964–1965	Six-cylinder production sports car
911/00	1969–1970	Four-speed transmission for Type 911T
911/01	1969–1970	2.2-liter engine for Type 911E; five-speed transmission
911/02	1969–1970	2.2-liter 180 hp engine for Type 911S
911/03	1969–1970	2.2-liter engine for manual European Type 911T
911/04	1969–1970	Type 911/01 engine equipped for Sportomatic
911/06	1969–1970	Type 911/03 equipped for Sportomatic
911/07	1969–1970	2.2-liter engine for manual American Type 911T
911/08	1969–1970	Type 911/07 equipped for Sportomatic
911/20	1970	2,247 cc racing engine for competition 911S
911/21	1971	2,381 cc racing engine for competition 911S
911/22	1970	Type 911/20 with carburetors instead of fuel injection
911/51	1971–1972	2.4-liter engine for American Type 911T
911/52	1971–1972	2.4-liter engine for Type 911E
911/53	1971–1972	2.4-liter engine for Type 911S
911/57	1971–1972	2.4-liter engine for European Type 911T
911/61	1971–1972	Type 911/51 equipped for Sportomatic
911/62	1971–1972	Type 911/52 equipped for Sportomatic
911/63	1971–1972	Type 911/53 equipped for Sportomatic
911/67	1971–1972	Type 911/57 equipped for Sportomatic
911/70	1971	2,494 cc racing engine for competition 911S
911/73	1972	2,466 cc racing engine for competition 911S
911/91	1973	2.4-liter CIS-injection engine for American Type 911T
911E	1968–1969	Fuel-injected model between Type 911T and 911S
911L	1967–1968	Top-line model in America; intermediate model in Europe
911R	1967	Lightweight racing model of Type 911S
911S	1966–1967	Higher-performance touring model of Type 911
911T	1967–1968	Type 911 model tuned for all-round road performance

1964 - 1973 MODELS BY YEAR, ENGINE TYPE, ENGINE NUMBERS, CAPACITY & KW/HP OUTPUT

Vehicle	Engine Type	Year	Engine Numbers	Capacity & Output
911 COUPE	901/01	65	900001>	2,0L /95 KW/127HP
911 COUPE	901/01	66	903551>	2,0L /95 KW/127HP
911 COUPE	901/05	66	907001>	2,0L /95 KW/127HP
911 COUPE	901/05	67	909001>	2,0L /95 KW/127HP
911 TARGA	901/05	67	911001>	2,0L /95 KW/127HP
911 S COUPE/TARGA	901/02	67	960001>	2,0L /117KW/157HP
911 T COUPE/TARGA	901/03	68	2080001>	2,0L /80 KW/107HP
911 T COUPE/TARGA/SPM	901/13	68	2180001>	2,0L /81 KW/109HP
911 L COUPE/TARGA	901/06	68	3080001>	2,0L /95 KW/127HP
911 L COUPE/TARGA/SPM	901/07	68	3180001>	2,0L /96 KW/129HP
911 S COUPE/TARGA	901/02	68	4080001>	2,0L /117 KW/157HP
911 S COUPE/TARGA/SPM	901/08	68	4180001>	2,0L /118 KW/158HP
911 COUPE/TARGA (USA/CDN)	901/14	68	3280001>	2,0L /95 KW/127HP
911 COUPE/TARGA/SPM (USA/CDN)	901/17	68	3380001>	2,0L /96 KW/129HP
911 L COUPE/TARGA (USA/CDN)	901/14	68	3280001>	2,0L /95 KW/127HP
911 L COUPE/TARGA/SPM (USA/CDN)	901/17	68	3380001>	2,0L /96 KW/129HP
911 T COUPE/TARGA	901/03	69	6190001>	2,0L /80 KW/107HP
911 T COUPE/TARGA/SPM	901/13	69	6193001>	2,0L /81 KW/109HP
911 E COUPE/TARGA	901/09	69	6293001>	2,0L /103 KW/138HP
911 E COUPE/TARGA/SPM	901/11	69	6298001>	2,0L /103 KW/138HP
911 S COUPE/TARGA	901/10	69	6398001>	2,0L /125 KW/168HP
911 T COUPE (USA/CDN)	901/16	69	6195001>	2,0L /80 KW/107HP
911 T COUPE/SPM (USA/CDN)	901/19	69	6198001>	2,0L /81 KW/109HP
911 T	911.03	70	610 0001>>	2,2L /92KW/123HP
911 T / SPM	911.06	70	610 3001>>	2,2L /92KW/123HP
911 E	911.01	70	620 0001>>	2,2L /114KW/153HP
911 E / SPM	911.04	70	620 8001>>	2,2L /114KW/153HP
911 S	911.02	70	630 0001>>	2,2L /132KW/177HP
911 T (USA/CDN)	911.07	70	610 5001>>	2,2L /92KW/123HP
911 T / SPM (USA/CDN)	911.08	70	610 8001>>	2,2L /92KW/123HP

continued

1964 - 1973 MODELS BY YEAR, ENGINE TYPE, ENGINE NUMBERS, CAPACITY & KW/HP OUTPUT

Vehicle	Engine Type	Year	Engine Numbers	Capacity & Output
911 T	911.03	71	611 0001>>	2,2L /92KW/123HP
911 T / SPM	911.06	71	611 9001>>	2,2L /92KW/123HP
911 E	911.01	71	621 0001>>	2,2L /114KW/153HP
911 E / SPM	911.04	71	621 8001>>	2,2L /114KW/153HP
911 S	911.02	71	631 0001>>	2,2L /132KW/177HP
911 T (USA/CDN)	911.07	71	611 4001>>	2,2L /92KW/123HP
911 T / SPM (USA/CDN)	911.08	71	611 9501>>	2,2L /92KW/123HP
911 TV	911.57	72	652 0001>>	2,4L /96KW/129HP
911 TV / SPM	911.67	72	652 9001>>	2,4L /96KW/129HP
911 E	911.52	72	622 0001>>	2,4L /121KW/162HP
911 E / SPM	911.62	72	622 9001>>	2,4L /121KW/162HP
911 S	911.53	72	632 0001>>	2,4L /140KW/188HP
911 S / SPM	911.63	72	632 9001>>	2,4L /140KW/188HP
911 TE (USA/CDN)	911.51	72	612 0001>>	2,4L /103KW/138HP
911 TE / SPM (USA/CDN)	911.61	72	612 9001>>	2,4L /103KW/138HP
911 TV	911.57	73	653 0001>>	2,4L /96KW/129HP
911 TV / SPM	911.67	73	653 9001>>	2,4L /96KW/129HP
911 E	911.52	73	623 0001>>	2,4L /121KW/162HP
911 E / SPM	911.62	73	623 9001>>	2,4L /121KW/162HP
911 S	911.53	73	633 0001>>	2,4L /140KW/188HP
911 S / SPM	911.63	73	633 9001>>	2,4L /140KW/188HP
911 TE (USA/CDN)	911.51	73	613 0001>>	2,4L /103KW/138HP
911 TE / SPM (USA/CDN)	911.61	73	613 9001>>	2,4L /103KW/138HP
911 TK (USA/CDN)	911.91	73	613 3001>>	2,4L /103KW/138HP
911 TK / SPM (USA/CDN)	911.96	73	613 9301>>	2,4L /103KW/138HP

TYPE 2000 ENGINE
(Internal Designation 901/01)

Right Front View

1. Air duct from blower to heat exchanger
2. Float chamber
3. Crankcase breather connector
4. Crankcase breather connector with flame trap
5. Oil pressure sensor
6. Oil cooler
7. Oil suction line connector
8. Thermostat
9. Clutch
10. Heat exchanger

Left Rear View

1. Actuating rod
2. Fuel supply line
3. Float chamber
4. Intake air silencer
5. Cooling air blower
6. Heat exchanger
7. Distributor
8. Twin fuel pump
9. Support
10. Exhaust muffler

CHAPTER 1 - ENGINE

1 Description
2 Routine maintenance
3 Engine removal and refitting
4 Removing and refitting cylinder heads
5 Servicing cylinder heads
6 Overhauling rocker gear and camshafts
7 Overhauling chain tensioner
8 Valve timing
9 Servicing lubricating system
10 The flywheel and clutch
11 Removing and servicing cylinders and pistons
12 Splitting crankcase, remove & refit crankshaft
13 Servicing crankshaft and connecting rods
14 Servicing intermediate shaft
15 Reassembling stripped engine
16 Torque converter oil pump
17 Testing after overhaul
18 Fault diagnosis

1 Description

In September 1964, excited Porsche enthusiasts welcomed the introduction of a completely new engine design. This was a superb piece of engineering—a six-cylinder unit destined for the 1965 cars. It had the designation '2000', with a capacity of 1991 cc and a power output of 130 bhp at 6100 rev/min. After two years in this form, 1967 saw the production of an additional hotted-up version known as the '2000S' which was rated at 160 bhp at 6600 rev/min. A third, and milder, version was introduced in 1968, to be known as the '2000T' and rated at 110 bhp at 5800 rev/min. Car model designations used the same letters for identification, being known as 911, 911S and 911T, but an additional model called 911L indicates one with exhaust emission control and optional Sportomatic transmission, the engine being in the '2000' class. 911E and 911T Lux models have fuel-injection systems and self-levelling suspension.

Since 1968, progressively more powerful engines have been fitted equipped with, amongst other things, different carburetters or modified fuel injection systems. In 1969 a 2.2 litre fuel injection unit replaced the existing 2.0 litre fuel injection units of the 'E' and 'S' types. The 'T' type was uprated also to 2.2 litres but was equipped with an emission controlled Solex-Zenith carburation system and, from 1970, an electric fuel pump; similar to the type used on the previous 'E' and 'S' models. The new uprated models were re-designated 'EC', 'SC' and 'TC'.

Improvements continued throughout the range but the greatest significant change was in 1971 when the power units were again uprated, this time to 2.4 litres with the 'T' type converted to fuel injection. A carburation system was retained and designated type 'TV'.

The cross-sectioned views of the engine in FIGS 1 and 2 show most of the outstanding features of this brilliant design and help to explain the reasons for the high power output. Six cylinders are arranged in two horizontally-opposed banks of three, each cylinder carrying its own aluminium head. The cylinders are of cast iron on the '2000T' but are of composite construction on the other models, the aluminium fins and barrels having a thin cast-iron bore to give excellent heat dissipation and a good wearing surface.

The cylinders are mounted on an aluminium crankcase which is split vertically. The crankshaft 4 runs in eight plain bearings, one between each throw, one to take thrust at the flywheel end and a sleeve type in the timing cover (see FIG 2). The connecting rods have split big-end bearing shells and bushed small-ends. Aluminium alloy pistons carry fully-floating gudgeon pins, two compression rings and one for oil control (see 15 in FIG 1).

Each aluminium head carries an inlet and an exhaust valve, these being set at a wide angle to each other. Valve guides are detachable and there are valve seat and sparking plug inserts. Rocker gear housings span each set of three heads, carrying the rockers 29 and camshafts 30, the latter running in three plain bearings. FIG 2 shows how the camshafts are driven by two duplex chains 14 from an intermediate shaft 13, this shaft being gear-driven from the crankshaft. Each chain is tensioned by a spring-loaded sprocket.

The intermediate shaft also drives twin oil pumps 18 and 19, pressure pump 19 supplying oil to the engine. The larger scavenging pump 18 picks up draining oil from the sump and returns it to a separate oil tank. Before oil from the pressure pump reaches the engine bearings it passes through an oil cooler. When the oil is cold a valve opens to allow oil to arrive at the bearings without passing through the cooler.

The air-cooling system is similar to that employed on Volkswagen cars, a belt-driven blower 7 producing large volumes of air which is ducted over the cylinders and heads by shaped covers. After passing through heat exchangers associated with the exhaust system, the hot air is available to warm the car interior through pipes and valves.

The flywheel 2 normally carries an orthodox diaphragm-spring clutch, but is replaced by a fluid torque converter when Sportomatic transmission is fitted. The flywheel housing is bolted to the transmission casing to provide integral construction of the power unit and drive. Such technical details as compression ratios, firing order and general fits and tolerances will be found in Technical Data at the end of this manual.

2 Routine maintenance

Before the summer and winter seasons or every 6000 miles, drain the engine oil while it is hot. The plug is part 16 in FIG 2, and it is also shown in FIG 3. Next remove the coverplate 4, followed by the gaskets and gauze strainer 1, 2 and 3. Clean strainer with brush and fuel, not fluffy rag. Remove all traces of old gaskets.

Fit gasket to strainer and replace strainer so that the opening exactly surrounds the inlet pipe inside the crankcase. Refit the second gasket and cover, tightening the nuts on spring washers. **Do not overtighten or the cover may be distorted.** Clean metallic particles from drain plug and refit, then fill up with oil to the upper mark on the dipstick. Use heavy duty oil SAE.30 in summer and SAE.20 in winter. Quantity required is 9 litres (15.8 Imp. or 19 US pints). For normal oil changes the quantity is the same for cars with Sportomatic transmission.

Oil filter:

The throwaway filter is mounted adjacent to the oil filler as shown in FIG 4. It cannot be cleaned and must be renewed every 6000 miles. Unscrew anticlockwise. Fit a new filter after verifying that the rubber seal and seating face are clean and undamaged.

Key to Fig 1

- 3 Crankcase
- 4 Crankshaft
- 5 Air cleaner
- 15 Connecting rod
- 20 Heat exchanger
- 22 Intake air horn
- 23 Idle adjusting screw
- 24 Accelerator pump
- 25 Float chamber vent
- 26 Throttle shaft
- 27 Float housing
- 28 Intake valve
- 29 Rocker arm
- 30 Camshaft
- 31 Piston
- 32 Exhaust valve
- 33 Valve spring
- 34 Oil drain tube
- 35 Suppressor

FIG 1 A transverse cross-section through the type 2000 engine

Key to Fig 2

1. Clutch and pressure plate
2. Flywheel
3. Crankcase
4. Crank shaft
5. Air cleaner
6. Air intake
7. Cooling blower impeller
8. Alternator
9. V-belt
10. Distributor drive gear
11. Crankshaft pulley
12. Exhaust muffler
13. Intermediate shaft
14. Camshaft drive sprocket I
15. Connecting rod
16. Oil drain plug
17. Oil strainer
18. Oil scavenging pump
19. Oil pressure pump
20. Heat exchanger
21. Heating air outlet

FIG 2 Longitudinal section through the type 2000 engine

FIG 3 Components of the oil strainer. Section on right shows how strainer surrounds oil pick-up pipe

Key to Fig 3

1 Gasket
2 Oil strainer
3 Gasket
4 Oil strainer cover plate
5 Sealing ring
6 Magnetic threaded plug

FIG 4 Arrow points to renewable oil filter, which is mounted on the oil tank

FIG 5 For checking purposes, use the cylinder numbering indicated. Firing order is 1, 6, 2, 4, 3, 5

Valve clearance:

Check this every 3000 miles. Correct clearance for both inlet and exhaust valves on all engines is .10 mm or .004 inch (cold). Check in firing order 1-6-2-4-3-5, the cylinder numbering being shown in **FIG 5**. Each cylinder must have its piston at TDC on the firing stroke with both valves closed. At this point it will be found that marks on the crankshaft belt pulley align with the crankcase joint as shown in the top view of **FIG 6**. Note that there are three marks 120 deg. apart.

Remove cylinder head covers. Turn belt pulley until both valves of No. 1 cylinder are closed and TDC mark (Z1) on the pulley lines up with the crankcase mark. Check clearance with feeler gauge. Adjust as in lower view of **FIG 6**, slackening the nut on the rocker adjuster and turning the adjuster with a screwdriver. Hold screw while tightening nut and check clearance again.

Continue checking by turning belt pulley clockwise to next mark at 120 deg. or one third of a turn. This should find No. 6 cylinder at TDC with both valves closed. Repeat procedure until all valves have been checked. In every case, make quite sure that the feeler is being inserted immediately above the valve stem tip.

Rocker arm shafts:

Check tightness every 6000 miles. Refer to **Section 6**.

Compression:

Check cylinder compressions every 6000 miles.

Blower belt:

Check tension every 6000 miles and adjust if necessary, referring to **Chapter 4**.

3 Engine removal and refitting

Porsche recommend the removal of the engine and transmission as a single unit. For most operations on the engine it is easier to work on it when it is out of the car, and as the crankcase must be split to attend to the crankshaft, removal is then essential. Proceed as follows:

1 Raise rear of car on firmly-based stands to a height which will permit removal of the engine downwards and to the rear.

2 Remove air cleaner and oil tank vent hose. Disconnect battery, then cables from ignition coil, alternator, fuel pump, oil pressure transmitter (see **FIG 7**), reversing light switch and starter motor. Remove earth strap. Detach alternator cables from body fasteners.

3 Detach throttle linkage from bell crank and remove hose from oil filler (see **FIG 7**). Drain engine oil. Detach hoses from oil tank. See **Chapter 6** for extra details when Sportomatic transmission is fitted.

4 Detach axle shafts (see **Chapter 7**). Detach hot air ducts from front ends of heat exchangers. Detach clutch cable from release lever.

5 Detach fuel hose from connector at float chambers. Remove cover from floor tunnel in passenger compartment. Pull rubber boot forward (see **FIG 8**). Cut safety wire and remove square-headed bolt, detach shift rod clutch from shift control lever.

6 Just take weight of engine on trolley jack. Release engine rear support and transmission support from body mountings (see **FIG 9**). Lower jack, keeping engine steady, and pull out rearwards. Detach engine from transmission, taking great care not to let the transmission input shaft hang in the hub of the clutch plate.

Refitting engine:

Adopt the reverse sequence, observing the following precautions:

1 Check transmission input shaft for runout (see **Chapter 6**). Check condition of clutch release bearing. If clutch plate was removed, make sure it is centrally disposed in flywheel and cover (see **Chapter 5**).
2 Put 2 to 3 cc (.06 to .09 fluidid oz) of multi-purpose grease in the pilot bush for the input shaft (see 4 in **FIG 27**). Put a smear of multi-purpose grease on the shaft splines and the bearing surface, in the starter shaft bush, and on the teeth of starter pinion and flywheel.
Grease must be applied sparingly, particularly on the input shaft splines in order to avoid contaminating the clutch friction linings. When tightening the axle halfshafts make sure they are filled with grease. (see **Chapter 7, Section 3**). Coat all of the oil hose connections with multi-purpose grease, but note that from engine number 903070 the oil connecting hoses are no longer used.
3 Clean mating faces of engine and transmission flanges. Keeping engine square with transmission, feed shaft through clutch plate hub, turning crankshaft by means of pulley with transmission engaged until splines are aligned. Push engine into place, being careful to put no strain on the shaft or clutch plate hub.
4 Start bottom screws in flanges first, then push transmission home against engine and tighten all bolts with equal torque.
5 After installation, check clutch free play. Do not reconnect battery until all cables are in place.

4 Removing and refitting cylinder heads

One bank of three heads with camshaft housing may be removed as a unit, or individual heads may be removed, with the engine out of the car.

Removing heads and camshaft housing as a unit:

1 Remove carburetters (see **Chapter 2**). Remove distributor cap with plug leads. Detach all cooling air ducts and covers. The alternator need not be removed.
2 Remove rear engine support and silencer. Remove heat exchanger (see **FIG 10**). Detach the hose between crankcase and chain housing cover. Remove chain cover. Remove chain tensioner (see **Section 7**). Remove camshaft sprocket nuts and pull dowel from one of vernier timing holes in sprocket using tool P.212 (see **FIG 21**). Lift spring retainer with a screwdriver and pull chain guide ramp from housing. **Do not turn camshaft or crankshaft or pistons may hit valves.**
3 Withdraw sprocket and flange. Remove key from camshaft. Remove three flange bolts and push out seal through slots in front of housing (see **FIG 11**). Detach chain housing from crankcase. Loosen cylinder head nuts with Allen key and lift off head and camshaft housing.
4 When refitting, remove the rockers to avoid distortion of the camshaft bearings (see **Section 6**).

Removing individual cylinder head:

Follow the preceding operations, but remove the rocker shafts and camshaft (see **Section 6**). Remove camshaft housing nuts and spring washers and the three socket-head nuts. Remove particular head required.

FIG 6 Adjusting valve clearances. Distributor rotor pointing to notch on body and pulley mark Z1 in line with crankcase joint with both valves closed, gives TDC on No. 1 cylinder (top view). Using feeler gauge to set valve clearance (bottom view)

FIG 7 Removing engine. Detach throttle linkage from bellcrank (left arrow). Remove oil breather hose (central arrow). Detach cable from oil pressure transmitter (right arrow)

FIG 8 Gearshift rod joint under tunnel cover in passenger compartment

FIG 9 Righthand and lefthand engine support mountings at rear (top view). Transmission support from below (lower view)

Refitting heads:

Perforations in cylinder head gaskets face cylinder. When camshaft housing is refitted, use sealing compound (Teroson Atmosit) on head faces. Fit housing and oil return pipes but do not tighten fixings. Tighten head fixings to 3.0 to 3.3 mkg (21½ to 24 lb ft). Tighten camshaft housing nuts evenly, inserting camshaft and checking free running. Use a torque of 2.2 to 2.5 mkg (16 to 18 lb ft).

Note that the cylinder head gaskets fitted to the 2.2 litre engine are different from those fitted to the 2.0 litre engine.

The upper cylinder flange of the 2.2 litre engine has a machined groove which accommodates a symmetric cylinder head gasket. The gasket consists of a U-section rolled aluminium ring which envelopes a tubular spring.

Heads for engines up to No. 900.727:

When renewing pistons or heads on these engines, use plasticine or a similar compound to check clearance between valves and pockets in piston crown. **Do not turn crankshaft until rocker gear has been fitted and timed correctly.** After turning several revolutions, remove head and check clearance. If less than .80 mm (.032 inch) the particular valve seat must be ground back until correct clearance is obtained.

5 Servicing cylinder heads

Heads with unserviceable guides, seats or plug inserts may be works reconditioned.

Removing valves:

Remove springs with suitable compressor. Note any washers under spring seats. Remove burrs from cotter grooves in valve stems and push out valves, storing them in correct order. After 6 May, 1965 the valve stem seal need not be removed when lifting off the spring seat.

Checking head:

Check tightness and condition of valve seats and plug inserts. Check both faces of head (see **FIG 12**). Distortion must not exceed .15mm (.006 inch). **The faces must not be machined.**

Check valve guide bores and measure valve stems. Clearance between inlet stem and guide must be .030 to .057 mm (.001 to .002 inch), and exhaust .050 to .077 mm (.002 to .003 inch). Defective guides cannot be renewed with normal workshop equipment. If facilities are available, heat head to 200°C (392°F) and drive out guide with a shouldered drift. Factory guides are oversize and must be machined until there is an interference of .031 to .06 mm (.001 to .0024 inch) between guide and head. Heat head again, put guide in freezer and then fit guide from camshaft side, using tallow as a lubricant. Correct position is shown in **FIG 13**. Ream bore to a diameter of 9.015 to 9.00 mm (.355 to .354 inch).

Renewing valve seat inserts also needs considerable skills and precision tools, so that the owner is recommended to entrust the work to a Porsche agent. The old seat is ground away until it becomes loose in the head and is then knocked out without damaging the recess.

FIG 10 Removing heat exchanger flange nuts with spanner P.217

FIG 11 Sealing ring 3 and thrust washer 4 determine the end float of camshaft

Key to Fig 11
1 Paper gasket
2 O-ring
3 Sealing ring
4 Thrust washer
5 Spacer
6 Camshaft sprocket flange

FIG 12 Checking joint face of head for flatness, using a straightedge and feeler gauges

This recess is then accurately measured for bore and a new seat turned on the outside until it will have an interference fit of .14 to .18 mm (.0055 to .007 inch) for an inlet seat and .16 to .20 mm (.006 to .008 inch) for an exhaust seat. The seats are driven in with a suitably shouldered drift after the heads have been heated to 200°C or 392°F. Let head cool slowly. Reheat to the same temperature and maintain for 2 hours. Allow to cool slowly. Renewal of valve guides and head seats calls for accurate grinding of the new seat to ensure that it is the correct width and is concentric with the guide. Width of inlet seat (see A in **FIG 13**) must be $1.25 \pm .10$ mm ($.050 \pm .004$ inch) and exhaust seat $1.55 \pm .10$ mm ($.060 \pm .004$ inch). Correct angle is 45 deg.

FIG 13 Correct position of valve guide with respect to valve spring seat in head. Width of valve seat is indicated at **A**

Checking valves, grinding-in:

Clean valves and check against dimensions in Technical Data. Renew valves with burned seats, worn stems, stem ends and cotter grooves. **Do not try to straighten bent stems.** If grinding with paste will not remove pitting have valve seatings ground on a machine to an angle of 45 deg.

Grind-in with a suction tool and water-soluble paste. Put a light spring under the valve head. With a smear of paste on the valve face, grind-in with a semi-rotary action, letting the valve rise now and then to turn it to a fresh position. Continue until valve and head seats are a smooth matt grey. Wash off all traces of compound and dry thoroughly. Hold valve in place and pour fuel into port. Leakage past valve will be evident.

Checking springs:

Correct lengths and loadings are in Technical Data. Variation on used springs may be 5 per cent. Clean first and check for cracks. If one spring of a pair is defective, renew both. Installed length is shown at 'A' in **FIG 14**. For most engines it is 36 ± .30 mm (1.42 ± .01 inch) but later 2000 engines after No. 911.001 have an installed length of 35 ± .3 mm (1.378 ± .012 inch). On 2000S engines for 911S cars, the installed length for inlet valves is 35.5 ± .50 mm (1.4 ± .02 inch) and for exhaust valves 35.0 ± .30 mm (1.378 ± .012 inch). For 2000T engines the length for both valves is 41.0 — .50 mm (1.614 — .02 inch).

Dimensions have been modified in relation to the valves on the 1969 models and the 2.2 litre engines. The installed lengths of the valve springs on the 2.2 and the 2.4 litre engines have also been revised. Refer to Technical Data for the new valve dimensions and to the following for the fitted dimensions.

Referring again to **FIG 14** note that dimension 'A' with particular regard to some of the 2.2 litre and all the 2.4 litre engines, should be as follows:

Model	911TV
Engine type	911/57
	911/67
From engine numbers	6520862(57)
	6529026(67)
Inlet valve	35 ± .30 mm
	1.378 ± .012 in
Exhaust valve	As inlet

Model	911T(USA)
Engine type	911/51
	911/61
From engine numbers	6120950(51)
	6129029(61)
Inlet valve	35 ± .30 mm
	1.378 ± .012 in
Exhaust valve	As inlet

Model	911E
Engine type	911/52
	911/62
From engine numbers	6220380(52)
	6229026(62)
Inlet valve	34 ± .30 mm
	1.338 ± .012 in
Exhaust valve	As inlet

Model	911S
Engine type	911/53
	911/63
From engine numbers	632XXXX >>
	633XXXX >>
Inlet valve	35.5 ± .30 mm
	1.398 ± .012 in
Exhaust valve	34.5 ± .30 mm
	1.358 ± .012 in

FIG 14 Installed length of outer valve spring at **A**, adjustment shims at **B** (lefthand view). Check **X** for length of valve stem projecting above spring seat (righthand view)

Reassembling head:

Before refitting the valves, check the dimensions as shown in **FIG 14**. Dimension X must be 45.85 to 47.05 mm (1.805 to 1.852 inch) for both valves with a wear limit of 47.55 mm (1.871 inch). If the valves are the correct length and dimension X is not within the limits, renew the head or have new seat inserts fitted.

It is important to refer to the last instruction in **Section 4** when dealing with engines up to No. 900.727, so that there is no risk of contact between valves and pistons.

Referring again to **FIG 14**, note that dimension 'X', with particular regard to the 1969 models and 2.2 litre engines from 1970 on, should read between 46.90 and 48.10 mm (1.846 and 1.929 inches); the extreme dimensions being the absolute limits.

Put a smear of oil on the stem and fit the valve in its correct position. Fit adjusting shims, spring seat, and a new stem seal. Fit springs and collar, putting the close-coiled end of the outer spring against the head. Compress springs and fit collets.

6 Overhauling rocker gear and camshafts

To remove the camshaft housing proceed as instructed under 'Removing head and camshaft housing as a unit' in **Section 4**, but do not detach chain housing. Remove rockers as instructed later in this Section. After the seal is removed, push the camshaft to the rear and then detach the housing without disturbing the cylinder heads. Remember that three of the housing fixings have socket heads. Lift off the spring washers before removing the housing.

The housings are interchangeable but the coverplate must be pressed into place according to the housing position. Clean off all gasket material from sealing faces and check security of head studs.

The camshafts:

These are handed and the correct positions are shown in **FIG 15**. Clean shafts and check for wear or damage. Inject oil or use compressed air to check that oilways are clear. Refer to **FIG 11** and check condition of O-ring 2 and thrust washer 4. Sealing ring 3 is a guide and must be renewed if play is excessive.

Camshaft drive:

With the chain tensioner and camshaft sprocket removed it will be possible to attend to the chain guide ramps. The positions are shown in **FIG 16**. The inner ones are removed as shown in **FIG 17** after detaching the chain housing. These ramps are attached by stud bolts, and removal is effected by lifting the spring retainers from the groove in the stud and then unscrewing. Check condition of ramps, springs and stud bolts.

When replacing, check that spring locates correctly in groove. Fit new gaskets between crankcase and chain housing. Refer to **Section 7** for details of overhauling the chain tensioner. Alignment of sprockets is covered in **Section 15**.

FIG 15 Lefthand and righthand camshafts and housings, showing differing cam positions

FIG 16 Positions of timing chain guide ramps

Refitting camshaft housing:

Apply a thin coat of sealing compound such as Teroson Atmosit to the cylinder head surfaces. Place housing and oil return pipes on heads, fit a few nuts and washers and tighten finger tight. Fit remaining nuts and tighten diagonally across the head. While doing this, have the camshaft in place and check that it turns freely. If it binds, try altering the sequence of nut tightening.

Refitting camshaft:

With shafts correctly located as shown in **FIG 15**, attach gasket 1 with grease (see **FIG 11**). Fit sealing ring 3 and O-ring 2 and tighten the three screws. Fit thrust washer 4 and spacer(s) 5. Fit key to shaft and press on sprocket flange 6. The rockers must be detached during all these operations.

Camshaft sprockets are interchangeable but are offset differently when fitted. The one for cylinders 1 to 3 must have the deeper recess visible and the one for cylinders 4 to 6 must have the shallow recess visible. Cylinder numbering is shown in **FIG 5**.

Removing and refitting rockers:

Mark rockers for correct reassembly. When removing rocker with valves in position, turn camshaft until rocker is free of pressure before trying to remove rocker shaft.

FIG 17 Lifting spring on chain guide ramp out of groove in mounting stud

FIG 18 Components of rocker shaft. Cones expand ends to secure shaft in housing

Key to Fig 18

1 Conical nut
2 Rocker arm shaft
3 Conical bushing
4 Allen-head bolt

FIG 19 Components of chain tensioner (left). Using wire probe to depress valve to bleed tensioner (right)

Key to Fig 19

1 Circlip
2 Piston
3 Valve seat
4 Ball
5 Ball valve cage
6 Spring
7 Spring guide
8 Chain tensioner housing

FIG 18 shows the method of securing the rocker shaft 2 by means of expander cones in each end. Tightening screw 4 causes the cones to expand the ends of the shaft inside the camshaft housing, locking it in place and making an oil-tight seal.

Undo screw with an Allen key and push out the shaft. Check shaft and rocker for wear. Oil parts during reassembly.

Refit marked rockers in original positions. Allen screws at end rocker shafts must have their heads facing cylinders 2 and 5 respectively (see **FIG 5**).

The shafts must be centrally located so that the grooves are recessed into the camshaft housing bores the same amount each side. This should be 1.5 mm (.06 inch). Use feeler gauges as follows:

Insert feeler between rocker and housing and locate shaft so that feeler drops into groove. Push on shaft at end farthest from groove until feeler is trapped. Withdraw feeler. Push shaft approximately 1.5 mm (.06 inch) further in and tighten Allen screw to 180 cm/kg (13 lb ft).

Adjust the valve clearances as instructed in **Section 2**. If the timing gear has been dismantled, adjust the valve timing as described in **Section 8**.

7 Overhauling chain tensioner—removal and refitting

Removal:

With engine removed from car, disconnect both oil supply hoses from crankcase to chain housing cover. Remove cover and turn engine to TDC on firing stroke of No. 1 cylinder (see top view of **FIG 6**). On lefthand side of engine, jam tensioner sprocket against chain with a block between spindle and crankcase. On righthand side tie sprocket arm to a cover stud above it, using wire. Remove tensioner, noting that plunger is under spring pressure (see **FIG 19**).

Overhauling:

Refer to **FIG 19**. Righthand view shows that spring-loaded piston action is damped hydraulically. Dismantle tensioner by holding piston down and prising out circlip 1 (see lefthand view). Release piston slowly and extract the ball valve parts. Valve seat 3 is a press fit in piston. Clean parts and check fit of piston in bore. Check action of valve. Reject corroded parts, particularly the spring. Reassemble in reverse order.

Hold tensioner vertically in vice and fill oil cup with engine oil. Depress ball with bent wire as shown on right in illustration. Press piston up and down, keep cup filled with oil and continue until no more air bubbles emerge. Hold piston at bottom of stroke with steel strip bent inwards at each end, to facilitate refitting. This must fit over piston and under tensioner body.

A tensioner with doubtful action must be tested. Use SAE.30 engine oil at approximately 20°C or 68°F. Arrange for a weight of 5.5 kg (12 lb) to rest squarely and centrally on the piston end. During 5 to 10 minutes the piston must not yield by more than 10 mm (.40 inch).

Refitting:

Do this in the reverse order of dismantling, removing the steel strip to release the piston when the tensioner is in place. Remove device used to keep sprocket pressed firmly against chain.

A redesigned chain tensioner with additional parts has been installed in the following models.

911T from engine numbers:
6190834, 6193106, 6195622 and 6198071
911E from engine numbers 6191723 and 6391688
911S from engine number 6298507.

The components of the new type chain tensioner are shown in **FIG 19A** and a comparison check with the earlier type will immediately convey the obvious differences. Dismantling operations are slightly revised as follows:

1 Remove the tensioner (see earlier unit description).
2 Using soft jaw vice adaptors clamp the mounting part of the unit in a vice, hold the spring retainer 16 down and extract the lockring 17 with a small screwdriver. Take out the retainer 16 and spring 15.
3 Withdraw the aluminium piston 12 with pliers and with a small screwdriver extract the lockring 11. The plunger 10 should be held with a finger whilst the lockring is being removed.
4 Slowly release the plunger and withdraw it, check that the intermediate piece 8 is not stuck inside the plunger. If so, free it by tapping the plunger on a piece of wood.
5 Take out the ball retainer 6, ball 7 and the intermediate piece 8 with the O-ring 9. Remove spring 5 and guide 4.
6 Check the condition of each individual part, renewing any that are suspect or defective; renew the O-rings anyhow. To check the action of the piston 12 in the cylinder, position it on the plunger shaft 10 and slide the assembly into the housing. They should move freely without drag. High spots may be removed with extra fine emery cloth but clean these thoroughly afterwards.
7 Since June 1970 a new intermediate piece 8 and O-ring 9 has been introduced, if available these parts should be fitted instead of the previous types.

Reassembling:

8 Position the O-ring 9 correctly on the intermediate piece 8, lubricate lightly and insert the assembly into the plunger 10 with ball 7 and retainer 6.
9 Fill the housing 1 with SAE 30 oil; insert the spring 5 into the plunger and position the guide 4; insert the plunger assembly into the oil filled housing and secure with the lock ring 11.
10 Bleed the tensioner as described for the earlier unit.
11 Using soft-faced jaws, secure the assembly in a vice as shown in **FIG 19B**. Fill the upper part of the housing with SAE 30 oil; fit the O-rings 13 and 14 to the piston 12 and position the assembly over the plunger shaft. Do not depress the piston at this stage.
12 Place the special gauge ring P214V over the plunger shaft to rest on top of the piston. Simultaneously, open the bleed screw and depress the gauge ring until the latter firmly contacts the top of the housing. As soon as contact is made tighten the bleed screw.
13 Fit the spring 15, retainer 16 and secure with lockring 17.
14 Check the operation of the assembly as described in the earlier tensioner reassembly procedure.

Refitting:

There is a slight difference in the method of refitting between a reconditioned tensioner and a new one:

To fit a reconditioned tensioner:

Before installing, compress the assembly, very slowly, between vice jaws fitted with soft-faced adaptors. (A quick compression will damge the O-rings). Secure the piston in the depressed condition with special tool P.214. Refit the tensioner before removing the tool.

To fit a new tensioner:

All new tensioners have a locking clamp installed which is shown as item 18 in **FIG 19A**. Leave the clamp in position, slide the assembly onto the sprocket wheel carrier shaft to a point when half of the plunger shaft head is covered by the tensioner arm and, at this point, turn the lockring 17 until the temporary clamp 18 can be removed. Push the tensioner fully home and secure.

Continue the reassembly operations as described for the earlier tensioner.

1. Housing
2. Copper washer
3. Bleeder screw
4. Spring guide
5. Plunger spring
6. Ball retainer
7. Ball (5 mm dia.)
8. Intermediate piece
9. O-ring
10. Plunger
11. Lock ring
12. Oil retainer piston
13. O-ring
14. O-ring
15. Oil retainer spring
16. Spring retainer
17. Lock ring
18. Clamp (supplied only with new chain tensioners to help installation)

FIG 19 A Components of new type tensioner

FIG 19 B Secure the assembly in a vice as shown, preparatory to bleeding the system

FIG 20 Checking valve timing. Outer arrows point to camshaft markings, central arrow to pulley mark Z1 aligned with crankcase joint

8 Valve timing

It is essential to check the valve timing if an engine has been completely dismantled or if the camshafts and drive gear have been overhauled. **It is most important that all operations of turning the crankshaft and camshafts with the drive disconnected are undertaken with great care.** Unless the pistons and valves are correctly timed there is a possibility that they will make contact when the top of each stroke is reached. If the slightest resistance to turning is noticed, stop at once, back off a little and reset the relative positions of camshafts and crankshaft.

Adjustment:

Preliminary timing is set as follows:
1 Refer to **FIG 20** and turn crankshaft so that pulley mark Z1 lines up with crankcase joint.
2 Camshafts are marked on the end with a punch. Turn these marks until they are vertically above camshaft centres (see outer arrows in illustration), taking the precautions mentioned at the start of this Section.
3 One hole in each camshaft sprocket will line up with one in the sprocket flange. Insert dowel (see **FIG 21**). Fit spring washer and tighten nut to 10 mkg (72 lb ft).

Accurate timing is obtained as follows:
1 Set inlet valve clearance of No. 1 cylinder to .10 mm (.004 inch). See **FIG 5** for cylinder numbering.
2 Set up a dial gauge as shown top left in **FIG 22**. The plunger must rest on the valve spring collar and be in line with the valve stem. Arrange for the plunger to extend a further 10 mm (.40 inch) as the valve opens. Zero the gauge.
3 Use a screwdriver to press the tensioner sprocket firmly against the chain, as shown, and block the tensioner in that position. Turn crankshaft through a complete turn so that No. 1 cylinder is now at TDC on the inlet stroke and the inlet valve should have started to open. Read the dial gauge. This will be the amount of inlet valve lift at TDC and figures for the various models are as follows:

2000 engine
(up to No. 909.927)
4.2 to 4.6 mm (.165 to .181 inch)
Desirable adjustment value 4.3 mm (.169 inch)

2000 engine
(Nos. 911.001 to 912.050 and 3180.001 to 3380.001)
3.0 to 3.3 mm (.118 to .130 inch)
Desirable adjustment value 3.15 mm (.124 inch)

2000S engine
(from Nos. 960.001 and 4080.001)
5.0 to 5.4 mm (.197 to .213 inch)
Desirable adjustment value 5.2 mm (.205 inch)

2000T engine
(from No. 2080.001)
2.3 to 2.7 mm (.091 to .106 inch)
Desirable adjustment value 2.5 mm (.098 inch)

2000L engine
(from No. 3380.001) 6.8 ± .10 mm (.268 ± .004 inch)

If the amount of lift shown by the gauge differs from these figures, adjust as follows:
1 Remove camshaft sprocket nut and spring washer. Withdraw dowel. Ensure that pulley mark aligns with crankcase joint.
2 Turn the camshaft with special tool P.202 as shown. Do this until the dial gauge shows the desirable adjustment value just specified.
3 Find the holes in sprocket and flange which line up and insert dowel. Fit washer and nut and tighten to correct torque.
4 Turn crankshaft two complete turns and check gauge reading. Readjust if necessary.

Repeat the procedure on cylinder No. 4 to set the timing of the other camshaft, making sure the tensioner sprocket is firmly pressed into the chain. When adjustment is completed, remove blocks used to maintain position of tensioners. Note in **FIG 22** that a screwdriver is being used to press the tensioner into the chain to take up all backlash.

9 Servicing lubricating system

The layout of the system is shown in **FIG 23**. There are two pumps 2 and 3. Pressure pump 3 draws oil from tank 9 and pumps it to thermostat 5. If the oil is cold it is prevented from passing through cooler 8 and is forced through passages to the various engine bearings. When the oil warms up, the thermostat opens and allows the oil to pass through the cooler 8 before it goes to the bearings. Draining oil collects in the crankcase and is drawn out by scavenge pump 2. It is then pumped to tank 9, passing through a fullflow filter 12 on its way.

Excessive pressure in the system will open relief valve 7 which allows some oil to escape into the crankcase. If this valve becomes blocked or otherwise inoperative a safety valve 4 will open under excessive pressure to ensure that there is no possibility of the hoses, the cooler or the filter being damaged.

Maintenance of the filter and the crankcase strainer has been covered in **Section 2**.

Key to Fig 23

1. Oil strainer in crankcase
2. Scavenge pump
3. Pressure pump
4. Safety valve (opening pressure $p = 8$ atü (113.7 p.s.i.))
5. Thermostat (opens to pass oil through cooler at approx. $80^\circ C$)
6. Oil pressure gauge
7. Pressure release valve (opening pressure $p = 5.4$ atü (76.8 p.s.i.))
8. Oil cooler
9. Oil tank
10. Perforated plate (to prevent foaming)
11. Bypass valve
12. Full-flow oil filter
13. Oil filler pipe
14. Oil temperature gauge
15. Crankcase breather into oil tank
16. Oil tank breather to intake air filter
17. Combined oil pressure and temperature indicator

FIG 21 Withdrawing dowel which aligns vernier hole in camshaft sprocket with that in flange

FIG 22 Valve timing check. Dial gauge records inlet valve lift while camshaft is turned with tool No. P202

FIG 23 Layout of lubricating system. Inset (top right) is a section through oil filter

FIG 24 Plug for oil pressure relief valve (bottom), plug for safety valve (top)

FIG 26 Removing oil cooler. Top view also shows pressure transmitter (top arrow) and thermostat (lower arrow)

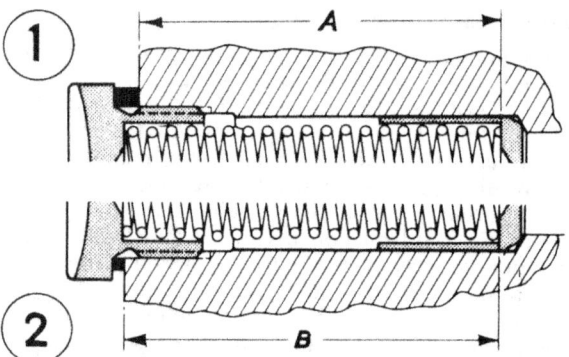

FIG 25 Length **A** should be 57.5 mm (2.26 inch) on engines up to No. 901282. The plug is fitted with a thick aluminium sealing washer (view 1). Later engines have thinner washer and dimension **B** is 59.5 mm (2.34 inch), as shown in view 2

On the 911S models, from 1969 onwards, an auxiliary oil cooler is fitted under the righthand front fender. The purpose, to ensure the oil temperature does not rise excessively when the engine is operating at high speeds or under heavy loads.

If the temperature of the oil flowing from the crankcase exceeds 87°C, a secondary thermostat opens to allow the oil to enter the front auxiliary cooler and return to the tank. If the returned oil still remains above 83°C, the primary thermostat opens to allow the overheated oil to enter the engine mounted cooler.

Removing:

1 Take off the righthand front road wheel and uncouple the hoses from the double-ended connectors where they join with the hoses from the cooler. An extra wrench will be required to hold the connector.

2 Slacken the louvred shroud support screws to loosen the shroud; remove the front righthand headlight assembly and possibly the horn, if access is still difficult to one of the cooler mounting bolts remove the mounting bolts and the oil cooler. Note that the oil lines inside the door rocker panel are not removable.

Refitting:

3 Use MolyKote or similar lubricant on the oil hose connectors and reassemble in the reverse order.

Servicing pressure relief and safety valves:

The location of the valves is shown by the arrows in **FIG 24**. The relief valve is on the bottom. Both are removed by unscrewing the plugs and withdrawing the springs and pistons.

Examine the pistons and remove score marks with care. Renew pistons if worn or beyond renovation. Check springs as follows:

The springs are identical, the fitted length varying to give the required lifting pressures. Free length is 70 mm (2.75 inch). Pressure at length of 52 mm (2.04 inch) should be 23 lb and at a length of 46 mm (1.81 inch) it should be 31 lb.

For engines up to No. 901.282 it is necessary to fit a special aluminium sealing ring to the plug for the pressure relief valve. This will give the required length of 57.5 mm (2.26 inch) as shown at A in view 1 of **FIG 25**. Measure with a depth gauge.

Later engines had modifications which made distance B in view 2 as 59.5 mm (2.34 inch). The sealing ring then became the same as that fitted to the safety valve plug.

When refitting the piston spring, make sure it does not scratch the bore.

Removing and refitting oil filter and oil cooler:

Instructions concerning the oil filter are to be found in **Section 2**. To remove the oil cooler with the engine in or out of the car, proceed as follows:

1. Remove upper coverplate, front coverplate and righthand coverplate. Refer to **FIG 26** and remove upper nuts (top view).
2. Hold hexagon of inlet pipe to prevent it turning and release union from cooler.
3. Remove lower nuts (bottom view). Lift cooler away, noting seals to crankcase. Always renew these.

When refitting cooler, make sure the seals are correctly seated and connect the inlet pipe, using the precautions taken to remove it.

Thermostat and oil pressure transmitter:

These are indicated by the arrows in the top view of **FIG 26**. To remove the thermostat, disconnect cable to transmitter (top arrow), disconnect hose from breather outlet and unscrew transmitter. Remove thermostat (two nuts).

Refit in the reverse order, fitting new O-rings. Offset holes in thermostat flange prevent incorrect assembly.

Oil pump removal and refitting:

The location of the pump can be seen on the left in **FIG 30**. Note how it is driven by the intermediate shaft (see 13, 18 and 19 in **FIG 2**).

The pump is removed after the crankcase halves have been parted. Arrows indicate the securing nuts. Remove pump with intermediate and connecting shafts. Withdraw pump from connecting shaft.

The pump cannot be repaired and must be renewed if faulty. Check action after cleaning and blowing out with compressed air. Run at moderate speed. Check sealing surfaces and renew seals.

Refit pump in the reverse order, inserting it complete with shafts and chains. Make sure the seals are correctly fitted and are not displaced. Secure with nuts and tabwashers.

Piston cooling:

From December 1970 all power units are equipped with oil spray jets for piston cooling. The jets are located in the crankcase cylinder bores drilled into the bearing webs.

The spray jet valves open when oil pressure reaches 42-56 lb/sq inch and oil from the six jets is sprayed against the pistons underside. With this system a reduction of approximately 55°C is achieved in the piston head temperature. The spray quantity is approximately 250 litres (55 UK gallons or 66 US gallons) per hour at 6000 rev/min.

Oil tank relocation:

Since the introduction of the 1972 models the oil tank is now repositioned in the righthand rear wheel housing, in front of the rear axle. The oil filler neck is also made accessible from the outside by relocating it under a hinged cover which is situated on the righthand rear fender. The oil filter housing is now separated from the tank and mounted on the righthand engine compartment wall.

Removing oil tank:

1. Take off the rear righthand road wheel.
2. Drain the oil from the tank and take precautions against spillage over the brake discs during draining and the removal of the tank.
3. Loosen the return hose clamps and retaining clamp, detach the return hose and on the 911S, the oil hose from the bottom of the tank.
4. Loosen securing strap and partially move the tank to disconnect oil line, breather hoses and oil level gauge wires; remove tank.

Refitting:

5. Refit in the reverse sequence of removal and ensure the plastic caps between tank and body, and the securing strap liner, are correctly seated. Coat hose connections with Molykote or similar lubricant.

10 The flywheel and clutch

Removing:

Part the engine and gearbox, then loosen the bolts securing the clutch. Do this a turn at a time, working diagonally to avoid distortion of the clutch cover. Lift away clutch cover and driven plate. With the flywheel secured against turning, use a long-handled wrench to remove the socket-head screws and lever the flywheel squarely off the crankshaft (see **FIG 27**). Note drive shaft bush 4 and spacer 5.

Reconditioning flywheel:

Check condition of starter teeth, clutch plate surface and centre boss where it mates with crankshaft. Renew flywheel if seriously defective, but have it machined if damage is slight. Gear teeth may be cut back slightly and clutch plate surface may be resurfaced by Porsche agents, who will know the necessary dimensions. From engine No. P901.639 the flywheel was reduced in width and the gear teeth were of finer pitch, the width of the rim being 39 mm (1.54 inch). Flywheels must be rejected if the clutch driving face is less than 11 mm (.433 inch) from the face of the centre boss.

Check condition and fit of input shaft bush. It may be renewed by pressing out from the front and fitting a new one from the back.

When inspecting the flywheel on the 2.2 litre models, note that the flywheel minimum thickness (taken from the narrowest section) should not be less than 8.50 mm (.335 inch); this also applies if any machining is required.

Before installing the flywheel, refer to **FIG 27** and ensure that the spacer washer 5 has a thickness of 3 mm (.118 inch) the retaining bolts 2 have an overall length of 35 mm (1.378 inch) and a head thickness of 8 mm (.315 inch).

Refitting:

Flywheels and crankshafts may be renewed separately without upsetting the balance. Holes for securing screws are staggered so that flywheel fits in one place only.

Mounting faces of crankshaft, flywheel and spacing washer must be free from oil. Lightly oil threads of screws and tighten them evenly and progressively to a torque of 15 mkg (108 lb ft). Put about 2 cc of graphite or molybdenum-disulphide grease in the input shaft bush. Centralize the clutch plate and refit the clutch cover as instructed in **Chapter 5**.

FIG 27 How flywheel is secured. Bush 4 supports rear end of gearbox input shaft

Key to Fig 27
1 Flywheel
2 Socket-head screws
3 Crankshaft
4 Bush and seal
5 Spacing washer

A — Cylinder height tolerance
B — Cylinder diameter tolerance
C — Manufacturer's mark

FIG 28 Location of cylinder marking for height, and bore diameter

11 Removing and servicing cylinders and pistons

Before removing the cylinders, mark them 1 to 6 as indicated in **FIG 5**. After removing the cylinder head, either in sets or individually, as described in **Section 4**, detach the air deflector plates and lift off the cylinders.

Removing pistons:

Mark each piston with the cylinder number and indicate how it faces with respect to the flywheel or front of the engine. Push rag into the crankcase apertures to prevent gudgeon pin circlips falling in as they are prised out with a thin screwdriver, using the slots provided. Pistons must be heated before gudgeon pins are pushed out. Electric heaters are available but hot water may be used to get each piston up to a temperature of 80°C or 176°F, taking care that water does not enter the crankcase. Remove pin and lift piston off connecting rod. Remove rings with special pliers.

Cylinder specifications (up to and inc 1967 models)

911T engines have cast iron cylinders, all other models having 'Biral' cylinders with iron bores and aluminium cooling fins as shown in **FIG 28**. Note how the tolerance groups are designated A and B. If the triangle encloses the figure 5 the height of the barrel from joint face to joint face is 82.2 to 82.225 mm (3.236 to 3.237 inch). If the figure is a 6 the height is 82.225 to 82.250 mm (3.237 to 3.238 inch). **All cylinders in a bank of three must be of the same height.** Specifications are as follows:

Designation B	Bore size
−1	79.99 to 80.00 mm (3.1492 to 3.1496 inch)
0	80.00 to 80.01 mm (3.1496 to 3.150 inch)
+1	80.01 to 80.02 mm (3.150 to 3.1504 inch)

Oversize:

−1.KD.1	80.49 to 80.50 mm (3.1689 to 3.1692 inch)
0.KD.1	80.50 to 80.51 mm (3.1692 to 3.1696 inch)
+1.KD.1	80.51 to 80.52 mm (3.1696 to 3.170 inch)

Use this table when assessing bore condition in association with the table of piston sizes which follows. Measure bore 30 mm (1.18 inch) up from the bottom. Cylinders may be rebored by any reputable workshop.

Piston clearance (1968 models onwards):

Measure piston at point indicated by D1 in **FIG 29**. Measure cylinder bore 30 mm (1.18 inch) up from bottom. Clearance of piston in bore should lie between limits of .035 to .055 mm (.0014 to .0022 inch) for 911L and 911T (Schmidt) pistons. It should be .025 to .045 mm (.001 to .0018 inch) for 911T (Mahle) pistons, and .045 to .065 mm (.0018 to .0026 inch) for 911S pistons.

Piston Type 911 S

Piston Type 911 L

Piston Type 911 T

FIG 29 Piston types **A, B** and **C**. For clearance checks, measure at D1

Piston specifications (up to and including 1967 models):

Clearance between piston and cylinder should be .055 to .075 mm (.0022 to .0029 inch). Wear limit is .10 mm (.0039 inch). Establish clearance by measuring with internal and external micrometers. Measure pistons at right angles to gudgeon pin about 2 mm below the bottom ring groove. Specifications are as follows:

Piston crown marking	Piston diameter
−1	79.925 to 79.935 mm (3.1466 to 3.1470 inch)
0	79.935 to 79.945 mm (3.1470 to 3.1474 inch)
+1	79.945 to 79.955 mm (3.1474 to 3.1478 inch)
Oversize:	
−1.KD.1	80.425 to 80.435 mm (3.1663 to 3.1667 inch)
0.KD.1	80.435 to 80.445 mm (3.1667 to 3.1671 inch)
+1.KD.1	80.445 to 80.455 mm (3,1671 to 3.1675 inch)

Pair this table off with the cylinder bore table to check wear. Standard pistons are marked −1, 0 and +1. **These are obtainable only as a set with matching cylinder.** Oversize pistons are available individually.

Cylinder specifications (1968 models onwards):

Designation B	Bore size
0	80.00 to 80.01 mm (3.1496 to 3.150 inch)
1	80.01 to 80.02 mm (3.150 to 3.1504 inch)
2	80.02 to 80.03 mm (3.1504 to 3.1508 inch)
Oversize:	
0.KD.1	80.50 to 80.51 mm (3.1692 to 3.1696 inch)
1.KD.1	80.51 to 80.52 mm (3.1696 to 3.170 inch)
2.KD.1	80.52 to 80.53 mm (3.170 to 3.1704 inch)

Use this table in conjunction with the following tables for the three types of piston shown in **FIG 29**. Note, however, that type C comes in two makes, Mahle and Schmidt, with differing dimensions.

Piston specification for 911L engine (1968 models onwards):

Crown mark	Diameter of piston B at D1 (tolerance ± .005 mm or ± .0002 inch)
0	79.960 mm (3.148 inch)
1	79.970 mm (3.1484 inch)
2	79.980 mm (3.1488 inch)
Oversize:	
0.KD.1	80.460 mm (3.1677 inch)
1.KD.1	80.470 mm (3.1681 inch)
2.KD.1	80.480 mm (3.1685 inch)

Piston specification for 911T engine (1968 models onwards—Mahle):

Crown mark	Diameter of piston C at D1 (tolerance ± .005 mm or ± .0002 inch)
0	79.970 mm (3.1484 inch)
1	79.980 mm (3.1488 inch)
2	79.990 mm (3.1492 inch)
Oversize:	
0.KD.1	80.470 mm (3.1681 inch)
1.KD.1	80.480 mm (3.1685 inch)
2.KD.1	80.490 mm (3.1689 inch)

Piston specification for 911T engine (1968 model onwards—Schmidt):

Crown mark	Diameter of piston C at D1 (tolerance +.006 −.007 mm or +.0002 inch −.0003 inch)
0	79.960 mm (3.148 inch)
1	79.970 mm (3.1484 inch)
2	79.980 mm (3.1488 inch)
Oversize:	
0.KD.1	80.460 mm (3.1677 inch)
1.KD.1	80.470 mm (3.1681 inch)
2.KD.1	80.480 mm (3.1685 inch)

Piston specification for 911S engine (1968 models onwards):

Crown mark	Diameter of piston A at D1 (tolerance ± .005 mm or ± .0002 inch)
0	79.95 mm (3.1476 inch)
1	79.96 mm (3.148 inch)
2	79.97 mm (3.1484 inch)
Oversize:	
0.KD.1	80.45 mm (3.1673 inch)
1.KD.1	80.46 mm (3.1677 inch)
2.KD.1	80.47 mm (3.1681 inch)

Piston and Cylinder specifications for 2:2 Litre engines

Model	911TC	911EC	911SC
Piston make	Schmidt	Marhle	Marhle	Marhle
Markings and cylinder diameter:				
0 (84.00-84.01 mm)	83.96 mm	83.97 mm	83.96 mm	83.95 mm
(3.3071-3.3075 in)	3.3055 in	3.3059 in	3.3055 in	3.3051 in
1 (84.01-84.02 mm)	83.97 mm	83.98 mm	83.97 mm	83.96 mm
(3.3075-3.3079 in)	3.3059 in	3.3063 in	3.3059 in	3.3055 in
2 (84.02-84.03 mm)	83.98 mm	83.99 mm	83.98 mm	83.97 mm
(3.3079-3.3083 in)	3.3063 in	3.3067 in	3.3063 in	3.3059 in
Oversize marks and cylinder diameter:				
0.KD1 (84.25-84.26 mm)	84.21 mm	84.22 mm	84.21 mm	84.20 mm
(3.3169-3.3173 in)	(3.3154 in)	(3.3157 in)	(3.3154 in)	(3.3150 in)
1.KD1 (84.26-84.27 mm)	84.22 mm	84.23 mm	84.22 mm	84.21 mm
(3.3173-3.3177 in)	(3.3157 in)	(3.3161 in)	(3.3157 in)	(3.3154 in)
2.KD1 (84.27-84.28 mm)	84.23 mm	84.24 mm	84.23 mm	84.22 mm
(3.3177-3.3181 in)	(3.3161 in)	(3.3165 in)	(3.3161 in)	(3.3157 in)
Tolerances	+.007 mm / .008 mm (±.0003 in)	±.005 mm (±.0002 in)	±.005 mm (±.0002 in)	±.005 mm (±.0002 in)
Dimension 'h'	15.0 mm (.590 in)	11.50 mm (.453 in)	2.50 mm (.098 in)	2.50 mm (.098 in)
Piston weight	393±4 g	380±3 g	385±3 g	375±3 g

Piston and Cylinder specifications for 2:4 Litre engines

Model	911T		911E	911S
Piston make	Schmidt	or Marhle		
Markings and cylinder diameter:				
0 (84.00-84.01 mm)	83.97 mm	(3.3059 in)	83.97 mm	83.95 mm
(3.3071-3.3075 in)			(3.3059 in)	(3.3051 in)
1 (84.01-84.02 mm)	83.98 mm	(3.3063 in)	83.98 mm	83.96 mm
(3.3075-3.3079 in)			(3.3063 in)	(3.3055 in)
2 (84.02-84.03 mm)	83.99 mm	(3.3067 in)	83.99 mm	83.97 mm
(3.3079-3.3083 in)			(3.3067 in)	(3.3059 in)
Oversize marks and cylinder diameter:				
0.KD1 (84.25-84.26 mm)	84.22 mm		84.22 mm	84.20 mm
(3.3169-3.3173 in)	(3.3157 in)		(3.3157 in)	(3.3150 in)
1.KD1 (84.26-84.27 mm)	84.23 mm		84.23 mm	84.21 mm
(3.3173-3.3177 in)	(3.3161 in)		(3.3161 in)	(3.3154 in)
2.KD1 (84.27-84.28 mm)	84.24 mm		84.24 mm	84.22 mm
(3.3177-3.3181 in)	(3.3165 in)		(3.3165 in)	(3.3157 in)
Cylinder/piston clearance	.023-.048 mm (.0009-.0019 in)		.025-.045 mm (.0010-.0018 in)	.045-.065 mm (.0018-.0025 in)
			.025-.045 mm (.0010-.0018 in)	
Dimension 'h'	12.5 mm (.492 in)		8.00 mm (.315 in)	2.5 mm (.098 in)
			2.5 mm (.098 in)	
Piston weight	375±4 g		376±3 g	354±3 g
			371±3 g	

Cylinder and Piston check 2.2 and 2.4 litre

1 Refer to **FIG 29 A** and check the D1 dimension, that is, at a location 2 to 3 mm (.080 to .12 inch) below the top reversal point of the top piston ring, to determine cylinder wear; if the measured dimensions is .10 mm (.004 inch) above its original size the cylinder is worn out.

2 Check the D1 and D2 dimensions to determine ovality in the cylinder, this is resolved by the difference of the two values of 'a' and 'b', which must not exceed .04 mm (.0016 inch).

3 Measure dimension D on the pistons from a point indicated by dimension 'h' in the table. If the dimension is .10 mm (.004 inch) below the original size the piston is worn out.

Gudgeon pins:

These must be a force fit in piston. Any pin which can be inserted easily into a cold piston must be replaced by one of larger diameter. Pins are colour-coded black or white and this marking will also be found on the inside of the piston boss. Piston bore and pin diameter are as follows:

White .. 22 mm (.866 inch), tolerance 0 to —.003 mm (—.0001 inch)

Black .. 22 mm (.866 inch), tolerance —.003 to —.006 mm (—.0001 to —.0002 inch)

When fitting gudgeon pins it is best to fit new circlips. Insert one circlip so that its opening faces to the piston crown or the skirt. Heat piston to 80°C or 176°F and push oiled gudgeon pin into place in one movement. **Do not stop on the way.** Make sure circlips are properly seated.

For correct clearance of gudgeon pin in small-end bush of connecting rod refer to **Section 13**.

Piston rings:

Ring gap should be .30 to .45 mm (.012 to .018 inch) with a wear limit of 1.0 mm (.04 inch). Use a piston to push ring about 20 mm up the cylinder bore from the bottom. Measure gap with feeler gauges. Too small a gap may be rectified by judicious filing. Check side clearance of rings in groove with feelers. Correct clearance is given in Technical Data.

Fit rings with marking 'TOP' uppermost and set gaps 120 deg. apart. Use piston ring pliers to avoid breakage.

Decarbonizing pistons:

Clean carbon off piston crown with soft tool, taking care not to scratch surface. Clean carbon out of ring grooves, taking care not to remove metal from the sides of the ring grooves. Check for markings which might indicate a bent connecting rod. These often show as scoring and heavy marking on one side of the piston below the gudgeon pin, with similar marking above the pin on the opposite side.

Refitting pistons and cylinders:

Refit the gudgeon pins as instructed in a preceding section. Lightly oil the pistons, rings and cylinder bores. Stagger the ring gaps evenly. Use a compressor on the rings. Making sure that the mating faces are clean, fit a new gasket to the base of each cylinder and slide the cylinders into place. Check that holding-down studs do not contact cylinder fins. Refit air deflector plates (see **FIG 35**).

FIG 29 A Check points of cylinders and pistons

FIG 30 Oil pumps and intermediate drive shaft. Arrow points to pump fixings

FIG 31 Special spring steel strips hold connecting rods and timing chain upright to facilitate assembly of crankshaft halves

FIG 32 Connecting rod dismantled, showing bearing shells

FIG 32 A Modification to No. 8 main bearing to improve oil sealing characteristics. All dimensions are in millimeters

12 Splitting crankcase, removing and refitting crankshaft

With cylinders and pistons removed and crankcase stripped of external parts, remove the chain guide ramps as described in **Section 6** under the heading 'Camshaft drive'. **FIG 17** shows the operation. Proceed as follows:

1. Remove oil strainer from base of crankcase. Remove flywheel (see **Section 10**).
2. Remove oil pressure relief and safety valves (see **Section 9**). Remove V-belt pulley. Remove cover at rear end of intermediate shaft (see **Section 14**).
3. Detach breather outlet nozzles and adjacent thermostat and oil pressure transmitter (see **FIG 26**).
4. Remove all nuts securing crankcase halves. This includes two cap nuts which are located inside the oil cooler mounting flange. Unscrew all through bolts. Remove nut inside the lefthand chain housing aperture.
5. Separate crankcase halves and lift out crankshaft. Remove nuts arrowed in **FIG 30** and lift away oil pump and intermediate shaft. Mark bearing shells if to be refitted.

Cleaning and inspection:

Clean off all jointing material. Flush out oil passages with solvent and compressed air. Check crankcase for cracks and damage. Check joint faces for flatness and freedom from burrs.

Examine groove round through-bolt hole in lefthand casing at No. 7 main bearing, counting from the front end. This must be clean and free from jointing compound.

Bolt crankcase halves together and check main bearing bores with internal micrometer. Standard bores for bearings 1 to 8 is 62.0 to 62.019 mm (2.4409 to 2.4417 inch). Bores may be machined at the factory and oversize bearing shells fitted. The bore then becomes 62.269 to 62.250 mm (2.4515 to 2.4508 inch). While the case is bolted together, check the bores for the intermediate shaft. Bearing 1 should be 29.8 to 29.821 mm (1.173 to 1.174 inch) and bearing 2 should be 24.0 to 24.021 mm (.945 to .9457 inch).

Note that there is a modification to the No. 8 main bearing incorporated on models TC, EC and SC from June 1970 on. The bearing has an oil pressure relief groove cut into it to improve the oil sealing characteristics between the bearing and the crankcase.

If the modification is not incorporated the bearing can be cut with a very fine tooth saw to the millimeter dimensions shown in **FIG 32 A**. Clean up after modifying.

Do not use gasket compound when installing the No. 8 bearing.

Reassembling crankcase:

Service the crankshaft as explained in **Section 13** and the intermediate shaft as in **Section 14**. Proceed as follows:

1. Refit oil pump and intermediate shaft (see **Section 9**). Fit main bearing shells 2 to 7 in both casings, locating the tags in the notches provided. Fit flanged shells for bearing 1. Check that oil holes coincide.
2. Oil bearings and fit crankshaft. At front end, coat outer diameter of seal with jointing compound and fit.
3. Use flat spring strips to hold connecting rods and timing chain in position as shown in **FIG 31**. Fit new sealing rings to oil pump and adjacent oil passage. Fit No. 8 bearing, using a new seal and O-ring (see **FIG 34** lower view).
4. Smear jointing compound thinly on joint faces, keeping it away from bearings and annular groove round No. 7 bolt hole. Before fitting the lefthand case, check all parts, see that none becomes displaced and lower the casing half into place. Make sure dowel locates bearing No. 8.
5. Fit through-bolts, fitting a double-chamfered washer under each head with smooth face to crankcase. Push on an O-ring and assemble bolt to crankcase. Fit another O-ring followed by a double-chamfered washer and cap nut.
6. The same washers, rings and nuts are used on the studs for No. 1 bearing. These are located on the lefthand side inside the oil cooler flange. Use a washer and nut on the stud for No. 7 bearing, to be found in the chain housing on the lefthand case. Tighten through-bolts and studs evenly to 3.5 mkg (25 lb ft).
7. Fit spring washers to all retaining studs. Tighten all nuts evenly and diagonally to 2.2 to 2.5 mkg (16 to 18 lb ft).

FIG 33 Main bearing journals on crankshaft are numbered 1 to 8, the flywheel end being on the left. End thrust is taken at bearing 1 as indicated at **A**

Renewing oil seal at No. 8 bearing:

Refer to the upper view in **FIG 34**. To renew the seal without dismantling the engine remove the pulley and push a small screwdriver carefully under the lip of the seal and lever out the seal. Take care not to mark the sealing surface of the crankshaft.

Coat a new seal with oil and refit it, using tool No. P.216. This is a steel cup which presses the ring into place by the action of a nut on a bolt which is screwed into the crankshaft.

Renewing oil seal at flywheel end:

This is possible without splitting the crankcase, after the flywheel has been removed. Displace the seal from its recess with a chisel and then prise it out with a screwdriver. Take care not to damage the sealing surface of the crankshaft. Lightly radius outer corner of recess, removing all swarf.

Take a new seal and lightly coat the outer surface with joint compound. Press the seal into place with tool P.215 so that it finishes flush with the crankcase. Oil the sealing lip and refit the flywheel.

13 Servicing crankshaft and connecting rods

Removal of the crankshaft has been covered in the preceding Section.

Remove connecting rods:

This is simply a matter of removing the big-end bolts, but make sure that the caps and rods are correctly marked for reassembly. **The bolts must be renewed at each overhaul.**

Check rod weights. They must not vary by more than 5 gr. (.176 oz). This is the weight of a complete rod without bearing shells, and is the one quoted when ordering spares. The rod components are shown in **FIG 32**.

The connecting rods and big-end sizes have been modified on the 1972 models. To identify them they have been assigned to weight groups and each weight group has a part number which is stamped on the connecting rods. The rods are weighed without the bearing inserts. The following is a list of weight variations for the 1972 models but bear in mind that the weight variation between the lightest and heaviest connecting rod in any engine must not exceed 9 grammes.

Connecting rod weight chart 1972 models

Weight (grammes)	Weight group	Part number
645 to 654	1	911-103-015(31)
654 to 663	2	911-103-015(32)
663 to 672	3	911-103-015(33)
672 to 681	4	911-103-015(34)
681 to 690	5	911-103-015(35)
690 to 699	6	911-103-015(36)
699 to 708	7	911-103-015(37)
708 to 717	8	911-103-015(38)

Removing oil seal from No. 8 bearing

FIG 34 Marking position of dowel hole on face of bearing housing to ensure correct location (bottom).

FIG 35 Cooling air shrouds fitted below cylinders (top view). Shrouds secured with clamps (lower view)

Check gudgeon pin in small-end bush. It should be a light push fit. Clearance between gudgeon pin and small-end bush should be not more than .020 to .039 mm (.0008 to .0015 inch). Data on oversize pins is given in the preceding Section.

Small-end bushes are renewable, the interference fit being such that the bush must be .014 to .055 mm (.0005 to .002 inch) larger in diameter than the bore in the eye of the connecting rod. The bore of the bush after reaming should be 22.033 to 22.020 mm (.8674 to .867 inch). The pin should then be a light push fit.

Bearing shells:

If scored or breaking up, these must be renewed. If a bearing has 'run', all oilways in the engine must be flushed through at high pressure to remove bearing particles. **Never attempt to rectify bearing clearances by filing or scraping the shells.**

Dismantling crankshaft:

Remove circlip and use a puller to draw off the distributor drive gear, spacer and timing gear as one assembly. Remove spring washer. Prise out Woodruff key.

Clean crankshaft and oilways and examine shaft for wear or cracks. Support shaft on V-blocks at bearings 1 and 7 and check for eccentricity. Bearing eccentricity at bearings 4 and 8 should not exceed .002 mm (.0008 inch). Bearing numbers are given in FIG 33. Standard diameters of main (d1) and connecting rod pins (d2) are 56.990 to 56.971 (2.244 to 2.243 inch). Of No. 8 bearing (d3) it is 30.993 to 30.980 (1.2202 to 1.2197 inch). Excessive wear may be cured by regrinding mains or crankpins to one of three undersizes, —.25, —.50 and —.75 mm and fitting the appropriate bearing shells. As the shaft needs heat treatment after grinding it is advisable to entrust it to a Porsche agent.

Referring to FIG 33 From 1972 onwards all models are fitted with a modified crankshaft which incorporates counterweights, also the stroke is increased to 70.4 mm and the crankpin diameter is decreased to 51.990-51.971 mm (2.0468-2.0461 inch). Refer to further information on the new crankshaft in Technical Data section.

Cylinder height:

Markings (all models):

No. 5 in triangle, standard	85.400-85.425 mm (3.3622-3.3632 in)
No. 6 in triangle, standard	85.425-84.450 mm (3.3632-3.3642 in)
R5, reconditioned	85.150-85.175 mm (3.3524-3.3533 in)
R6, reconditioned	85.175-85.200 mm (3.3533-3.3543 in)

Main bearing and crankpin clearances:

Clearance of main bearings 1 to 7 must lie between .030 and .088 mm (.001 and .0034 inch). Clearance for big-end bearings is the same. Clearance for main bearing No. 8 should be .048 to .104 mm (.002 to .004 inch). End float is .110 to .195 mm (.004 to .0076 inch).

Check by measurement the bore of shells when assembled and the diameters of main and big-end journals. Alternatively, use 'Plastigage' between the assembled bearings and check the width of the squashed material against the gauge supplied, to determine the clearance. Remember that main bearing shells may become loose in the crankcase bores and this may be cured by machining, and then fitting shells which are oversize on outside diameter (see **Section 12**).

Reassembling crankshaft:

Having carefully removed any scoring where the gears are pressed onto the shaft without actually impairing the fit, slide on the spring washer and insert the key. Heat the gear to 150°C or 302°F in an oil bath or on a hotplate and push it onto the shaft with its shoulder facing forward. Fit the spacer and distributor drive gear after heating the gear to 100°C or 212°F. Check that gears are tight when cool and fit circlip.

Inject oil through the crankshaft passages and fit the connecting rods. Make sure the shells are correctly located in the rod and cap, oil the bearing and assemble cap to rod so that the identification numbers coincide. Fit new bolts and tighten to a torque of 5 mkg (36.2 lb ft). If bearing seems tight, tap big-end lugs with a copper hammer to settle cap and rod together. When lubricated the rods should fall freely under their own weight.

14 Servicing the intermediate shaft

This is shaft 13 in FIG 2 and its function is to drive the two camshafts through sprockets 14. The front end of the shaft is coupled to oil pumps 18 and 19. A crankshaft gear immediately behind No. 7 main bearing drives the intermediate shaft.

Great care is needed when servicing the shaft to ensure satisfactory meshing of the gears. Firstly, the shaft and gear must be renewed as an assembly because the gear is machined in situ to make sure it is concentric with the shaft. Secondly, there was a change in design during production and gears and crankcases must be paired together, due to an alteration in shaft centres.

First-type intermediate shaft assembly

Nominal distance between crankshaft and intermediate shaft is 104 mm. Deviation from this dimension is stamped on the rear face of the lefthand crankcase-half adjacent to the alternator mounting. The gears have the deviation from pitch radius of the teeth stamped on the sides. Deviation values are in 1/100 mm. Gears must be mated so that the installed tolerances are nil, with a maximum clearance of 1/100 mm.

Second-type intermediate shaft assembly:

An identifying number, either 0 or 1, will be found on the rear face of the lefthand crankcase-half adjacent to the alternator mounting. The gears are stamped in the same way.

When the crankcase number is 0, fit a pair of gears stamped 0. The gear backlash will then be .029 to .049 mm (.001 to .002 inch). It is permissible to fit a No. 1 crankshaft gear with a No. 0 intermediate gear, the backlash then being .016 to .042 mm (.0006 to .0016 inch). It is also permissible to fit a No. 0 crankshaft gear with a No. 1 intermediate gear, the backlash being .017 to .043 mm (.0007 to .0017 inch).

If the crankcase number is 1, fit a pair of gears stamped 1. Backlash will be .012 to .041 mm (.0005 to .0016 inch). It is permissible to fit a No. 0 crankshaft gear with a No. 1 intermediate gear to give a backlash of .025 to .049 mm (.001 to .0019 inch). Also permissible is a No. 1 crankshaft gear and a No. 0 intermediate gear, the backlash being the same.

Servicing shaft:

Bearing clearance in crankcase must be .020 to .054 mm (.0008 to .002 inch). Wear limit is .10 mm (.004 inch). Shafts which have seen much service should have the internal bore cleaned of residue. Access is by removal of the aluminium plug at the rear end. This is drilled and tapped and a bolt used to withdraw it, a piece of tubing 1 inch long and slightly larger in bore than the diameter of the plug, being used as a spacer. Clean the bore of the shaft and press in a new plug, taking care not to damage the oilway.

Fitting shaft to crankcase:

Being satisfied with the condition of the gear teeth and the bearing surfaces of the shaft, place the shaft in the crankcase, complete with pump but without timing chains. Check for freedom of movement. Altering position of connecting shaft splines may cure binding. When satisfied remove shaft without altering position of connecting shaft, fit the chains and continue with crankcase assembling as instructed in **Section 12**.

End float of intermediate shaft:

Later engines have no provision for adjustment of end float because the rear bearing has renewable inserts with thrust flanges. When fitting the inserts, take care to locate the tabs in the crankcase notches.

On earlier engines, end float is controlled by a thrust plate secured to the rear face of the crankcase. One paper gasket must always be fitted, and adjustment made with shims, before the chain housings are fitted.

Through the chain aperture, lever the sprocket forward to take up all play in the shaft and install the plate with gasket and a thread of 'Plastigage' between the contact faces. Lever the shaft to the rear, remove the plate and measure the 'Plastigage'. Alter shims until the correct end float of .08 to .12 mm (.003 to .0047 inch) is obtained.

The Porsche method of checking uses a dial gauge fitted to a plate which takes the place of the thrust plate so that the plunger can bear on the end of the intermediate shaft to record end float directly.

When reassembling a stripped engine, do not install the thrust plate until the timing sprockets have been checked for alignment as instructed in the following Section.

15 Reassembling a stripped engine

1 Fit the intermediate shaft and oil pump as instructed in **Sections 14** and **9**. Fit a new oil seal and O-ring to the housing for bearing No. 8 and mark the position of the dowel pin hole on the housing face as indicated by the arrow on the right in **FIG 34** (lower view). Fit the assembly to the crankshaft.

2 Fit main bearing liners, making sure oil holes coincide in righthand crankcase half. Coat all bearing surfaces with oil or molybdenum disulphide compound. Fit assembled crankshaft into righthand crankcase half (see **Section 12**), making sure that the dowel for No. 8 bearing housing is in the correct hole.

3 Fit lefthand crankcase half. Fit flywheel (see **Section 10**). Check that crankshaft turns freely, but ensure that the timing chains cannot jam.

4 Fit pistons (see **Section 11**). The deeper recess in piston crown is for the inlet valve, so that it must face upwards. Fit the cylinders, holding each in place with two opposite nuts and spacers. Fit head gaskets with perforated face to cylinder. Assemble valves in heads.

5 If cylinder heads and camshaft housings are assembled together, fit these on the cylinders, at the same time inserting the oil return tubes into the recesses in crankcase and in camshaft housings. The tubes must be initially prepared by fitting them with new O-rings which are oiled to facilitate entry.

6 Fit the washers and nuts and tighten them evenly and diagonally to a torque of 3 to 3.3 mkg (21½ to 24 lb ft). Make sure the camshafts do not bind as the nuts are tightened (see **Section 4**).

7 If cylinder head and camshaft housings are to be refitted separately, follow the instructions in **Section 6** and take the same precautions to ensure that the camshafts do not bind. The rocker arms and shafts must not be installed. In all operations where the crankshaft and camshaft are not correctly timed together, take particular care not to continue turning either of them if the valves can be felt to contact the piston crowns or serious damage could result. Alter the relative positions and try again with extreme caution.

8 Refit the camshafts and rockers as described in **Section 6**. Fit chain guide ramps in crankcase, making sure the springs locate properly in the stud grooves. Fit the chain housings, then the sealing flanges round the sprocket ends of the camshafts. These operations are covered in **Section 6** where instructions will also be found for refitting the camshaft sprockets.

FIG 36 Checking camshaft drive sprockets for correct alignment, using a straightedge and depth gauge

FIG 37 Pipe connections to torque converter oil pump on cars fitted with Sportomatic transmission. Pump is driven by front end of lefthand camshaft

FIG 38 Cover removed from torque converter oil supply pump to show rotors (Sportomatic transmission)

9 The next task is to align the sprockets correctly. The diagram in **FIG 36** shows a straightedge in use for this purpose. The coverplate over the rear end of the intermediate shaft must be removed to reveal a small hole just below. Push the intermediate shaft and camshafts forward as far as possible and use a depth gauge to measure from the straightedge to the face of the drive sprocket, as shown by the central A in **FIG 36**. Keeping the straightedge firmly pressed against the crankcase face, check the distance shown by the righthand A. Any difference must not exceed .25 mm (.01 inch). Check the second camshaft as indicated by the lefthand A, note that 54.8 mm (2.157 inch) must be added to compensate for the offset.

10 If checking reveals any misalignment of the sprockets, correct this by adding or removing spacers (see **FIG 11**). Fit the chains and ramps, followed by the tensioners (see **Section 7**). Adjust the valve timing according to **Section 8**.

11 It is preferable not to invert the engine once the tensioners are fitted because of the oil scoop in each tensioner. For this reason it is often more convenient to fit the heat exchangers before installing the tensioners. Now install the distributor body, fitting a new O-ring to the neck. With cylinder No. 1 at TDC, set the distributor as described in **Chapter 3**.

12 Install chain housing covers, but first check condition of seals for oil supply to the camshafts. Each seal is pressed into its cover and a defective one must be prised out and a new one pressed into place. Refit the oil supply pipes from crankcase to chain covers.

13 The diamond flange on the lefthand chain cover carries the mechanical fuel pumps (when fitted). At least two gaskets and an intermediate plastic flange must be fitted between the lowest point of the eccentric nut and the mounting surface of the pump. Distance from the mounting face must be measured with a depth gauge. It must be 51.4 mm (2.024 inch).

14 Refit the remaining parts in the reverse order of dismantling. Centre the clutch driven plate before fitting the pressure plate (see **Chapter 5**). The rear engine support leaf spring must be horizontal when fitted. Place a straightedge along the carburetter connecting plate so that it projects over the support. Measure from the top edge of the support spring to the straightedge on both sides of the engine and adjust until the measurements are the same.

16 Torque converter oil pump

If the car is fitted with Sportomatic transmission, there is a camshaft-driven oil pump to supply the torque converter. It is mounted in line with the lefthand camshaft as shown in **FIG 37**.

Testing pump:

Oil flow should be 3 litres (5¼ pints or 3.2 US quarts) per minute at a maximum pressure of 29 lb/sq in. Check action of pump by disconnecting the oil return pipe from the torque converter at the oil tank while the engine is running. Oil should flow from the pipe if the pump is working.

If an engine is run while it is out of the car, connect the pump to a supply of oil in a container to keep the system full of oil. **Never run the pump dry.**

Removing pump:

Remove rear wheel on lefthand side. Remove lefthand heat exchanger. Detach pipelines (see arrows in **FIG 37**). Remove pump.

Dismantling and reassembling pump:

Remove cover (see **FIG 38**). Drive dowel pin out of shaft and remove rotors. Remove relief valve cover (two nuts) and lift out spring and plunger.

Clean parts and inspect for wear or damage. Renew rotors as a pair. Fit inner rotor and shaft. Press dowel pin into shaft until it is midway. See that cover dowel protrudes 4 mm (.16 inch) above joint face. Fit outer rotor with bevelled edge leading. Oil parts liberally. Fit cover on a new gasket and tighten down with temporary bolts. The rotors should turn freely. Remove bolts and then fit relief valve, putting the O-ring in the cover.

Refitting pump:

Before doing this, check the driving pins in the end of the camshaft. They are roll-pins and must be fitted in such a way that the pump driving pin cannot rest on the roll-pin slots. The pins must project 8 mm (.315 inch) from the camshaft end.

Install the pump on a new gasket, setting the driving shaft pin between the camshaft roll-pins. Fit heat exchanger using new gaskets, tightening the bolts and nuts uniformly.

17 Testing after overhaul

Before starting the engine, check the contact breaker points and the ignition timing (see **Chapter 3**). Check fan belt tension (see **Chapter 4**). Fill up with correct Heavy Duty oil to upper mark on dipstick (approximately 9 litres, 15¾ pints or 9½ US quarts).

Use the starter for a few revolutions without switching on the ignition. Start the engine and check the oil pressure at once. It must rise immediately and failure to do so will starve the bearings of oil. The red ignition warning light should go out when a fast idling speed is reached.

Let the engine warm up at 2000 to 3000 rev/min until it reaches a temperature of 60°C approximately. Check all joints and oil pipe connections for leakage and inspect the oil filter and oil cooler. Adjust carburetter (see **Chapter 2**). Check oil level in tank at idling speed. The oil pressure at a temperature of 80°C at 5000 rev/min should be 78 to 200 lb/sq in. Set ignition with a stroboscopic lamp.

After running for some time, check that the rocker shafts are tight, tighten the cylinder head nuts, check the valve clearance and check the fan belt tension.

18 Fault diagnosis

(a) Engine will not start

1 Defective ignition coil, carbon brush in distributor cap not contacting rotor arm
2 Faulty distributor capacitor (condenser)
3 Dirty, pitted or incorrectly set contact breaker points
4 Ignition wires loose, insulation faulty
5 Water on sparking plug leads
6 Battery discharged, corrosion of terminals
7 Faulty or jammed starter
8 Sparking plug leads wrongly connected
9 Vapour lock in fuel pipes
10 Defective fuel pump(s)
11 Overchoking or underchoking of carburetters
12 Blocked fuel pump filters or carburetter jets
13 Leaking valves
14 Sticking valves
15 Valve timing incorrect
16 Ignition timing incorrect
17 Engine flooded with fuel

(b) Engine stalls after starting

1 Check 1, 2, 3, 4, 5, 10, 11, 12, 13 and 14 in (a)
2 Sparking plugs defective or gaps incorrect
3 Retarded ignition
4 Mixture too weak
5 Water in fuel system
6 Fuel tank vent blocked
7 Incorrect valve clearances

(c) Engine idles badly

1 Check 2 and 7 in (b)
2 Air leaks at manifold joints
3 Carburetter idling adjustment wrong, jets blocked
4 Over-rich mixture
5 Worn piston rings
6 Worn valve stems or guides
7 Weak exhaust valve springs

(d) Engine misfires

1 Check 1, 2, 3, 4, 5, 8, 10, 12, 13, 14, 15 and 16 in (a), 2, 3, 4 and 7 in (b)
2 Weak or broken valve springs

(e) Engine overheats

1 Weak mixture, ignition over-advanced
2 Fan belt slipping
3 Defective oil thermostat
4 Oil cooler blocked or choked with dirt
5 Loss of cooling air through badly fitted covers

(f) Low compression

1 Check 13 and 14 in (a), 6 and 7 in (c) and 2 in (d)
2 Worn piston ring grooves
3 Scored or worn cylinder bores

(g) Engine lacks power

1 Check 3, 10, 12, 13, 14, 15 and 16 in (a), 2, 3, 4 and 7 in (b), 6 and 7 in (c) and 2 in (d). Also check (e) and (f)
2 Leaking joints and gaskets
3 Fouled sparking plugs
4 Automatic ignition advance not working
5 Exhaust system blocked

(h) Burnt valves or seats
1 Check 13 and 14 in (a), 7 in (b) and 2 in (d). Check (e)
2 Excessive carbon in head

(j) Sticking valves
1 Check 2 in (d)
2 Bent or scored valve stems, defective guides
3 Defective stem seals
4 Incorrect valve clearance

(k) Excessive cylinder wear
1 Check 11 in (a) and check (e)
2 Dirty or insufficient oil. Wrong grade
3 Piston rings wrongly gapped, gummed or broken
4 Bent connecting rods
5 Dirt under cylinder mounting flanges

(l) Excessive oil consumption
1 Check 6 and 7 in (c), check (k) and 3 in (j)
2 Ring gaps too wide
3 Oil control rings ineffective
4 Scored cylinders
5 Oil level too high
6 External oil leaks
7 Incorrect grade of oil

(m) Crankshaft or connecting rod bearing failure
1 Check 2 and 4 in (k)
2 Blocked oilways
3 Bent or worn crankshaft
4 Bearing shells wrongly fitted
5 Worn oil pump, defective lubricating system
6 Loose bearings or connecting rod caps

(n) High fuel consumption
1 Car in poor mechanical condition
2 Bad driving habits, excessive acceleration in low gears
3 Incorrect ignition or carburetter adjustments
4 Flooding float chamber, fuel leakage
5 Incorrect jet sizes
6 Carburetter accelerating pump wrongly adjusted

(o) Engine vibration
1 Mounting failures
2 Loose alternator mounting
3 Fan out of balance
4 Clutch and flywheel unbalanced
5 Misfiring due to mixture, ignition or mechanical faults

NOTES

CHAPTER 2 - FUEL SYSTEM

1 Description of system
2 Routine maintenance
3 Checking fuel system
4 Servicing mechanical fuel pumps
5 Servicing electric fuel pumps
6 The Solex carburetter
7 Servicing Solex carburetter
8 The Weber carburetter
9 Servicing Weber carburetter
10 The fuel tank
11 Fuel injection
12 Fault diagnosis

1 Description of system

Engines up to No. 907.000 have six Solex carburetters, type 40.PI (see **FIG 1**). After that number the installation changes to a triple-throat Weber carburetter on each bank of three cylinders (see **FIG 13**). Starting with the 1969 models, 911E and 911S cars have a fuel injection system which is fully described in **Section 11**.

The Solex system differs from orthodox layouts because the supply of fuel needs an electric pump and two mechanical pumps. The electric pump (see **FIG 3**) passes fuel from the tank to a separate float chamber below each bank of three carburetters. Each mechanical pump (see **FIG 5**) takes fuel from its own particular float chamber and pumps it to a spill-tube fuel well in the body of each one of a set of three carburetters. This well is on the right in **FIG 7**, the fuel level in the spill-tube controlling the fuel level in the jet system to the left of it. Surplus fuel overflows from the tube and returns to the float chamber. This method provides a constant level of fuel to the jets, whatever the driving conditions.

The mechanical pumps are mounted on the lefthand chain housing cover, being operated by a cam nut on the camshaft and a plunger reciprocating in the mounting flange. **FIG 5** shows that the pumps are of the normal diaphragm type with inlet and outlet valves.

The electric pump for the Solex system is shown in **FIG 3**. A pumping piston is reciprocated by a solenoid and spring, current control being made by a magnetic contact breaker.

Each triple-throat Weber carburetter assembly has two float chambers and an accelerating pump. **FIG 13** includes a section through one of the carburetters and shows how fuel is drawn from the float chamber.

The mechanical pumps are not needed for the Weber installation and fuel is pumped by the Hardi electric pump shown in **FIG 6**. This has a pumping diaphragm which is reciprocated by an electric magnet and a throw-over contact breaker, inlet and outlet valves controlling the flow.

In 1970 both the fuel pump and carburetters for the 911T were modified. A Bosch electric fuel pump and the Weber carburetters were substituted by two Zenith, triple throat down draught types; similar to the Webers but modified to pass the emission control regulations. It was then re-designated the 911 TC. When the power units were uprated to 2.4 litres a new 911T was introduced equipped with an improved fuel injection system which was duplicated on the existing 'E' and 'S' models. The 911 TC was uprated also, still with the same type carburetters, and redesignated 911TV.

2 Routine maintenance

Cleaning mechanical pump filters:

Refer to **FIG 2**, unscrew the cover bolt and withdraw the cover, gasket and filter gauze. Remove dirt from filter with a brush and fuel. **Do not use a fluffy rag.** Clean out the filter recess in the body. Refit filter, gasket and cover, making sure that the gasket is in good condition and properly seated. Run the engine and check for leaks.

Cleaning Bendix electric pump filter:

Refer to **FIG 3** and remove the bottom cover 7 by turning it to release the bayonet catches. Remove filter 5, clean it with a brush and fuel and then with compressed air. Clean the bottom cover and magnet and check that gasket 6 is in good condition. Reassemble parts, turning cover clockwise to its stop. Run the engine and check for leaks.

Cleaning Hardi electric pump filter:

Refer to **FIG 6** and remove lower plug to release filter 10. Clean filter with a brush and fuel. **Do not use a fluffy rag.** Check condition of gasket for plug and reassemble. Run engine and check for leaks.

Cleaning air filter:

The filter body contains a large paper element which becomes clogged according to road conditions, so that servicing periods cannot be fixed. It is better to service too frequently, if in doubt. Refer to **FIG 4**, release the spring clips indicated and remove the filter cover. Extract the element. If it is seriously loaded with dust it is best to renew it. **Do not attempt to clean the element with a solvent and do not oil it.** The best method of cleaning is to tap it lightly, at the same time blowing dry compressed air through it from the inside.

Clean the inside of the casing with an oily rag. Do not use cotton waste or anything of a fluffy nature. Check the condition of the gasket. When reassembling, fit the cover so that the mark on it points to the upper lefthand clip.

Cleaning Weber carburetter fuel filters:

There are two banjo bolts securing the fuel feed pipe to each bank of three carburetters (see **FIG 17**). Remove the bolts for access to the tubular filters. Clean filter gauze with a brush and fuel. Renew gaskets if faulty.

Setting hand throttle lever:

From 1968 models onwards, a hand throttle lever is incorporated in the handbrake mounting on 911L, 911S and 911T-Sportomatic cars. This is the small lever with the round knob. This knob is a push fit.

To adjust the friction of the lever pivot, remove the handbrake boot and turn the pivot nut. Correct setting, using a spring balance at right angles to the hole in the lever on the underside is that the lever should not begin to move until a pull of 6 kg (13 lb) is recorded.

There is a hole in the tunnel just below the knob of the lever and this will reveal a clamping collar on the throttle control rod. Correct adjustment is such that the engine should be running at 4000 rev/min with the lever fully opened. Adjust by resetting the position of the clamp.

FIG 1 One of the six Solex carburetters, type 40.PI, as fitted to engines up to No. 907.000

FIG 2 Removing one of the filters on twin mechanical fuel pumps

3 Checking fuel system

If faulty operation is suspected, check as follows:
1 Check that there is fuel in the tank. Make sure the vent hole in the filler cap is clear.
2 Detach fuel hose from carburetter, operate starter (or switch on ignition) and see if fuel spurts from hose. If fuel is pumped, check pump pressure and cleanliness of all jets and fuel passages. Also check floats and float needle valves.
3 If fuel is not pumped, check pump filters, pump valves, tightness of diaphragm flange screws and electrical connections. Check contacts of throw-over breaker in Hardi pump. Check fuel feed pipes from tank and use compressed air to clear possible obstructions. Do not pass compressed air through pumps.

4 Servicing mechanical fuel pumps

Details of the pumps can be seen in **FIG 5**. As the plunger is forced inwards by a cam nut on the camshaft it pulls down the diaphragms by pressing on the rockers or actuating arms. The resulting suction above each diaphragm induces fuel to enter the pumping chambers through the inlet valves. On the return stroke, spring pressure below each diaphragm forces fuel out of the outlet valves and so to the carburetters, the inlet valves being closed. The function of the pumps is to draw fuel from the Solex float chambers and deliver it to each of the six carburetters.

Removing and refitting pumps:

This is a simple matter of pulling off the fuel hoses and removing the bolts from the pump flange. When refitting the pumps, use a new flange gasket, reconnect the hoses and check for leaks by running the engine.

Overhauling pumps:

1 Remove covers and filters (screens). From each pump flange remove six fillister-head screws and lift off upper bodies.
2 Remove screws and detach pump flange with plunger. The actuating arm pins are held in place by lock rings. Remove one ring and drive out the pin for each pump, which will release the arms and springs.
3 Lift off the diaphragms complete with actuating rods, springs and seals.
4 Working inside the upper bodies, remove the inlet valves by unscrewing one screw from each retainer. The outlet valves cannot be removed.

Clean all the parts in fuel and check for wear and corrosion. Suck and blow on the outlet valves to check their operation. Check condition of diaphragm, diaphragm springs and seal. **Do not stretch the spring in an attempt to modify pump performance.** Check for wear of the actuating arms and pivot pins. Check fit of plunger in flange. Renew worn parts.

FIG 3 The Bendix electric fuel pump showing the bottom cover removed for access to the filter

Key to Fig 3

1 fuel outlet 2 Electrical terminal
3 Fuel inlet   4 Pump housing
5 Fuel screen 6 Gasket
7 Cover with filtering magnet

Check seats of inlet valves, assemble valves and suck and blow to test them for correct action.

Reassemble pumps in the reverse order. When joining the pump halves, make sure that the diaphragm is not creased and then tighten the screws diagonally, a turn at a time. Renew the cover gasket if faulty or leaking. Fit a new gasket to the pump flange. Lubricate the plunger and check that its seal is working.

Checking pump flow:

Pumps are tested one at a time, the pump not under test being connected to both banks of carburetters by a T-piece. The object of the test is to determine the rate of flow under a certain amount of outlet pressure. This pressure is arranged by connecting a vertical length of tubing to the outlet of the pump being tested. The top of the tube must turn over into a suitable container, and the total vertical lift of fuel must be 650 mm (25.6 inch).

With the engine running at 3000 rev/min, the pump must deliver not less than 800 cc (27 fl oz) of fuel in one minute. Check both pumps by changing over the T-piece and the vertical tube.

5 Servicing electric fuel pumps

The Bendix pump:

This is the one illustrated in **FIG 3**. A central brass tube houses an inlet valve at the bottom, a spring and a sliding piston of steel containing a fuel transfer valve. At rest, the piston is at the top of its stroke and its presence affects the field of a trigger magnet on the outside of the brass tube. The trigger magnet tilts and closes electrical contacts. Lower down there is a solenoid coil round the outside of the tube. When the ignition is switched on, the closed contacts allow current to flow through the coil which produces a powerful magnetic field. This pulls the piston down against the spring and fuel flows through the transfer valve into the bore above the piston. With-

FIG 4 Arrows point to spring clips which secure the air filter cover

drawal of the piston from the trigger magnet field causes it to tilt in the opposite direction and open the contacts. The solenoid becomes de-energized and the piston is forced upwards by the spring, pushing fuel out through the outlet connection. At the same time, suction below the piston induces fuel to flow into the bore below the piston past the inlet valve. This operation continues all the time fuel is needed.

Much of the pump assembly is sealed and the electrical components work in helium gas to prevent contact erosion. Overhauling is restricted to removal of the bottom cover and filter for cleaning. It is, however, possible to remove the valve carrier from the central brass tube (3 screws). It will then be possible to check the pump parts, the valves and the spring. The first check in the case of faulty operation is on the electrical connection to the pump to ensure that it is sound. Failure of the sealed part of the pump calls for the attention of an electrical service station dealing in this type of Bendix pump.

FIG 5 Section through twin mechanical fuel pumps. The plunger is reciprocated by a cam on the end of one of the camshafts

FIG 6 The Hardi fuel pump

1 Valve housing
2 Diaphragm
3 Armature
4 Pressure rod
5 Diaphragm spring
6 Magnet housing
7 Breaker points
8 Condenser
9 Plastic cap
10 Filter
X Contact adjusting screw

The Hardi pump:

This is illustrated in **FIG 6**. The main parts are a valve housing 1 and a magnet housing 6. These are secured together with a diaphragm 2 in between. A pressure rod which is attached to the diaphragm passes through the magnet housing and is connected to a throw-over mechanism incorporating a contact breaker 7. The valve housing carries inlet and outlet valves and connections.

Assuming that the contact points are closed and the ignition is switched on, the magnet is energized and it attracts a polepiece or armature 3 which is secured to the diaphragm. Consequent suction in the chamber of the valve housing induces fuel to flow in through the inlet valve. The movement of the diaphragm and pressure rod eventually causes the contact breaker mechanism to throw-over and the contacts separate. The breakdown in magnetism allows spring 5 to push the diaphragm towards the valve housing, the inlet valve closes, the outlet valve opens and fuel is pumped to the carburetters. The action is repeated so long as fuel is required.

Removing and refitting Hardi pump:

Disconnect fuel pipe banjos. Detach cable from terminal on pump cover. Remove mounting bolts and detach earth lead. Check mounting grommets.

When refitting pump, make sure that the electrical connections are clean and tight, and check that the banjo gaskets are sound. Switch on and check for leaks. Rapid action without pumping fuel may be due to air leaks on the suction side. Sluggish action may be due to a blocked filter or trouble with the valves. Another cause of faulty operation may be dirty contacts. These are cleaned by drawing a strip of paper between them while pressing them together.

Overhauling Hardi pump:

1 Remove outlet connection from valve housing and extract valve assembly 1A.
2 Separate housings (six screws). Unscrew diaphragm 2 by turning anticlockwise. Collect spring, and also impact washer on pressure rod.
3 Remove plastic cap 9. Remove breaker adjusting screw X, condenser 8 and breaker platform. Make a careful note of the electrical connections.
4 If necessary, release the throw-over mechanism by pushing out the pivot pin.

Clean and examine the parts. Check valve assembly 1A by sucking and blowing. Check the diaphragm for cracks. Parts 2, 3 and 4 are an assembly and must be renewed as such. Check breaker points 7 and renew pivot pin if worn. This pin is hardened and a genuine spare must be used.

Reassemble in the reverse order, putting a tiny drop of oil on the breaker pivots. **Oil must not reach the contact points.**

Fit the diaphragm and spring, screwing the pressure rod into the contact breaker trunnion. Press on the diaphragm so that the points are open and adjust the contact gap to 1.2 mm (.05 inch) by turning the adjusting screw. The diaphragm spring must have its large end against the magnet housing. **Do not try to alter pump performance by stretching the spring.**

Continue to screw in the diaphragm rod until the contacts will no longer open when the diaphragm is pressed in towards the magnet housing. Now turn the diaphragm anticlockwise until a point is reached where the contact points will just begin to open when the diaphragm is pressed in. From this point, unscrew the diaphragm a further 300 deg. or five holes in the edge of the diaphragm. Fit the body halves together and tighten the screws diagonally and evenly. The electrical connections must be clean and tight. After switching on, check for leaks.

Bosch electric fuel pump:

The 1970 911T models are equipped with a Bosch electric fuel pump which is similar to the one fitted to earlier 911E and S models.

On the 1971 models the electric fuel pump is repositioned. The new location is between the transverse tube and rear axle trailing arm on the lefthand rear side of the vehicle. The removal procedure is as follows:

1 Locate the pump and take off the cap nuts that retain the support bracket.
2 Partially withdraw the pump and bracket, loosen the hose clamp and separate the pump and bracket.
3 Slacken the hose retaining clamps and pull the hoses off the pump. Plug the hoses or block them off with clamps to prevent fuel spillage. Note that the inlet is marked 'S' and the return is marked 'R'.
4 Disconnect the terminals.

Refitting:

5 When refitting in the reverse sequence coat both terminals with Lithium grease to prevent corrosion and make sure the rubber boot is properly seated.

6 The Solex carburetter

FIG 1 is an external view of the carburetter and **FIGS 7, 8** and **9** show some of the main principles of operation. In **FIG 8**, the central part of the section shows how the jets are mounted in a carrier which is readily removable. The darker shaded passages indicate the fuel level, and this is maintained by the height of the spill-tube in the well on the right. Surplus fuel which overflows will return to the float chamber by the tube illustrated.

FIG 8 shows how the carburetter operates in the lower speed range. At idling speed there will be no flow from the fuel line and diffuser, and the throttle valve will be almost closed, so that emulsion will flow from the orifice below the volume control screw but not from the passages just above.

In power metering, as shown, fuel flows, in part, from the main jet into the chamber containing the mixing tube and air correction jet 3. The emulsion formed by fuel and air issues from the fuel line and diffuser to mix with the incoming air in the right proportions for correct combustion.

Where rapid throttle opening during acceleration calls for an enriched supply of mixture, the diaphragm pump comes into operation as shown in **FIG 9**. The pump connecting rod is attached to the throttle control and operates the pump lever. Fuel is forced through the passages shown until it lifts the upper ball valve on the left, to squirt from the injector tube into the stream of incoming air 2. The pump recuperates as the diaphragm flexes to the right and draws in fuel through the lower ball valve, the upper valve closing. When full power is needed at large throttle openings, additional fuel is provided by the enrichment nozzle shown in **FIG 7**.

7 Servicing Solex carburetter

Idling adjustment:

Run the engine until the oil temperature is approximately 60°C and remove the air filter. Check ignition timing and contact breaker gap. Check that ball joints in carburetter linkage are properly seated. Disconnect links from operating shafts (see righthand arrow in **FIG 10**). Accurate setting is best achieved with a synchronizing device which fits on the air intake, but careful work with a length of rubber or plastic hose will give reasonable results. One end of the tube is held to the ear and the other placed on the lip of the air intake in the same position every time. The hiss which is heard must be of the same intensity for all carburetters. With either device, set the engine to run at 1200 to 1400 rev/min and synchronize the throttle valves to give equal results. Adjust the idling mixture screws (see **FIG 1**) so that the engine runs smoothly. Readjust the throttle stops (central arrow in **FIG 10**) to set the idling speed to 900 ± 100 rev/min. Use the synchronizing tester or listening hose to check that each throttle opening is correct and then readjust the idling mixture screws.

When satisfied that all carburetters are correctly synchronized, reconnect the operating links, adjusting the length so that the ball joints fit without preload. Refit the air filter and try a minor adjustment of the idling mixture screws. Check the throttle return damper. The plunger travel should be approximately 4 to 5 mm (.16 to .20 inch).

FIG 7 Diagrammatic section through Solex carburetter, type 40.PI. Note how the fuel level is controlled by the height of the spill-tube above the fuel feed

FIG 8 Throttle partly opened on the Solex carburetter, type 40.PI. All jets are producing air and fuel emulsion

FIG 9 Opening throttle actuates accelerator pump to inject fuel into main air stream to enrich the mixture on Solex carburetter, type 40.PI

FIG 10 Solex installation, type 40.PI. Lefthand arrow points to float chamber. Central arrow indicates throttle stop. Righthand arrow points to link connecting bellcrank shaft to throttle shaft

FIG 11 Solex carburetter, type 40.PI. Checking fuel delivered by accelerator pump to injection nozzle

FIG 12 Solex carburetter, type 40.PI. Four screws secure cover for pump diaphragm. Arrow on left points to retaining pin for pre-atomizer. Lower arrow on right points to adjustment for pump operating rod

Throttle valve adjustment:

Unsatisfactory idling may sometimes be due to damaged idling screws or to lack of unison in throttle closing. Remove the idling adjustment screws and check that the points are smooth and not bent. Equal closing of the throttle valves is obtained by turning the knurled nut in the centre of each throttle lever link.

Adjusting injection quantity:

Refer to **FIG 11**. Remove air filter and throttle shaft connecting link. Earth the body of an electric fuel pump and mount the pump on the blower housing. Disconnect float chamber hose from mechanical fuel pump and connect it to electric pump inlet. Disconnect carburetter hose from mechanical pump and connect to electric pump outlet. Connect terminal 1 of electric pump to terminal 15 on the ignition coil.

Switch on ignition and check that both electric pumps are working. Wire a small graduated test tube as shown in the illustration and hold it under the injection nozzle or tube (see **FIG 7**). Move throttle linkage twice from stop to stop and check quantity of fuel collected. Correct quantity should be .40 to .50 cc in summer and .55 to .65 cc in winter (Northern hemisphere). Adjust at the two nuts indicated by the arrow in the bottom righthand corner of **FIG 12**. Pump jet size does not affect injection quantity. The quantity must be the same for all carburetters.

Checking float level:

Withdraw mechanical pump hose from float chamber, using a container to catch draining fuel. Push a short piece of clear plastic hose on the float chamber connector and turn it up at right angles so that the open end is well above the joint line. Switch on the ignition and watch the fuel level rising in the plastic tube. When it is steady, measure the distance from the fuel level to the machined underside of the intake duct. The correct figure is 15 to 20 mm (.60 to .79 inch). If level rises above 15 mm the float must be renewed.

Removing individual carburetter:

1 Remove air filter and duct. Detach link connecting throttle actuating shafts.

2 Withdraw vent hose from float chamber bowl. Remove air inlet horns and base plate (six nuts).

3 Release particular carburetter from flange, lift off carburetter and cover the intake to prevent dirt entering.

When installing, clean the flange faces and fit a new gasket. Make sure the gasket does not overlap the inlet duct. Adjust the throttle link so that the throttle closes fully (see 'Throttle valve adjustment'). Adjust the idling speed.

Removing carburetters and inlet duct:

1 Remove air filter and duct. Disconnect ball joints from throttle levers and remove throttle control rod and connecting links.

2 Remove the bellcrank shaft connecting the two banks of carburetters. The righthand joint is solid, but the lefthand joint is mounted on a spring leaf. Pull this outwards to remove the shaft.

3 Disconnect fuel hoses to float chamber and carburetters. Disconnect inlet duct from cylinder head flanges and remove the assembly complete. Cover the inlet ports in the heads. Refit in the reverse sequence. Adjust the idling.

Dismantling and reassembling:

Refer to **FIG 1** and remove the cover. Withdraw jet carrier (two screws-white arrows). Unscrew jets and shake out mixing tube. Remove idling mixture adjustment screw. The pre-atomizer can be seen in the same illustration. Unlock and slacken the retaining screw indicated by the lefthand arrow in **FIG 12** and lift out the pre-atomizer and venturi. Remove pump rod nuts (bottom righthand arrow in **FIG 12**). Remove pump cover (4 screws). Remove diaphragm and spring.

Clean all parts in fuel and pass compressed air through the jets. Do not use needles or wire for cleaning jets as any enlargement will lead to inaccurate metering. Check fit of throttle shaft in body as air leaks will upset performance. Check that throttle disc closes to a light-tight fit. Check diaphragm and renew if cracked or if rivet is loose. Shake body to check that both ball valves are free. The idling mixture screw must have a point which is smooth and not bent. Check sizes of jets against those given in Technical Data.

Main jet:

These must be stamped with the prefix 'X'. In the case of hesitancy or flat spots with carburetters of early type having covers of an older design, try a main jet X125 instead of the X130 jet fitted.

Idle air bleed and metering jet:

The idle air bleed bore is now machined in the jet carrier. The original hole for the idle air bleed is blocked with a plug. Check the tapered seating of idle metering jet g (see **FIG 7**). Renew faulty parts.

Reassembling:

Do this in the reverse order to dismantling. When fitting the jet carrier make sure that the bottom gasket does not obstruct the idle mixture bore. Renew the O-ring at the top if it is deformed or stretched. Tighten the carrier screws alternately and a quarter of a turn at a time so that the gasket is not damaged. Poor sealing at this point causes abnormally high fuel consumption.

Tuning:

If the engine is run without the air filter there is considerable risk of a carburetter fire.

Large variations in altitude call for differing main jets. Change jet calibration by 6 per cent for each 1000 m (3280 feet) variation. Example - jet size at 400 m (1312 feet) is 125. At 1400 m (4592 feet) it should be 117.5.

Throttle linkage:

Regular lubrication of all joints will make for smooth operation. Place a small quantity of high melting point grease in the ball joint cups. Lubricate all moving joints with engine oil and put a drop or two on each accelerator pump linkage.

To remove and install the linkage under the floor, remove the mat to reveal the opening in the floor panel. Detach the throttle control from the ball joint at the front bellcrank. Withdraw the gearshift lever and fixture. Withdraw handbrake lever. This will leave room for access to the throttle linkage retaining clamps, which can now be removed. From under the transmission, detach the throttle control from the ball joint in the rear bellcrank. Withdraw the control rearwards.

Install in the reverse order, lubricating all ball joints and bellcrank pivots. Tighten ball joint locknuts securely.

Solex carburetter 1970 and later vehicles:

The 1970 and 71 models of the 911T are equipped with two triple throat Solex-Zenith 40 TIN type carburetters. The North American version embodies a mixture enrichment for overrun to meet the emission control standards. The engine types fitted with this system are the 911-03, 911-06, 911-07 and 911-08; the last two types specifically for the North American market. For the carburetter specifications refer to the Technical Data at the end of this manual.

The same types of carburetter are continued on the 1972 911 TV models with slight modifications to the size of jets. The engine types effected are the 911-57 and 911-67. These latest Solex-Zenith carburetter specifications are also included in the Technical Data.

The new Zenith carburetters have very similar physical characteristics to the triple throat, downdraught Weber carburetters fitted to earlier models, each having two float chambers and three venturi, one venturi to each cylinder. Each throat has an accelerating pump jet but unlike the Weber the jets on the Zenith are adjustable. The individual throttle valve shafts are interconnected by couplings with a lever attached at one end that has overall control when activated by the pedal; a pivot attached to the lever operates a rod that engages the accelerating pumps. An auxiliary enrichment system on the Zenith keeps the emissions to a minimum. The components parts of the Zenith 40TIN are illustrated in in exploded form in **FIG 12A**.

Removing and refitting:

1 Take off the top part of the air cleaner assembly complete with hoses.
2 Uncouple the fuel line and the actuating rod from the throttle valve lever.
3 Unscrew the retaining nuts, take off the spring washers and on the righthand carburetter disconnect the wire from the solenoid valve.
4 Disconnect the vacuum line and lift the multiple carburetter off the engine.
5 As a precaution cover up the intake stack openings.
6 Refit in the reverse sequence noting the following:
  Clean gasket surfaces and fit a new gasket and ensure the blanks in the gasket match the openings in the intake stack. Tighten retaining nuts evenly.
  On the righthand carburetter, reconnect the solenoid wire.
  Adjust the idling speed (see next heading).
  After installing air cleaner push the condensation drain hose onto the bottom part of the cleaner assembly.

Adjusting the idle speed:

Referring to **FIG 12B** each mixing throat has its own idling system and fuel is drawn from the float chamber via the main jet circuit, it is then metered by the idle jet and mixed with air drawn in through the idle air jet. The emulsified fuel is channelled through the casting and out of the discharge port below the closed throttle valve. The flow through the discharge port is regulated by the idle mixture control screw 9. Just above the throttle valve are the transition discharge ports from which emulsfied fuel is drawn during the initial opening of the throttle valve, to ensure a smooth transition during the interim between idle speed and high speed. The screw 7 regulates the flow of air that bypasses the throttle valve when it is in the closed position.

FIG 12 A Components of Solex-Zenith carburetter Type 40 TIN. If dismantling is necessary follow the numerical sequence

Nr.	Description	Qty.
1	Self-locking nut	6
2	Velocity stack	3
2a	Gasket	3
3	Clamp pan	1
4	Gasket	1
5	Threaded plug	2
6	Ring gasket	2
7	Float needle valve	2
8	Gasket	2
9	Hollow bolt	2
10	Gasket	2
11	Filtering screen	2
12	Connector	1
13	Gasket	2
14	Fillister head screw	12
15	Lock washer	12
16	Carburetor cover	1
17	Gasket	1
18	Round head screw	4
19	Float, complete	2
20	Pre-atomizer	3
21	Retaining clip	3
22	Venturi	3
23	Air correction jet	3
24	Emulsion tube	3
25	Pump inlet valve	6
26	Injection tube	3
27	Plug	3
28	Fuel jet for enrichment valve	1
29	Enrichment solenoid	1
30	Gasket	1
31	Fillister head screw	4
32	Lock washer	4
33	Pump shaft	
34	Round head screw	12
35	Pump cover	3
36	Diaphragm	3
37	Pump spring	3
38	Hollow bolt	1
39	Gasket	1
40	Fuel line, complete	1
41	Gasket	1
42	Fillister head screw	4
43	Lock washer	4
44	Fillister head screw	2
45	Lock washer	2
46	Enrichment valve top	1
47	O-ring	1
48	Diaphragm	1
49	Diaphragm plunger	1
50	Spring	1
51	Enrichment valve bottom	1
52	Idle jet	3
53	Air bypass control screw	3
54	Threaded plug	3
55	Auxiliary mixture control screw	1
56	Jet housing	3
57	Gasket	3
58	Main jet	3
59	Idle mixture control screw	3
60	Spring	3
61	Idle speed adjusting screw	1
62	Spring	1
63	Nut	1
64	Lock plate	1
65	Cam track	1
66	Spring washer	1
67	Carburetor housing	1

Key to Fig 12 A

FIG 12 B Schematic illustration of idling system

Key to Fig 12 B
1. Main jet housing
2. Double float
3. Fuel inlet line
4. Float needle valve
5. Float chamber
6. Main jet
7. Air bypass control screw
8. Throttle valve
9. Idle mixture control
10. Threaded plug
11. Idle jet
12. Idle air bleed

① Fuel inlet
② Induction air flow
④ Idle air inlet

FIG 12 C Adjustment screws

Key to Fig 12 C   a Idle speed   b Idle mixture control
c Air bypass control

Before adjusting the idle speed ensure the ignition timing and points gap are correct and bring the engine to operating temperature; oil temperature approximately 80°C. Close the hand throttle lever.

1 Take off the air cleaners and uncouple the actuating linkage from the cross-shaft.
2 Refer to **FIG 12 C** and for an initial workable setting screw the mixture controls screws (b) fully in—do not bottom too hard—and unwind them two and a half (2½) times.
3 Close the air-bypass control screws (c).
4 Start the engine and connect the P227 synchrotester, or any other suitable synchronizer, to the carburetters and make an initial adjustment to the carburetters serving the No. 1 and No. 4 cylinders by turning the idle speed screws (a) to obtain an idle speed of 1000 rev/min.

5 Synchronize cylinders 1-3 and 4-6 by adjusting the air by-pass control screws (c). It is very important to note two things at this stage. If there is one throat with a higher rate of air flow than the remaining two in the same bank—measured with all the air by-pass screws closed—the air by-pass screw on that particular throat must remain closed whilst the other throats of that cylinder bank are adjusted. And secondly, the air by-pass screws should be opened as little as possible.
6 Turn the idle mixture control screws (b) inwards to obtain a lean mixture, at which point the engine will begin to run unevenly, then unwind them slowly to a richer mixture until the engine gives the smoother performance.
7 If the idling speed changes after the last operation, readjust the screws (a) to obtain an equal air flow in the left and right banks and a conducive idling speed of 900±50 rev/min.
8 The exhaust emission CO value must now be checked if the vehicle is operating in CO value restricted areas. If the equipment is not available it should be done as soon as possible at the nearest service agency. The CO value should not exceed 3.5±.5%. Adjustment is made on the mixture control screws (b).
9 Reconnect the linkage, ensuring that the ball joints engage without preload and the cross-shaft does not stick or bind.

Auxiliary enrichment for overrun conditions:
Refer to FIG 12 D:

This system is not incorporated in all models, only those where emission control laws exist. The purpose of this system is to provide all cylinders with a correct amount of clean emulsified fuel to ensure combustion during overrun. Normally, most vehicles under closed throttle conditions, when the wheels are overrunning the engine, will burn or only partially burn the inducted and badly proportioned mixture in the cylinders. The result is a very high hydrocarbon emission in the exhausted gases.

The system comprises an auxiliary mixture valve 16, a solenoid valve 10 and a rev/min transducer. During overrun conditions at engine speeds above 1350 rev/min, the transducer activates the solenoid valve 10 and allows the high vacuum to reach the diaphragm 18 of the mixing valve. This causes the valve to open and release a flow of correctly proportioned air-fuel mixture into the induction manifolds..

Key to Fig 12 D
1. Velocity stack
2. Injection tube
3. Accelerator pump
4. Adjusting screw
5. Threaded plug
6. Fuel inlet
7. Float needle valve
8. Accelerator pump inlet valve
9. Double float
10. Enrichment solenoid
11. Vacuum line
12. Throttle valve
13. Air control screw
14. Connecting hose
15. Hollow bolt for vacuum line
16. Mixing valve
17. Flow rate adjusting screw
18. Diaphragm
19. Auxiliary mixture control screw
20. Nut
21. Stud

FIG 12 D Schematic illustration of overrun system

At overrun conditions below 1350 rev/min the mixing valve closes and the idle mixture circuit takes over.

When the throttle valves are reopened—acceleration—a micro switch on the throttle control linkage shuts off the enrichment device.

The two auxiliary enrichment valve assemblies are situated in the mixing throats that serve the No. 2 and No. 5 cylinders. Adjustment is possible, but tricky, and requires special testing equipment including a synchronizer and a gas analyzer in situ whilst the adjustments are being carried out. This is an operation that must be given to the service agency.

Adjusting injection quantity:

1 Refer to **FIG 12 E** (see - injection adjustment - section 7) to adjust the quantity noting the following and do not adjust whilst the engine is hot.
2 Adjust the screws (a) to bring the three actuating levers perfectly vertical. Loosen the adjusting nuts (b).
3 Check the pumps charging the venturi for Nos. 1 and 4 cylinders. First, turning the screws (b) until they just touch the pump plungers.
4 Measure the injection quantity as described in section 7 which should be, in this instance, .5±.1 cc per stroke. Adjust as necessary.
5 Adjust the remaining pumps.

FIG 12 E Accelerating jet adjustment screws

Key to Fig 12 E
a Actuating lever adjustment   b Actuating finger adjustment

NOTES

1 Pre-atomizer
2 Mixture delivery port
3 Air correction jet
4 Emulsion tube
5 Float
6 Float chamber
7 Float needle valve

Key to Fig 13

8 Float valve needle
9 Float pivot
10 Main metering jet
11 Fuel port
12 Emulsion tube well
13 Venturi

FIG 13 Diagrammatic sections through Weber triple-throat carburetter as fitted to engines after No. 907.000. There are two float chambers

8 The Weber carburetter

FIG 13 is a section through a Weber triple-throat assembly, each of the three carburetters feeding its own cylinder. The assembly is provided with two float chambers supplied by an electric fuel pump. The three views in **FIGS 13, 14** and **15** will help in understanding the operating principles.

During idling, fuel is drawn from well 12 through port 22 to idle metering jet 23 to mix with air from bleed 24 (see **FIG 14**). The mixture passes through port 21 to port 19, control screw 20 metering the quantity delivered to the intake. Above throttle valve 18 are two transition ports 15 which will also deliver mixture as the valve starts to open (see righthand view). To equalize air flow into the three carburetters at idling speeds, adjustment screws 16 are provided.

For normal operation, refer to **FIG 13**. From float chamber 6, fuel flows through main jet 10 and port 11 to emulsion tube well 12. Mixing with air from jet 3 it flows through holes in emulsion tube 4 and is delivered into pre-atomizer 1 and venturi 13 by way of port 2.

For accelerating, refer to **FIG 15**. Opening the throttle causes link 33 to operate cam 32 which presses diaphragm 30 to the left by means of lever 31. Fuel is forced past valve diaphragm 28 through port 37 (one for each carburetter) through opened valve 26 to discharge nozzle 25 and so into the throat of each carburetter to enrich the mixture. Retraction of the pump diaphragm to the right closes the valves and allows fuel to be drawn into the pumping chamber from the float chamber by way of check valve 36. This action takes place when the throttle is closing.

9 Servicing Weber carburetter

Adjusting idling:

Follow the instructions given for Solex carburetters in **Section 7**. If the intake air flow differs from throat to throat, turn the air adjustment screws 4 one of which is shown on the right in **FIG 16**. One idle mixture control screw 5 is shown in the same illustration.

Checking and adjusting float level:

The operation is shown in **FIG 16**, the gauge being P.226. Remove plug from float chamber to be checked and fit the gauge. Car must be standing level. Run engine at idling speed, when the fuel level should be between the two marks at the top of the glass. If level is incorrect, remove plug indicated by arrow in **FIG 17**, unscrew float needle valve from inside and fit a thicker gasket to raise the level or a thinner one to lower it. If this is not enough, slight bending of the float lever will help.

If the gauge is not available, the following figures may be useful in determining where the level should be. Distance from top of float to top edge of float housing without gasket should be 12.5 to 13.0 mm (.49 to .51 inch). Fuel level, when pump pressure is 3.6 lb/sq in, should be 20.5 to 21.0 mm (.81 to .83 inch) from top edge of housing. Variations of these figures are as follows:

Fuel level 20.75 ± 1 mm (.82 ± .04 inch) for 2000S cars starting with engine number 408.0773 (with Sportomatic, 418.0144). Also for 2000T cars fitted with type 40.IDT.3.C and 40.IDT.3.C1 carburetters and 2000 engines equipped with Exhaust Emission Control.

Checking pump injection quantity:

This operation will be similar to the one suggested in **Section 7** for the Solex carburetter. Note, however, that it is not possible to adjust the pump to alter the quantity injected.

Correct quantity per carburetter per stroke is .80 cc with a permissible variation of ± .20 cc. This variation is reduced to ± .10 cc on 2000S cars starting with engine number 408.0773 (with Sportomatic, 418.0144). On 2000T engines with type 40.IDT.3.C and 40.IDT.3.C1 carburetters the quantity is .50 ± 1 cc per stroke. This also applies to 2000' engines with Exhaust Emission Control.

Removing and refitting carburetters:

1 Remove hoses from air filter and oil filler. Withdraw air filter element. Unclip ducts from carburetters and lift off the air filter assembly.

2 Detach fuel hoses. Disconnect throttle control links from throttle levers.

3 Remove nuts from carburetter flanges and lift off assembly. **Take great care that the spring washers do not fall into the inlet ports.** Cover the ports to exclude dirt.

When refitting the carburetters, use new gaskets on the inlet flanges. Clean the flanges and make sure that the gasket does not overlap the port. Adjust the throttle control so that the throttle valves can be fully closed and adjust the idling speed.

FIG 15 Throttle opens and actuates diaphragm pump on Weber carburetter. Pump delivers fuel to discharge nozzle to enrich the mixture

Key to Fig 15

6 Float chamber
25 Pump discharge nozzle
26 Check valve
27 Disc
28 Diaphragm
29 Spring
30 Diaphragm
31 Lever
32 Cam
33 Connecting link
34 Lever
35 Port
36 Inlet check valve
37 Delivery port

FIG 14 Lefthand section shows delivery of idling mixture on Weber carburetter. Righthand view shows additional mixture being delivered by transition ports as throttle starts to open

Key to Fig 14

12 Emulsion tube well
14 Passage
15 Transition ports
16 Air adjustment screw
17 Air port
18 Throttle valve
19 Idle mixture discharge port
20 Idle mixture control screw
21 Delivery port
22 Fuel delivery port
23 Idle metering jet
24 Idle air bleed

FIG 16 Weber carburetters. Float level gauge P.226 attached to side of float chamber. Level is marked on glass tube

Key to Fig 16

1 Main jet carrier
2 Idle metering jet
3 Venturi setscrew
4 Air adjusting screw
5 Idle mixture control screw

FIG 17 Top cover of Weber carburetters showing fuel feed detached. Arrows point to plugs over the float needle valves

FIG 18 Dismantling details on Weber carburetters

Key to Fig 18   1 Air correction jet   2 Accelerator pump
check valve   3 Pre-atomizer   4 Float pivot pin

Dismantling carburetters:

1 Remove carburetter top (see **FIG 17**). Detach fuel feed assembly, as shown. Remove plugs arrowed and unscrew float needle valves from inside.

2 Refer to **FIG 16** and remove main jet carrier 1, air adjustment screw 4, the stop screw adjacent to screw 4, the idle metering jet 2, and the venturi setscrew 3 from each carburetter.

3 Refer to **FIG 18**, unscrew air correction jet 1 and withdraw the emulsion tube. If it sticks, push in a tapered drift to gain a hold. Remove check valve and nozzle 2.

4 Withdraw pre-atomizer 3 followed by the venturi (see 13 in **FIG 13**). Remove float pivot pin 4 and withdraw float.

5 Remove pump cover 4 nuts). Remove diaphragms, disc, springs and valve (see **FIG 15**).

Clean all parts with fuel and compressed air. **Do not push wire or a needle through the jets, as enlargement will affect performance.** Jets are stamped with an identifying number. Correct sizes are given in Technical Data. The idle air bleed is drilled into the body and cannot be renewed. Check fit of throttle valve spindles in body. Excessive wear will allow air to upset the correct mixture. Throttle valve must close to a light-tight fit. Check pump diaphragms and renew if deteriorated. Renew idle and air adjustment screws if tips are deformed or broken.

Reassembling:

Do this in the reverse order of dismantling. Wire the setscrews which secure the venturis. Adjust so that the throttle valves close completely and refit controls so that there is no strain. Adjust for correct idling. Lubricate all ball joints.

10 The fuel tank

To remove the tank, work under the car at the front to remove the drain plug, having a container handy to catch the fuel. Detach both fuel lines. Remove spare wheel and padding from front compartment. Pull off the vent hose and the fuel gauge cable. Remove fuel filler hose and after removing three Allen screws, lift the tank up and away.

When refitting the tank, renew the support gasket if damaged. Clear the vent hose with compressed air. Detach fuel line from electric pump, use compressed air to clear the pipes and then reconnect.

NOTES

11 Fuel injection system

The fuel injection pump can only be adjusted with an exhaust emission analyzer. During the emission test, the CO components in the exhaust gases are measured.

The CO rating is also influenced by the general engine condition (timing, valve clearance, compression, spark plugs, etc.), by proper correlation of the throttle valves and injection pump, the operating temperature and the intake air temperature. Incorrect measurements will result if these conditions are not within tolerances.

FIG 19 Layout of fuel injection system fitted to 1969 models of 911E and 911S cars

Key to Fig 19

1 Fuel delivery pump
2 Fuel tank
3 Fuel filter
4 Solenoid for cold starting unit
5 Injection valve
6 Injection line
7 Injection pump

This was introduced on 911E and 911S cars, starting with the 1969 models. **FIG 19** shows the layout diagrammatically.

The object of the system is to inject an exact quantity of fuel into the desired inlet port to produce correct combustion. Chief advantages are greater power, improved acceleration, easier cold starting and lower fuel consumption.

A pump with six plungers 7 is driven by belt from the lefthand camshaft. Fuel is supplied to the pump by another pump 1, delivery being through a filter 3. The six plungers are operated by a camshaft and they force fuel at a pressure of 220 to 265 lb/sq in into pipes which are connected to injectors 5. Injection is timed so that fuel is discharged from an injector onto an inlet valve just as it begins to open.

The throttle valves are connected together and are also linked to the pump control lever. To compensate for changes in air pressure, engine speed and variations in load there is a centrifugal governor connected to the pump control rack, and movement of the rack is also controlled by a barometric cell, a thermostat, an enrichment solenoid and a shut-off solenoid. All these devices work to compensate for the variations and to ensure that the correct quantity of fuel is injected to suit the requirements. The arrangement of the parts is shown in **FIG 20**.

Cam 13 is moved axially by governor 14 and turned by the accelerator pedal. Sensor 1 transfers movement to control rack 9 in the injection pump. Barometric cell 5 compensates for changes in ambient air pressure in the same way as an aneroid barometer. Thermostat 4 responds to engine cooling air temperature to enrich the mixture for cold starting. Enrichment solenoid 3 is controlled by time-limit and temperature-limit switches so that it gives a rich mixture for starting, over a 2-second period or for longer at low temperatures. Shut-off solenoid 16 is controlled by a throttle valve microswitch and a rev/min transducer to stop fuel delivery from the injection pump when coasting in gear.

The action of the compensating devices is cumulative and is transferred to the pump rack by connecting levers.

Key to Fig 20

1. Sensor on contoured cam
2. Control rack head
3. Enrichment solenoid
4. Thermostat
5. Barometric cell
6. Check valve
7. Plunger unit
8. Toothed segment
9. Control rack
10. Roller tappet
11. Camshaft
12. Governor control lever
13. Contoured cam
14. Centrifugal governor
15. Idle adjusting screw
16. Shut-off solenoid

FIG 20 Control and compensating units on fuel injection system. These govern fuel injection quantity through the control rack

Key to Fig 21

1. Thermostat
2. Compensating lever
3. Thermostat connecting sleeve
4. Cross-arm
5. Support
6. Guide stud
7. Barometric cell
8. Guide
9. Injector line fitting
10. Check valve
11. Plunger unit
12. Fuel inlet
13. Toothed segment
14. Plunger spring
15. Engine oil return
16. Engine oil inlet
17. Pump drive wheel
18. Support flange
19. Camshaft
20. Roller tappet
21. Contoured cam spring
22. Contoured cam
23. Sensor
24. Centrifugal governor weight
25. Idle speed adjustment
26. Shut-off solenoid
27. Access to control rack head
28. Enrichment solenoid

FIG 21 Cutaway view of fuel injection pump

Injection pump:

This is illustrated in **FIG 21**. The compensating parts shown in **FIG 20** may also be seen in this view, together with the pump camshaft 19, the roller tappets 20, the injection plungers 11 and toothed segments 13 which engage with the rack to control the volume of fuel injected.

There are six cylinders and plungers 11, the plungers being reciprocated by roller tappets operated by the camshaft. The plungers may be turned by the rack, and as they are provided with cut-off lands, timing of fuel inlet duration to the pumping cylinder is obtained. The plunger land acts as an inlet valve in conjunction with a port in the side of the cylinder. Fuel is forced from the pump cylinders into pipelines connected to the injectors in the engine cylinder heads. At a pressure of 220 to 265 lb/sq in, check valves in the injector nozzles open and fuel is sprayed onto the opening inlet valves.

Modifications:

In 1972 the 911T was converted to a fuel injection system but with added improvements which are embodied also in the 'E' and 'S' types. Some of the main improvements include, a different type injection pump that has a wider contoured cam and modified weights and springs. Also a different throttle valve housing and intake manifold, whereby the throttle valve stops in the housing are relocated to the lever side. The new air intake velocity stacks are manufactured from plastic, which now forms a single unit with the lower air assembly; fuel for cold starting is fed directly into each individual velocity stack. The new discharge nozzles are bonded and cannot be repaired they must be renewed with a complete injection nozzle. Finally, a new induction air preheating system has been installed to reduce the exhaust emission values and at the same time provide an even induction air temperature, particularly in the lower engine speed ranges.

12 Fault diagnosis (fuel injection systems)

Symptom	Cause	Remedy
Hard starting when engine is cold	Improper starting procedure	Pull hand throttle valve up to stop at all outside temperatures. Do not use accelerator pedal when starting vehicle. When the engine starts, run for a short period in the preset hand throttle position. Then step on accelerator pedal until engine is running at approximately 4500 rpm. Release accelerator pedal and push hand throttle lever back until engine runs at approx. 1200 - 1400 rpm. If the engine speed increases as the temperature increases, set the hand throttle lever back accordingly until it rests against the bottom stop. If the engine does not start after 10 - 15 seconds, wait for 10 seconds and start again.
	Enrichment solenoid does not activate. Starting relay defective, Time limit relay for enrichment solenoid defective or response period too short.	Check electrical connections and voltage. Replace enrichment solenoid starting relay, as well as time limit relay, if necessary.
	Thermo-limit switch for cold starting device at outside temperatures below -10°C ($+14^\circ$F).	Replace thermo-limit switch.
Hard starting when engine is hot	Improper starting procedure	Before starting a hot engine, the ignition should be turned on for approximately 5 seconds so that any vapor that may have formed in the system will be flushed out. Depress accelerator fully while starting.
	Enrichment solenoid does not activate.	Check connections and voltage on enrichment solenoid.
	Starting relay defective	Replace starting relay.
	Control rod remains in starting position.	Check to see that control rack is released after approximately 2 seconds. Check relay, enrichment solenoid and time limit relay, replace if necessary.
	Time control switch defective	Replace time control switch.

continued

Symptom	Cause	Remedy
Rough engine idle	Idle air control on throttle valve housing incorrectly adjusted.	Adjusting air control screws with synchrometer P 235 (at 3000 rpm).
	Timing off.	Adjusting firing point (idling speed $0°$ to $-2°$, at 6000 rpm $30° - 32°$).
	Restricted warm air flow to thermostat (engine excessively oily).	Eliminate restriction in lines, replace lines.
	Thermostat on injection pump defective (engine excessively oily).	Replace thermostat.
	Injection valves defective	Check injection jet, replace valve if necessary.
	Compression of individual cylinders varies	Check compression or pressure loss and make required adjustment.
	Cold weather starting device does not shut off.	Check cold weather starting device.
Engine won't start	Fuel delivery pump inoperative	Check power supply, replace pump if necessary.
	Fuel delivery pump running but with insufficient or no delivery	Check hose connections (suction-pressure-bypass), check voltage and current draw on electrical connections. Check fuel filter, replace if necessary.
	Starting relay defective	Replace starting relay
	Thermo-time switch defective	Replace thermo-time switch
	Control rack stuck	Replace injection pump
	Time limit relay switch defective	Replace time-limit relay
Engine won't start at temperatures below $-10°C$	Cold starting device not operating	Check electrical connections, check voltage on electrical connections.

continued

Symptom	Cause	Remedy
Engine misfires	Ignition system not in order	Check ignition system
	Fuel filter contaminated	Replace filter element
	Injection valves not in order	Check injection valves, replace if necessary
	Insufficient delivery of fuel delivery pump	Check delivered quantity, check hose connections as well as electrical connections on pump, install new pump if necessary
Poor transition during acceleration with warm engine (jerking and backfiring)	Injection pump adjustment not in order	Check adjustment with exhaust gas tester, adjust if necessary
	Improper linkage correlation	Check coordination and linkage correlation, adjust if necessary
Backfiring under overrunning conditions	Throttle valve housing not synchronized	Synchronize throttle valve housing with synchrometer P 235
	Micro switch out of adjustment	Adjust micro switch, replace if necessary
	Rpm transducer defective	Replace rpm transducer (speed switch)

12 Fault diagnosis (carburetter systems)

(a) Fuel delivery nil or erratic

1 Tank vent blocked
2 Fuel pipes blocked
3 Air leaks on inlet side of pumps
4 Pump valves stuck or faulty
5 Pump diaphragm or spring faulty
6 Blocked pump filter

(b) Electric pump inoperative

1 Faulty electrical connections
2 Contact points dirty or out of adjustment (Hardi)
3 Breakdown of solenoid

(c) Engine will not start with adequate fuel supply and ignition working

1 Check (b)
2 Mechanical fuel pumps not working
3 Engine flooded by repeated throttle opening with engine not running

(d) Uneven idling

1 Faulty ignition
2 Idling speed adjusting screw damaged
3 Jets blocked
4 Sparking plugs fouled
5 Air leaks into inlet duct

(e) Uneven running

1 Check 5 in (d)
2 Mixture too rich or too weak
3 Incorrect idling adjustment, throttles not synchronized
4 Lower gasket of jet carrier not sealing (Solex)
5 Float chamber vent hose blocked

(f) Hesitancy or 'flat spots'

1 Check 4 and 5 in (d) and 3 in (e)
2 Incorrect injection quantity

(g) Engine stalls on sudden throttle closure

1 Check 3 in (e)
2 Throttle damper ineffective (Solex)

NOTES

CHAPTER 3 - IGNITION SYSTEM

1. General description
2. Routine maintenance
3. Ignition problems
4. Removing and refitting distributor
5. Ignition timing
6. Servicing distributor
7. Sparking plugs
8. Capacitive Discharge (CDS) ignition system
9. Fault diagnosis

1 General description

The ignition system comprises a battery, an ignition coil, a distributor and the sparking plugs. The distributor is driven by a spiral gear on the rear end of the crankshaft (see **Chapter 1**), and cams on its rotating shaft open the points of a contact breaker. At each moment of breaking, high-tension electricity is induced in the coil and this is fed back to the central terminal in the distributor cap. Connected to this terminal is a spring-loaded brush which bears on the brass electrode of a rotor arm at the top end of the distributor shaft. As the shaft revolves, the rotor segment comes opposite each one of six brass terminals in the cap in turn. It does not actually touch the terminals but high-tension electricity is able to jump the small gaps. The terminals are connected by leads to the sparking plugs in the correct firing order (see Technical Data).

The 911T model is fitted with a Marelli distributor, type S112.AX and the other models with a Bosch distributor, type JF.DR6. Automatic centrifugal advance mechanism is incorporated in both types, but the Marelli is unique because the cam weights are not in the usual position below the contact breaker but are housed above it (see **FIG 1**). If a car is equipped with exhaust emission control the distributor has vacuum control in addition to the centrifugal mechanism (see assembly 34 in **FIG 4**).

The Marelli S 112 AX distributor

The Marelli distributor can be easily distinguished from the Bosch distributors due to a different shape of housing and higher distributor cap.

2 Routine maintenance

Marelli distributor:

Every 6000 miles apply a thin smear of grease to the contact breaker cams. At the same intervals, check the ignition timing (see **Section 5**) and check the contact breaker gap. To check and adjust the gap, refer to **FIG 1**.

Remove rotor (two screws, upper view). Turn crankshaft by means of pulley until a cam has lifted the breaker arm to give the maximum gap between the contact points. Measure the gap with feeler gauges as shown in the lower view. If the gap is not .4 ± .03 mm (.016 ± .001 inch), loosen the front retaining screw of the fixed contact plate, adjust until the gap is correct and re-tighten screw. **After every adjustment, always check the ignition timing** (see **Section 5**).

FIG 1 Removing rotor arm on Marelli distributor (top). Adjusting gap between contact breaker points (bottom). Arrow points to distributor securing nut

Marelli distributor (1972 models):

Note that the rotor on the new Marelli distributor is retained by a screw, loosen the screw to remove the rotor. The clearance of the contact breaker gap remains the same, however, it is important to check also the dwell angle and if necessary readjust the gap to obtain a correct dwell angle of 40±3 deg. Accurate dwell angle testing equipment is normally available only to the service agents although there may be some cheaper, and possibly less accurate, testers obtainable through some retail markets.

Check the ignition timing after adjusting the dwell angle; this is most important.

FIG 2 Adjusting contact breaker points gap on Bosch distributor. Loosening fixing screw (left) and checking gap with feelers (right)

FIG 3 Rotor arm vertically above notch on rim of distributor body to give TDC on No. 1 cylinder

Bosch distributor:

Every 6000 miles, remove cap and rotor arm and apply a thin smear of non-corrosive, high temperature grease to the cams (see arrow in lefthand view of **FIG 2**). Take care no grease gets onto the contact points.

Every 6000 miles check the contact points gap and adjust if necessary. Remove cap and rotor arm and turn crankshaft pulley until a cam has fully raised the breaker arm. Check gap with feeler gauges as shown in righthand view of **FIG 2**. Correct gap is .40 mm (.016 inch). To adjust gap, loosen screw indicated, insert screwdriver in slot adjacent and twist it between the two pips on the base plate to move the contact plate. On early models, turn the eccentric screw. Tighten screw when gap is correct. **Always check the ignition timing after adjusting the points gap** (see **Section 5**).

Since April 1970, for the 911TC models, a Bosch distributor was fitted if optionally preferred. The advance curve of 35 deg. BTDC at 6000 rev/min remained the same. The distributor type is Bosch 0231 159 008 J.FDR(R).

Distributor cap and contact breaker:

At regular intervals, remove the cap and clean it thoroughly. The inside surfaces must be clean and dry. Check central brush by pressing it in. It should spring out again. Slight erosion of the brass terminals is normal.

If dirty, clean the contact points with fuel on a cloth. Slight corrosion may be rectified with a fine file, but the mating surfaces must be quite flat and must meet squarely. The best cure for contact breaker troubles is to fit a new set.

Sparking plugs and leads:

Check plug gaps every 6000 miles. As Bosch W265.P21 plugs have platinum electrodes, gap adjustment should be unnecessary. Gap should be .35 mm (.014 inch). Check the gap for other makes by referring to Technical Data. Electrodes must be clean and bright and the gap must be adjusted by bending the outer electrode only. Have carbon deposits removed in a sand-blasting machine and then have plugs checked under pressure.

Check sparking plug leads for cracks and deterioration. Insulation failure may sometimes be seen as a bluish discharge when running the engine in the dark.

3 Ignition problems

If the engine refuses to fire, check HT (high-tension) lead between centre of distributor cap and ignition coil for good contact. Pull lead out of cap and hold about 6 mm ($\frac{1}{4}$ inch) from a good earth (not a carburetter). Keep fingers away from end of lead and operate the starter. Sparks should jump the gap.

If no sparks, connect a 12-volt test bulb between terminal 1 on the distributor body and a good earth. Switch on ignition and operate starter. If light goes on and off, the coil primary is in order. If lamp stays alight while engine is turning over, check contact breaker points for dirt or too wide a gap. If lamp does not light, there may be a break in the coil primary or the points may not be opening properly. Check for loose cable connections, earthed wire to distributor and try substituting a coil which is known to work. Make sure contacts close and that breaker spring is not broken.

Failure to trace an ignition fault should lead to a check of the ignition timing and the fuel system, followed by mechanical checks on the engine.

4 Removing and refitting distributor

On all types, remove nut and washer indicated by arrow in the lower view of **FIG 1**. Do not slacken long clamp bolt or timing will be lost. Lift out distributor. Check gear and shaft for wear. Fit new sealing ring on neck.

To refit, turn crankshaft pulley until Z1 mark is aligned with crankcase joint or mark on blower rim (see **Section 5**). Piston of No. 1 cylinder should then be at TDC on the firing stroke. Set rotor arm on distributor so that it points in the direction of the rear edge of the blower while inserting neck of distributor in crankcase. The arm will move as the gears engage. Slacken the long bolt on the split clamp plate and turn the distributor to the left until the contact breaker just opens. The tip of the rotor arm should then be vertically over a notch on the rim of the distributor body. This position is shown in **FIG 3**. Check the timing as instructed in the following Section.

5 Ignition timing

Marelli:

Having set the contact breaker gap correctly, set the basic ignition timing at TDC on the firing stroke of No. 1 cylinder as described at the start of the preceding Section. Run engine up to operating temperature and connect a stroboscope. Note before starting the engine, that there are two marks on the crankshaft pulley rim to the right of the TDC mark (Z1). These indicate positions 30 deg. and 35 deg. BTDC when aligned with the crankcase joint or mark on blower rim. Gradually increase engine speed and watch the Z1 mark move to the left. At 6000 rev/min the 35 deg. mark should be in-line with the joint or mark.

When the setting is correct at this speed there may be a change in the basic setting but this does not matter. With engine stationary the basic timing may be up to 3 deg. ATDC. Make adjustments by slackening clamp plate bolt and turning distributor.

Bosch:

With correct breaker gap, set basic timing as described in **Section 4**. Check the timing at 6000 rev/min as instructed in the preceding notes on the Marelli distributor. For 2000S engines the 30 deg. BTDC mark on the pulley must line up with the crankcase joint or mark on blower rim, and basic timing at a standstill may be a minimum of 5 deg. BTDC. For other 2000 engines except 2000T, the timing should be the same at 6000 rev/min but may be out by a maximum of 5 deg. ATDC at a standstill.

If the car is fitted with exhaust emission control (EECS) it will also be fitted with a Bosch distributor incorporating vacuum control. The basic timing must be carried out with a stroboscope so that it is 3 deg. ATDC at 850 to 950 rev/min. At 6000 rev/min it should be 30 deg. ± 2 deg. BTDC. If the ignition point is not within the tolerances given, the 3 deg. ATDC setting may be altered in the range 2 to 5 deg. ATDC. Make adjustments by slackening the clamp plate bolt and turning the distributor body.

Note that engines from No. 902.029 onwards have a distributor with a basic timing of 5 deg. BTDC. The distributor is marked with a yellow dot or may be stamped 5 deg. v.OT (5 deg. BTDC). This type of distributor may be fitted to earlier engines as a replacement unit.

Marelli and Bosch (1972 models on):

Regarding the checking of the ignition timing by a stroboscope timing light, the distributors of the 1972 models have slightly different advance curves.

With the vacuum hose connected, at 900 ± 50 rev/min the mark on the left side of the Z1 mark, which is the 5 deg. ATDC mark, must line up with the mark on the fan housing. Adjust, if necessary, as previously described.

The idle speed timing adjustment must be checked and corrected before the maximum advance curves are checked, the latter being checked with the vacuum hose disconnected.

At 1000 rev/min—5 deg. BTDC
At 1500 rev/min—10 deg. BTDC
At 2000 rev/min—20 deg. BTDC
At 4000 rev/min—27 deg. BTDC
At 6000 rev/min maximum advance should be between 32 and 35 deg. BTDC.

Pulley marks:

Marks on the crankshaft pulley rim give a timing BTDC when to the right of the Z1 mark (TDC). For 5 deg. BTDC make a mark 5 mm (.197 inch) to the right. Intermediate marks may be set out using similar calculations.

Timing with test lamp:

Basic ignition timing may be carried out using a test lamp between side terminal 1 on the distributor body and an earth. Turn on the ignition switch. Slacken clamp plate bolt and turn distributor clockwise until points are closed. The Z1 pulley mark must be aligned with the crankcase joint or mark on blower rim. Turn distributor slowly in opposite direction until points open and light goes on. Tighten clamp bolt. The rotor arm must be over the distributor body notch as mentioned at the beginning of **Section 4** and the timing will then be correct for No. 1 cylinder. Proceed to set the timing with a stroboscope as instructed earlier in this Section.

In all these adjustments, remember that alterations to the points gap will affect the ignition timing.

6 Servicing distributor

Marelli:

It is necessary to remove the distributor to renew the contact breaker parts. Detach wire from terminal 1 on side of distributor and also remove cap and plug leads as an assembly. Remove nut holding clamp plate to crankcase and lift distributor away. Do not disturb the long bolt in the clamping plate. Take rotor off (see upper view in **FIG 1**). Remove breaker set complete with stationary plate. After fitting a new breaker, adjust the gap and then check the ignition timing.

Renew rotor if electrode is badly eroded or if plastic part is cracked. Check action of centrifugal weights and springs, renewing faulty parts.

It is difficult for the normal owner to check the capacitor (condenser) for faults. Symptoms may be poor performance, difficult starting and rapid contact point erosion due to arcing which the capacitor is designed to prevent. Substitution with a new condenser is the quickest and easiest method of checking.

Bosch:

FIG 4 is representative of the components of the Bosch distributor fitted to Porsche 911 cars. There may be some variations between early and late models but none which make servicing difficult when following the instructions. Note that the vacuum unit 34 is fitted only to cars with exhaust emission control (EECS).

To renew the contact points, remove cap 4 and rotor 3. Loosen nut of terminal assembly. Remove lock ring from pivot of moving contact arm (part of 1). Lift off arm. Remove screw and lift off fixed contact plate (part of 1). Renew points which are pitted or badly worn. A kit is inexpensive and engine performance will suffer if defective points are overlooked.

Check the distributor cap for dirt and cracks. Black 'tracking' marks on the inside surface may be due to insulation breakdown. Renew cap if brass terminals are eroded, but note that slight erosion is normal. Renew rotor arm if electrode is badly eroded. Check carbon brush in centre of cap. When pressed in it should spring out again.

FIG 4 Component parts of typical Bosch distributor.

Check action of centrifugal advance mechanism 8, 9 and 10. Turn rotor arm clockwise till it stops and then release it. If the mechanism is free and the springs in order, the arm should return smartly to its original position.

Dismantling Bosch distributor:

Remove side terminal and screws and lift out contact plate 7. Make a careful note of the exact positions of insulating washers on terminal. Remove vacuum unit if fitted. Lift out camshaft 10 and centrifugal mechanism. Drive out pin 31, pull off gear 14 and push drive shaft out of body after removing any burrs. Note position of metal and fibre thrust washers. **Do not put body in solvent, or self-lubricating qualities of bushes 12 and felt 13 will be impaired.** Have bushes and shaft renewed if worn.

Check condition of gear and thrust washers. Check pins, springs and weights of centrifugal mechanism. Check vacuum unit under suction to see that diaphragm is sound. Renew all faulty parts.

Reassemble in the reverse order of dismantling, making sure that the thrust washers and insulating washers are correctly positioned. Put a drop of oil on the weight pivots and oil the felt pad inside the top end of the camshaft. Put a tiny drop of oil on the contact breaker pivot, but be careful to keep all lubricants from the contact points.

7 Sparking plugs and leads:

Correct sparking plugs for the various models are listed in Technical Data. Carry out routine maintenance and adjustment as instructed in **Section 2**.

To check the appearance of the plugs, remove them as soon as the engine has stopped after running under operating conditions. Do not let the engine idle.

If the deposits at the firing end are white, the plug has been running at a high temperature possibly due to weak mixture. Light tan-coloured deposits indicate the use of the correct grade of plug and good operating conditions. Fluffy black deposits are caused by rich mixture, but if the deposits are wet and black it is a sign of oiling up due to piston or cylinder wear.

HT leads (1972 models on):

The ignition lead lengths have been changed for the 1972 models and it is important that the lead lengths are maintained to ensure the radio is free from interference.

No. 1 HT lead—330 mm (13 inch)
No. 2 HT lead—390 mm ($15\frac{11}{32}$ inch)
No. 3 HT lead—510 mm ($20\frac{5}{64}$ inch)
No. 4 HT lead—880 mm ($34\frac{21}{32}$ inch)
No. 5 HT lead—900 mm ($35\frac{7}{16}$ inch)
No. 6 HT lead—990 mm (39 inch).

8 Capacitive Discharge (CDS) ignition system

General description:

Since 1971 all 911 models are equipped with a Capacitive Discharge Ignition System (CDS). The advanatages of this system over the conventional induction coil system are that it eliminates current leakage, such as through carbon or lead deposits; there is a higher voltage available for cold starting; there is no voltage drop at high speeds and practically no wearing of the contact breaker points.

The components of the system are shown in **FIG 5** and a schematic wiring diagram in **FIG 6**. The housing of the CDS unit is made from light alloy, cast with cooling fins to help dissipate heat generated by the system. The voltage transformer looks very similar to a conventional coil, but there the similarity ends as the resistance, voltage gain ratio and inductivity completely differ; the transformer has been specially designed and constructed to match the specific electrical characteristics of the CDS unit.

Referring to **FIG 6** when the ignition is switched on the DC converter 5 increases the battery voltage from 12 volts to 450 volts and changes the storage capacitor 7 through periodic impulses at a frequency of approximately 3000 Hz., which produces a high pitched whistle in the DC converter. When the contact breaker points 3 open the igniter trigger unit 8 releases an impulse to the thyristor base 9 which becomes conductive. The storage capacitor then discharges through the thyristor and the voltage transformer 10, causing a high voltage surge on the secondary side that is carried through to the distributor and thence to the sparking plugs. With this system the voltage rise at the sparking plug occurs much faster and current losses, that occur with most conventional systems, are vitually eliminated.

Beginning with the 1972 Type 911 Vehicles, the distributor fitted may be either Bosch or Marelli, both have the same characteristics but they are different to the ones previously fitted, although engine governors continue to be used. A centrifugal weight built into the rotor of each distributor short circuits the secondary side of the ignition system at a predetermined cut off speed. The distributors are identical throughout the new ranges of models with the exception of the rotors which have different cut-off speeds. Refer to the Technical Data section to obtain the correct type for each model.

Checking the CDS ignition system:

To ensure personal safety and to prevent damage to the CDS unit, the following rules should be observed when performing tests.

(a) Do not attach instruments or components such as a suppressor, test light or stroboscopic timing light to terminal 15, it carries 460 volts.

(b) The ignition voltage transformer cannot be replaced with a conventional induction coil and neither can it be wired or tested as a coil.

(c) Do not stop the engine by placing a jump wire or any other conductor between terminal 15 and earth.

(d) Disconnect the battery earth straps when working on a CDS unit.

(e) Ensure the ignition is switched off before connecting or disconnecting wires and always make sure the dust cover is properly installed on terminal 15.

(f) If a battery is being recharged in situ, the supply and earth straps must be disconnected.

(g) Do not use a battery boost quick charger to start the engine.

(h) Ensure the battery is properly connected, i.e. positive to positive and negative to negative.

(i) Do not touch the leads of the voltage transformer shortly after its removal, there still may be a charge between terminal 'A' and earth which cannot be released by grounding. Do not touch the leads when operating the CDS unit on a test bench or in the car without the transformer; in such cases where the storage capacitor is defective due to an inter-terminal short.

FIG 5 Components of Capacitive Discharge System

Key to Fig 5
1 CDS unit
2 Ignition voltage transformer
3 RPM sensor

FIG 6 Schematic wiring diagram of CD system

Key to Fig 6

1 Ignition switch
2 Battery
3 Breaker points
4 CDS unit
5 DC converter (amplifier)
6 Rectifier
7 Storage capacitor
8 Ignition trigger unit
9 Thyristor (load-sensitive switch)
10 Ignition voltage transformer

Checking system in vehicles:

1 First check the breaker points and all electrical connections.

2 Switch on the ignition. The CDS unit should make a whistling sound, if not, remove the connection from the CDS unit and connect a voltmeter between terminal 'B' (centre terminal of connector) and earth. With the ignition switched on it should read at least 11 volts. It is possible for this reading to be recorded and there is still no whistling sound when the connector is re-plugged in. In these instances and where there is no reading, the CDS unit must be renewed.

3 If the whistle is audible, check terminal 4 for high voltage by disconnecting the HT lead from the voltage transformer and connecting a spark monitor, adjusted to a 10 mm (.40 inch) spark gap. Crank the engine with starter and if there is no spark or if it occurs only infrequently, complete checks 4 and 5.

4 Remove all connections from the transformer. With an ohm meter measure the resistance in the primary coil between terminals 1 and 15. It should be between .4 and .6 ohms. Measure the resistance in the secondary coil between terminals 1 and 4; the value should be between 650 and 790 ohms.

5 Check the CDS unit current draw. Connect an ammeter into wire 15, at the coupling from the ignition switch. Disconnect the distributor terminal 1 wire to prevent an incorrect reading. The current draw should be between 1.0 and 1.9 amps, if not, renew the CDS unit. Voltage at the unit between terminal 'B' and earth must be at least 11 volts, this can be measured by connecting an additional voltmeter between the ammeter input (+ terminal) and earth. After completing the test, reconnect the distributor terminal 1 wire.

6 The rev/min sensor can be checked only with an ohmmeter. The measured resistance between terminals 'A' and 'B' must be within a range of 170-210 ohms and between terminals A and C, 200 to 300 ohms.

9 Fault diagnosis

(a) Engine will not fire

1 Battery discharged
2 Contact breaker points dirty, pitted or out of adjustment
3 Distributor cap dirty, cracked or 'tracking'
4 Carbon brush inside distributor not in contact with rotor arm
5 Faulty cables or loose connections in the low-tension circuit
6 Distributor rotor arm cracked
7 Faulty coil or coil lead to distributor
8 Broken contact breaker spring
9 Contact points stuck open
10 Faulty capacitor (condenser)
11 Faulty ignition switch

(b) Engine misfires

1 Check 2, 3, 5 and 7 in (a)
2 Weak contact breaker spring
3 Plug or coil high-tension leads cracked or perished
4 Loose sparking plugs
5 Sparking plug insulation cracked
6 Sparking plug gap incorrect
7 Ignition timing too far advanced or retarded

CHAPTER 4
COOLING, HEATING AND EXHAUST EMISSION CONTROL

1 Description of cooling system
2 Routine maintenance of cooling system
3 Removing and refitting blower
4 Removing and refitting covers and deflectors
5 Silencer and heat exchangers
6 Heating system and controls
7 Exhaust emission control system
8 Fault diagnosis

1 Description of cooling system

The air required for engine cooling is produced by a belt-driven blower (see 7 in **FIG 2** in Chapter **1**).

The air is propelled forward into a large glass-fibre reinforced plastic cover which extends sideways to carry it to the two banks of cylinders and cylinder heads. The bowed outline of this cover can be seen immediately above the crankcase and cylinders in **FIG 1** Chapter **1**). After passing down between the fins of the cylinders and heads, some of the air is deflected upwards by shrouds or deflectors as shown in **FIG 35** Chapter **1**).

2 Routine maintenance of cooling system

This is confined to adjustment of the driving belt for the blower and alternator. The method is shown in **FIG 1**.

Check tension by pressing belt inwards about midway between the pulleys. Light thumb pressure should deflect it 15 to 20 mm (.60 to .80 inch). A belt which is too tight puts a greater strain on the alternator bearings and is more liable to break. A slack belt may slip, causing overheating problems and lower output from the alternator.

To adjust tension, remove nut from blower pulley shaft. A steel bar with pegs, similar to tool No. P208, can be used to engage the holes in the pulley flange to hold it still. Remove washer and any spacers which may be fitted. Remove the belt flange.

Removal of spacers from between the pulley flanges will tighten the belt and vice versa. Spacers from between the flanges must be added to those outside so that the total number of washers remains unaltered. A belt which is so stretched or worn that only one spacer remains between the flanges must be renewed. A belt must not run on the bottom of the pulley groove.

Tighten pulley nut to 29 lb ft torque. Check the belt tension. If a new belt is fitted, check the tension after 50 miles of running, as the belt will stretch slightly.

Never remove a belt by levering it over the pulley with a screwdriver. Belts contaminated with oil may be cleaned in a detergent solution and rinsed in water. Any signs of cracking or of frayed edges call for renewal.

3 Removing and refitting blower

The blower is mounted on the alternator shaft and the assembly must be removed complete (engine in or out of car). Details of the mounting can be seen in **FIG 2** in chapter **1** and **FIG 2** this chapter. Proceed as follows:
 1 Remove screws securing upper air channel. Remove belt (see **Section 2**).
 2 Slacken clip surrounding blower housing. Pull housing and alternator to the rear. Mark cables for correct position before detaching from alternator.
 3 Refit in the reverse order, making sure that dowel for blower housing is correctly located.

4 Removing and refitting covers and deflectors

The arrow in **FIG 3** points to the top cover or upper air channel. To remove it, first detach the carburetters and intake pipes (see **Chapter 2**). Next, remove the rear coverplate and the fuel pipes which pass over the blower housing (see **FIG 2**). Remove the air hoses to heat exchangers and the hot air ducts on both sides of the engine. Remove the front coverplates (see **FIG 3**). Remove the side coverplates.

The deflector plates or shrouds between the cylinders cannot be removed until the camshaft housings are taken off (see **Chapter 1** and **FIG 35** Chapter **1**). These plates are held in place with spring clips.

When refitting the shrouds, ensure that the spring clips hold them securely. Secure the coverplates so that there are no gaps where air can leak out and reduce cooling efficiency.

5 Silencer and heat exchangers

The position of the silencer is shown in **FIG 2** Chapter **1**, note retaining clip. Remove silencer, take out the two flange bolts and the bolts from the clips. Check for leaks and deterioration. Refit in reverse order, using a new gasket. Tighten flange bolts gradually and alternately.

To remove the heat exchangers, detach the air intake pipes and the connecting hoses between exchanger and heater control box (see **FIG 4**). Remove the heat exchanger securing bolts and the exhaust flange nuts (see **FIG 10** Chapter **1**). Check for damage, distorted flanges or cracks. Refit, using new gaskets and tighten the fixings evenly and alternately.

6 Heating system and controls

FIG 4 shows the heating system. Fresh air is drawn in by blower 2 and some is diverted through offtake pipes 3 into the casings of heat exchangers 4. The exhaust pipes pass through these casings and the air becomes heated (see part 20 in **FIG 1** Chapter **1**). Connecting hoses carry the air to control boxes 8, and then through ducts and air silencers to the various distribution points. The heater controls are so arranged that air still passes through the heat exchangers even though flaps prevent hot air from reaching the car interior (see shutter slots in **FIG 5**).

FIG 1 The tension of the blower belt is adjusted by altering the number of washers between the pulley flanges

FIG 2 The blower housing viewed from above, showing the fuel pipes secured to the cooling air casing

FIG 3 The arrow points to the cooling air casing, as seen from the flywheel end of the engine

Servicing heater controls (first type):

To remove cables, detach rear ends from control box levers shown in **FIG 5**. Remove tunnel cover and release gearlever mounting (3 screws). Remove heater control lever knob and lift off gearlever. Release control lever bracket (2 screws), ease lever forward and pull cables out of tunnel (see **FIG 6**).

When refitting, pass cable through correct hole in lever until the bend is reached. The greased cables must pass through the larger (lower) aperture. They must not cross. Fit the lever mounting and push the lever to the closed position (right forward). Attach the rear ends of the cables to the control box levers and check that flaps work smoothly and open and close to their fullest extent. Refit the gearlever.

Lever adjustment (first type):

Refer to **FIG 7**. The upper view shows the friction adjustment by means of nut 8. To adjust, hold bracket in a vice as shown in the lower view. Tighten nut to 50 cm/kg or 3.6 lb ft torque and slacken off one turn. Attach a spring balance to the inner hole in the lever and pull at right angles. Lever should not start to move until the pull is 10 ± 1 kg (22 ± 2.2 lb). Adjust by turning nut.

Servicing heater control (second type):

From 1968 models onwards, the heater control lever is fitted to the handbrake mounting (see **FIG 8**). The small lever is a hand throttle control. To remove the rear end of the control cables, refer to the instructions for the earlier type. Remove tunnel cover and handbrake lever boot. Release handbrake mounting from tunnel. Lift mounting and release spring clip on lower end of handbrake lever so that the pin through the equalizer bar may be removed. Pull the heater cables out of the guide tubes and control lever.

Check friction of control lever as described for the earlier type. Friction faces must be dry and free from grease. Fit cable, and grease with multi-purpose lithium-based lubricant. Make sure cables do not cross and insert longer cable in lefthand tube. Refit handbrake equalizer bar so that cables are correctly positioned. Tighten handbrake mountings to 2.5 mkg (18 lb ft). Refit rear ends of cables as described earlier. Do not forget to install the dust caps for the guide tubes. Check action of flaps.

7 The exhaust emission control system

A diagrammatic representation of the system is given in **FIG 9**. Known as 'EECS', it must, by law, be fitted to cars operating in America. The principle is that unburnt gases in the exhaust are injected with air from a pump. The oxygen in the air causes after-burning of the gases which considerably reduces the poisonous pollutants which would otherwise pass out into the atmosphere.

A pump 2, is belt-driven from one of the camshafts. Air is delivered from the pump to a regulating control valve 3 for each bank of cylinders. The valves incorporate a pressure relief valve and a check valve, the relief valve releasing excess air back to atmosphere. The check valve prevents exhaust gas flowing back into the air supply hoses if the pump stops working, probably through a broken belt. At conditions of high negative pressure in the induction system due to closed throttles and a steep down-grade, the mixture is liable to be excessively rich. To overcome this there is a dashpot compensator 10 which opens the throttles slightly in such circumstances.

The distributor 11 is fitted with a vacuum control unit so that a retarded ignition at low speeds calls for increased throttle opening to give a better mixture during deceleration.

FIG 4 How heated air is supplied to the car interior. The heavier arrows indicate hot air after it has left the heat exchangers

Key to Fig 4
1. Slots in rear engine hood
2. Axial cooling air blower
3. Offtake pipes
4. Heat exchangers
5. Exhaust pipes
6. Exhaust muffler
7. Connecting hoses
8. Heat control box
9. Heater pipe
10. Heated air muffler
11. Windshield defroster nozzle
12. Rear window defroster nozzle
13. Sliding valves
14. Fresh air unit
15. Pivoted lever
16. Self-powered heater
17. Air intake for self-powered heater

Routine maintenance:

Check belt tension. It should yield about 10 mm ($\frac{1}{2}$ inch) when pressed inwards at a point midway between the pulleys. Adjust by loosening the mounting bolt on the righthand side of the pump and the bolt on the lefthand side as shown in **FIG 10**. Lift pump by hand to tighten belt. Do not use force or the mounting may be deformed. Tighten the two bolts to a torque of 4 mkg (29 lb ft). Check hose connections. Always slacken off the adjustment before removing a belt.

Checking vacuum control unit of distributor:

Turn the crankshaft pulley until the Z1 mark is visible. This represents TDC when aligned with the mark on the blower housing. Make another mark to the left of TDC which corresponds to an angle of 3 deg. ATC.

Run the engine at idling speed and use a stroboscope to flash the pulley. The 3 deg. ATC mark should align with the mark on the blower housing. There is a permissible tolerance of between 2 and 5 deg. ATC. When checked at 6000 rev/min the ignition timing should be 30 deg. $\pm$ 2 deg. BTC. If adjustment at idling speed is not satisfactory, correct the timing at 6000 rev/min within the tolerance of $\pm$ 2 deg.

After setting the ignition timing, adjust the idle speed and check the adjustment of the throttle valve compensator.

Ignition timing:

Check contact breaker gap and make sure the dwell angle is 38 $\pm$ 3 deg. Run engine up to temperature and connect a stroboscope to No. 1 sparking plug lead. Loosen distributor clamping plate so that distributor can be turned by hand. Run engine at 6000 rev/min and flash the crankshaft pulley. Turn the distributor until the 30 deg. BTC mark on the pulley rim lines up with the mark on the blower housing. Tighten clamp plate and check timing.

FIG 5 The rear end of a heater control cable, showing connection to lever for control box valve. Shutter slots are open when heated air is not required in the car interior

FIG 6 Removing the gearlever mounting plate (top). Lower view shows heater control bracket

FIG 7 Section through frictional mounting of heater control lever. Lower view shows spring balance checking friction setting. Adjustment is made at nut 8

Key to Fig 7

1. Lever knob
2. Heater lever (LH steering)
3. Friction disc
4. Shim
5. Hexagon screw
6. Cup spring
7. Lever mounting bracket
8. Hexagon self-locking nut

FIG 8 Later type of handbrake mounting for heater control lever. The shorter lever is for throttle control

Removing and refitting air pump:

1 Detach hoses from pump.
2 Remove bolts attaching pump to mounting.
3 Remove belt and lift pump away.

The pump must not be dismantled. Turn the pulley and check that the pump turns freely in an anticlockwise direction. A new pump may squeak a little when turned, and there may be slight drag, but this is not important.

Refit the pump in the reverse sequence and tension the belt as explained at the beginning of 'Routine maintenance'.

Removing and refitting regulating valve:

Refer to **FIG 11**, disconnect the hose, remove the flange bolts and lift the assembly away from the engine rear shield. Remove the two long through-bolts and separate the three valve parts.

Check the condition of the flowback and pressure relief valves. Renew worn parts. Renew the rubber diaphragm in the flowback check valve if the edges are torn or frayed. Use new gaskets when reassembling, fitting the valve housings so that their arrows point outwards, with the pressure relief valves pointing downwards.

When refitting the valve assembly, fit gaskets under the flanges, and O-rings on the relief valve nozzles.

Removing and refitting pressure lines:

Remove regulating valve as just instructed. Remove heat exchanger hoses and then remove the heat exchangers. At the exhaust ports, unscrew the unions as shown in **FIG 12**, withdraw the connecting pipes and then unscrew the injector bodies.

Refit the bodies with new gaskets. Check condition of pipes and then fit them so that they cannot chafe against other parts. Check hoses for leaktight fitting.

Removing and installing camshaft pulley:

1 Remove engine transverse support and silencer. Remove regulating valve from rear shield (see earlier section).
2 Remove rear shield and pump belt. Do not lever belt over pulley flanges but slacken pump mounting bolts.
3 Remove retaining bolt and draw pulley off camshaft extension.

When refitting the parts in the reverse order, make sure the belt is correctly tensioned (see 'Routine maintenance').

Removing and fitting pulley bearing:

This is mounted in the lefthand camshaft chain cover. Remove the pulley as just explained, remove the retaining nuts and withdraw the bearing cover. Use a puller to draw the bearing off the camshaft, after removing the chain cover.

Clean the parts and check condition of bearing when unlubricated. Check the oil seal in the cover and renew if leaking. Oil sealing lip after fitting in cover. Refit bearing on camshaft after lubricating.

Fit chain cover on a new gasket. Fit bearing cover on a good gasket. Refit the pulley and tension the belt correctly.

EXHAUST EMISSION CONTROL SYSTEM
FOR TYPE 2000 ENGINE

FIG 9 Diagrammatic layout of the exhaust emission control system

Key to Fig 9

☐ AIR TUBES
▨ VACUUM PRESSURE TUBES
1 AIR CLEANER
2 AIR PUMP
3 PRESSURE RELIEF AND CHECK VALVE
4 EXHAUST PORT
5 CYLINDER HEAD
6 MUFFLER
7 INTAKE MANIFOLD
8 CARBURETOR
9 BUTTERFLY VALVE
10 COMPENSATOR DASHPOT
11 DISTRIBUTOR

Servicing throttle valve compensator and vacuum pipes:

Remove hose from compensator (10 in **FIG 9**). Detach connecting rod ball joint socket, release compensator from mounting bracket and lift away.

The vacuum lines are a push fit on the connections. The pipe from the compensator goes to a T-piece with branches to intake ports of cylinders 1 and 3. Branches from cylinders 1 and 4 go to a T-piece which is connected to the distributor vacuum control unit. Check that pipes are in sound condition and not chafed through.

FIG 10 The slotted adjustment for tensioning the air pump belt on the EECS system

FIG 11 EECS regulating valve showing mounting flanges

FIG 12 Removing pressure pipe from exhaust port connection

FIG 13 Throttle valve compensator showing return lag adjusting screw (top arrow). At idling speed there must be slight clearance between levers (lower arrow)

Adjusting compensator and linkage:

Before embarking on any adjustments, check that the ignition timing and carburetter idling are correctly set. Run the engine up to operating temperature and then check the compensator adjustment as follows:

Shut the throttle quickly from an engine speed of 3000 rev/min. Engine speed should then fall to around 1000 rev/min within 4 to 6 seconds. If this is not so, loosen the side screw which locks the adjusting screw indicated by the top arrow in **FIG 13**. Turn the adjusting screw right in.

Accelerate the engine quickly and shut off to draw the compensator rod up into the device and check the engine speed at once. It should be 2000 to 2200 rev/min. If speed is greater, lengthen the rod, if it is lower, shorten the rod, but make sure there is always slight clearance between the levers as indicated by the lower arrow when the engine is idling again.

Now adjust the time lag taken for the engine speed to drop. It must lie between 4 and 6 seconds, so turn the adjusting screw to the left to reduce the lag and to the right to increase it. In case of difficulty, check that the compensator is not sticking when the engine oil temperature is at least 200°F, or the indicator needle is in the green sector. Keeping the time lag to the upper limit will reduce exhaust back-firing to a minimum.

Testing the EECS system:

1 Check ignition timing and compensator adjustment. Adjust carburetters.
2 Remove hose connecting air pump to regulating valve.
3 Connect exhaust gas analyzer and check carbon monoxide content at idle speed. It should be approximately 4.5 per cent.
4 Reconnect the pump hose, run the engine at idling speed and check for carbon monoxide. The figure should be approximately 1 to 1.5 per cent.

8 Fault diagnosis

(a) Engine overheats

1 Blower belt slipping
2 Cooling air leaking from cover joints
3 Crankcase, oil cooler and cylinder fins caked with dirt
4 Carburetters out of tune, ignition wrongly timed
5 Exhaust system blocked
6 Air deflectors or shrouds wrongly fitted

(b) Heating system ineffective

1 Check 1 in (a)
2 Control cables broken or out of adjustment
3 Control box valves stuck
4 Hoses disconnected or leaking

NOTES

CHAPTER 5 - CLUTCH

1 General description
2 Routine maintenance
3 Removing and refitting clutch cable
4 Removing and dismantling clutch
5 Clutch driven plate
6 Refitting clutch
7 Servicing release bearing and fork
8 Fault diagnosis

1 General description

The clutch is of the single dry-plate variety incorporating a diaphragm spring (see **FIG 1**). The cover 1 is bolted to the front face of the flywheel 6 and carries diaphragm spring 4 on pins and fulcrum rings. The outer edge of the spring bears on pressure plate 2 and spring pressure traps driven plate 3 between the faces of the flywheel and the pressure plate. The driven plate is splined to the gearbox input shaft 7 and thus transmits drive from the flywheel to the gearbox. When the clutch pedal is depressed, release bearing 5 presses on the diaphragm spring. As the spring becomes dished the outer edge moves in the opposite direction by reason of the fulcrum rings. In consequence, pressure on the pressure plate is relieved, the driven plate is no longer trapped and there is no drive from the flywheel to the input shaft and gearbox. The dark shaded parts of the driven plate are friction linings which are riveted in place. The hub of the plate incorporates shock-absorbing springs to eliminate snatch.

1970 models:

From the beginning of 1970 the cable control of the 911 models has been redesigned, and accommodated in a modified diaphragm spring clutch; to reduce the effort required and ensure a smoother engagement. A section through the latest clutch system is shown in **FIG 1A**.

Referring to **FIG 1B** the forward end of the new clutch cable is attached to the pedal by an adjustable fork end, and at the rear end to an integrally cast lug on the transmission housing. The outer cable housing is adjustable and is supported at the centre tunnel rear panel and the clutch throwout fork. It is routed in an upward arc through a guide bracket that prevents the cable moving sideways but allows it to move vertically and towards the throwout fork.

When the pedal is depressed the cable is tensioned and because it is fixed firmly to the transmission housing the pressure is then exerted on the cable housing. The housing reacts against the rear wall of the centre tunnel and is forced to move in the direction of the throwout fork. As it approaches its fully extended condition it reacts also against the throwout fork pushing the end away from the centre tunnel rear panel. When the gap between the end of the fork and the tunnel rear panel has increased by about 15 mm (.60 inch) the clutch is fully disengaged.

1972 models:

The clutch operating system was again redesigned for the 1972 models. The throwout fork and clutch lever are mounted on a shaft which is splined on both ends and located within the transmission tunnel. The fork and lever are secured to the shaft by lockrings and the lever is now pulled by the inner cable instead of being pushed by the cable housing. The driven plate disc hub splines have been reduced in number from 24 to 20 and the force in the pressure plate has been increased to between 650 and 720 kg (1430 to 1584 lb).

FIG 1 Section through clutch, flywheel and releasing bearing

Key to Fig 1 1 Cover 2 Pressure plate 3 Driven plate 4 Diaphragm spring 5 Release bearing 6 Flywheel 7 Input shaft

2 Routine maintenance

Accurate setting of free play at the clutch pedal is essential. The amount of play before the clutch starts to disengage must be 20 to 25 mm ($\frac{3}{4}$ to 1 inch). Too little clearance may cause clutch slip and too much may cause rapid wear of the gearbox synchronizing cones.

Clearance may be adjusted at either end of the clutch cable. The top view in **FIG 2** shows the location of the adjustment at the release lever where it protrudes from the transmission casing. Loosen the locknut and turn the adjusting nut until pedal pad free play is correct. When satisfied, tighten the locknut. See 'Removing release bearing' (**Section 7**) for details of free play when pedal is fitted with a return spring.

The adjustment at the clutch pedal is shown in the lower view of **FIG 2**. Turn back the mat and rubber cover at the front end of the floor tunnel. Loosen locknut, disengage spring clip and withdraw clevis pin. Turn clevis and fit pin to check pedal pad free play. Do not let cable end protrude in clevis fork. Tighten locknut, make sure spring clip is secure and smear cable threads with grease.

After adjusting, check the pedal travel. Run the car until the gearbox is at operating temperature, depress the clutch pedal fully, and after a short pause, engage reverse gear. This should happen silently. If this is not so it will be necessary to move the pedal stop shown in **FIG 3**. After removing the rubber mats, slacken the two socket-head screws and slide the stop up or down as required. Tighten the screws and check engagement of reverse gear again.

To adjust the clutch on the 1970-71 models:

1 Loosen the cable housing locknut (situated to the rear of the casing integral lug) and turn the adjusting nut to obtain a free play in the clutch pedal of 20 to 25 mm (.80 to 1.0 inch). To check, measure the travel of the pedal as it is pulled upwards. Tighten the locknut without turning the cable housing.
2 When the clutch pedal is fully depressed the throwout fork should move approximately 15 mm (.60 inch) to disengage the clutch fully. If it does not move this distance the clutch pedal stop must be adjusted.
3 Referring to **FIG 3A** if the cable rests at the bottom of the guide bracket, as shown, when the pedal is fully depressed, adjust the inner cable at the fork end. To check the location of the cable in the fork end, use slide calipers and measure from the end of the cable to the outer face of the locknut as shown in **FIG 3B**. The correct measurement should be between 17 and 22 mm (.70 and .90 inch).
4 If, after adjusting, the cable still rests on the bottom of the guide bracket, lengthen the inner cable at the fork end.

FIG 1A Section through clutch, 1970 models
Key to Fig 1A
1 Cover
2 Pressure plate
3 Driven plate
4 Diaphragm spring
5 Release bearing
6 Flywheel
7 Input shaft
8 Release lever

FIG 1B Location and attachment of clutch cable assembly, 1970 models

5 If the arc of the cable is too large, as shown by the example in **FIG 3C** with the cable coming out of the top of the guide bracket in the pedal released position, the inner cable must be shortened at the fork end.

To adjust the clutch on the 1972 models:
1 Refer to **FIG 3D** and move the self-locking nut to obtain a free travel in the pedal of 20 to 25 mm (.80 to 1.0 inch). Check the free movement as described for the 70-71 models.

3 Removing and refitting clutch cable

At the front end of the floor tunnel, peel back the mats and tunnel cover. Loosen clevis locknut and release spring clip to remove clevis pin (see lower view of **FIG 2**). Unscrew clevis and locknut. Take hold of the rear end of the cable at the release lever (see top view in **FIG 2**) and pull the cable out of its guide. Check condition of cable, guide and rubber bellows.

Before refitting, smear cable with grease and push into place from the rear. Fit release lever nut and locknut, connect clevis at front end and set the clearance (see **Section 2**).

FIG 3A Typical example of the cable resting on the bottom of the guide bracket with pedal fully depressed. To remedy, adjust the inner cable at the pedal fork end

FIG 3B With slide calipers measure from the end of cable to outer face of locknut

FIG 2 Clutch cable adjusting nut and locknut at release lever (top). Lower view shows adjustment of cable at pedal shaft

FIG 3C Typical example of the cable ejecting itself from the guide bracket when the pedal is fully released. To remedy, adjust the inner cable, to shorten, at the pedal fork end

FIG 3 Location of adjustable stop used to set clutch pedal travel

FIG 3D Adjusting the pedal free travel, 1972 models

FIG 4 Clutch cover assembly. Top arrow points to inner ends of diaphragm spring leaves which take thrust of release bearing. Pressure plate face indicated by lower arrow

FIG 4A One of the screwed rivet heads seen through the starter aperture

FIG 4B Using an Allen wrench on three screws to relieve tension on the throwout bearing

4 Removing and inspecting clutch

Removing:

Remove the engine and separate from gearbox (see both **Chapter 1** and refer to this section for the later type clutch). Do not let weight of transmission hang on input shaft and keep it square to prevent damage to clutch driven plate.

Release clutch cover from flywheel (six bolts). Loosen bolts diagonally a turn at a time to release the spring pressure and to avoid distorting the cover. Lift off cover assembly and driven plate.

Note that modifications to the clutch have resulted in changing some of the procedures when dismantling.

Separating transmission from engine:

Engine and transmission removed:

1 Remove the starter and referring to **FIG 4A** turn the flywheel to bring one of three equally spaced rivet heads into sight through the starter mounting aperture.
2 Install a spacer sleeve on each of the three rivet heads secured with a M6 x 12 Allen screw. By tightening the three screws evenly as shown in **FIG 4B** the diaphragm spring will be lifted to release the tension on the throwout bearing.
3 Refer now to **FIG 4C** and with a screwdriver inserted through the opening in the transmission housing, turn the throwout bearing 90 deg. until the throwout fork lever can be slid past the bearing.
4 Proceed normally to separate the transmission from the engine.

Reconnecting transmission to engine:

1 When the transmission has been secured to the engine, refer to **FIG 4D** and with a screwdriver as shown turn and guide the throwout bearing into engagement with the fork lever.
2 Take out the three Allen screws and spacers.

Removing clutch:

1 Remove the three Allen screws and spacers if still installed.
2 Loosen the pressure plate mounting bolts evenly and progressively until the pressure plate can be lifted off.
3 Refer to **FIG 4E** and lay the assembly down as shown, press down on the plate and thrust washer and remove the circlip with pliers.
4 Do not clean the throwout bearing in solvent otherwise the prepacked grease will be washed out.

FIG 4C Turning the throwout bearing through 90 deg.

Inspecting:

Clean the parts and examine for wear or damage. Refer to **FIG 4** and check spring leaves for scoring by the release bearing (top arrow). Scores up to .30 mm (.011 inch) in depth are permissible.

Check face of pressure plate (lower arrow). Cracks, deep scores, burn marks or uneven wear call for renewal. Note that the clutch must be renewed as an assembly and there is no point in dismantling it by removing the rivets. Use a straightedge and feelers to check the flatness of the pressure plate face. Concavity up to .30 mm (.011 inch) is permissible. Check all rivets for security and check the cover and springs for cracks. Examine the fulcrum rings and rivet heads where they contact the diaphragm spring. If worn, renew clutch. Put molybdenum disulphide grease on fulcrum rings where they contact the diaphragm spring.

5 Clutch driven plate

Examine friction linings. Renew plate if linings are worn, broken or contaminated with oil. Thickness of plate should be 10.1 —.40 mm (.40 —.015 inch) as shown at 'A' in **FIG 5**. Renew plate if thickness is much less than 9 mm (.354 inch).

Mount plate on a mandrel between centres and check runout with a dial gauge (see **FIG 5**). Maximum permissible runout is .60 mm (.023 inch). It will be noticed that the steel disc is divided into leaves and the linings are riveted to these alternately. The leaves are bowed and offset to provide a cushioning effect and the offsetting must be evenly balanced. Compressed thickness of the plate should be 9.20 ± .20 mm (.362 ± .007 inch) and the wear limit is 8 to 7.80 mm (.314 to .307 inch).

Commencing June 1971 these dimensions have been revised, though only modestly. The uncompressed thickness of the driven plate assembly, shown at 'A' in **FIG 5**, should be 9.8 ± .40 mm (.386 ± .016 inch). The wear limit uncompressed should be 6.5 mm (.256 inch), if uneven wear has occurred renew the assembly anyhow. The run-out restriction remains the same.

Check hub splines for wear. Plate should slide freely on input shaft without undue play. Check shock-absorbing springs for wear and breakage.

The linings may have a high polish and be perfectly capable of transmitting power. If the grain of the lining material is visible the linings are good, but if the linings are a dark brown, with an opaque glaze, they are probably contaminated with burnt oil and the plate must be renewed. It is not advisable to try riveting linings into place. Renew the whole plate.

FIG 4E Press down on the plate and thrust washer to remove the circlip with pliers

FIG 4D Turning the throwout bearing into engagement with the fork lever

FIG 5 Driven plate spun on mandrel between centres to check runout with dial gauge. 'A' is the uncompressed thickness over linings

FIG 6 Clutch secured to flywheel (top). Dowel pins and dummy input shaft used to centre clutch when refitting (bottom).

FIG 7 Top arrows indicate clearance between clutch release lever and gearbox housing with lever pulled in direction of lower arrow

FIG 8 Later type of clutch release bearing showing plastic guides 1 and bearing 2

6 Refitting clutch

It is assumed that the clutch face of the flywheel has been checked for cracks, scoring and wear. Details for the restoration of a worn surface have been given in **Chapter 1**.

It will be evident from an examination of the clutch section in **FIG 1** that the driven plate hub must be truly centred in the flywheel or the gearbox input shaft will not be able to pass through the hub splines so that the pilot or spigot will enter the bushing in the flywheel boss. Centralizing is assured by using a mandrel which may be the rear end of an old input shaft or, for a one-off job, a wooden dowel turned so that the smaller diameter is a snug fit in the flywheel bush and the larger diameter is a good fit in the driven plate splined hub.

Fit the driven plate, using the temporary mandrel. One can be seen in use in the lower view of **FIG 6**. About 2 cc of molybdenum disulphide grease should be pressed into the flywheel bushing before fitting the mandrel. Fit the clutch cover assembly to the flywheel using centralizing pins as shown. Fit the bolts and tighten them diagonally a turn at a time so that the cover is not distorted. Use spring washers and tighten to a torque of 3.5 mkg (25 lb ft).

Remove the mandrel, apply a smear of grease to the input shaft splines and pilot and refit the transmission to the engine as explained in **Chapter 1, Section 3** and also this chapter - see **Section 4**. Finally, check the clutch release lever setting as shown in **FIG 7**. Pull lever in direction of arrow. Distance between lever and gearbox housing must be at least 20 mm (.80 inch) as indicated by top arrows. Adjust clearance as in **Section 2**.

7 Servicing release bearing and fork

The bearing is part 5 in **FIG 1**. Note, however, that a new release bearing No. 901.116.081.11 was fitted as follows:

911 from 12th January, 1967
911S from beginning of production

The new bearing may be used as a replacement for the original type. It is essential to fit plastic guides No. 901.116.825.11 to the new-type bearing, as shown in **FIG 8**. Use fine emerycloth on the plastic guides if the bearing is not a free fit in the release fork.

Removing release bearing:

With transmission detached from engine, release socket-head bolt as shown in **FIG 9** and remove release lever and bearing, after unhooking return spring. This spring is not fitted to models with the modified release bearing and it will be found that there is a spring fitted to the clutch pedal shaft to keep the pedal pressed towards the toe board. In this case the clutch pedal free play is checked by pulling the pedal away from the toe board.

Servicing release fork and bearing:

The fork is carried on a ballpin as shown in **FIG 10**, the earlier version being on the left. This plain-shanked pin was cemented into the housing and was fitted up to transmission number 102082 or 222706. Clean the parts and check ballpin and bush for wear.

Do not use solvents on the release bearing, as it is packed with grease. Renew the bearing if dirt has entered or if it sounds noisy when turned.

Refitting release fork and bearing:

If screwed ballpin was removed, refit it using a good sealing washer and tighten to a torque of 2.1 to 2.3 mkg (15 to 16½ lb ft). Smear molybdenum disulphide grease in the ballpin bush and on the rubbing surfaces of the release bearing. Refit the bearing and fork and tighten the socket-head bolt to a torque of 1.0 mkg (7 lb ft).

8 Fault diagnosis

(a) Noisy clutch

1 Worn pilot bush in flywheel boss
2 Worn release bearing
3 Broken springs in driven plate hub
4 Broken driven plate disc or linings

(b) Clutch judder

1 Defective engine and transmission mountings
2 Pressure plate face worn and uneven
3 Diaphragm spring distorted
4 Driven plate disc distorted
5 Grease or oil on linings

(c) Dragging or incomplete release

1 Excessive clutch clearance
2 Driven plate or input shaft running out of true
3 Driven plate segments or linings unevenly set
4 Input shaft spigot bearing tight
5 Stiffness of clutch pedal, cable or release mechanism
6 Sticky linings
7 Distorted clutch cover or pressure plate

(d) Slipping

1 See 3 and 5 in (b)
2 Lack of free play in clutch pedal
3 Linings burned or broken, contact faces defective

FIG 9 Releasing clutch withdrawal fork. Allen key is loosening dowel pin

FIG 10 Plain shank of early withdrawal lever ballpin (left). Later type of screwed ballpin (right)

Key to Fig 10

1 Ball pin   2 Sealing washer   3 Threaded insert

NOTES

INTRODUCTION TO CHAPTER 6 - TRANSMISSION

General

The transmission and differential, contained in one housing, is bolted to the engine and forms a unified power transmission assembly located at the rear of vehicle. The assembly is mounted in rubber on supports attached to the forward part of the transmission and rear of engine. The power transmission unit can be removed or installed only as a whole assembly.

Transmission Housing

The housing -a tunnel type case- is made of die-cast light alloy. A cast iron insert is cast into the center web of the case to support the bearings.

Transmission

The transmission has five forward speeds and one reverse. A servo-lock synchronization is incorporated in all forward speeds. The forward speed gears and Gear II of the reverse gear twin cluster are in constant mesh; silent operation is achieved through the use of helical gears.

The 4th and 5th speed gears on the input shaft are arranged as free-wheeling gears; due to this arrangement, the two gears remain stationary in the neutral gear speed resulting in less gear noise at idling.

Gear Ratios

Due to the 5-speed transmission it was possible to provide close ratios between the gears and thus achieve excellent acceleration and top speed characteristics.

The individual gear ratios are shown in the transmission diagram opposite. This diagram is a handy reference showing the relative engine rpm, vehicle speed, and gear ratio.

Example:
With engine RPM (left vertical column) at 5000, a third speed gear ratio of 23:28, effective vehicle speed is 69 MPH (bisecting lines of the horizontal 5000 RPM line and the third speed diagonal). Similar readings can be made at any place on the diagram.

Function of Synchromesh in Shifting Gears

Shifting of gears is effected by way of the floor-mounted gearshift lever through a shift rod leading to the transmission through the chassis center tunnel. The reverse gear engages by sliding a gear into reverse speed position. The forward speeds are engaged through the servo-lock synchromesh units. The servo-thrust force in the synchromesh units varies according to the prevailing friction, i.e., the greater the difference in the gears' speed, the more friction is created. The synchromesh units permit a rapid synchronization of the given gears with the minimal application of force at the gearshift lever.
For better understanding of the function of the synchromesh units, the following outline will first deal with the mechanical process that takes place when shifts are made with the transmission at standstill.

When a gear is shifted with the transmission at standstill, the selector fork moves the sliding sleeve from its neutral position towards the selected gear and proceeds to engage it with the toothed engagement ring of the selected gear. As this takes place, the synchronizing ring is compressed within the sliding sleeve and, upon completion of the move, snaps to rest within the machined groove on the inner race of the sliding sleeve, locking itself in that position.

Fig. 1

In the static process it is necessary to overcome only the static resistance created by the spring tension of the synchronizing ring as it is compressed in its diameter by the sliding sleeve.

When gears are shifted while in motion, entirely different conditions prevail. The purpose of the synchromesh units is to equalize the speeds of the input shaft or pinion shaft and the respective gear on a given shaft; this is possible only by way of a mechanical clutch, i.e., the synchromesh unit. This clutch must be able not only to synchronize the gear speeds through friction, but also keep the sliding sleeve from clashing with the toothed ring on the selected gear (clutch carrier) as long as the gears run at unequal speeds.

When shifting gears, the engine clutch must be fully disengaged since the clutch plate is part of the mass to be synchronized and must be accelerated or decelerated, as the case may be.

When a gear is shifted while driving, the selector fork guides the sliding sleeve off the synchronizing ring of the engaged gear, through the neutral position, and on to the point of contact between the internal teeth of the sliding sleeve and the beveled edge of the synchronizing ring of the next gear. As this contact is made, friction created by the unequal gear speeds drags the synchronizing ring to one side, against the brake band energizer. The floating brake band energizer thus slides against a brake band whose other end rests against the brake band stop. Since the brake band stop keeps the brake band from sliding away under the pressure of the band energizer, it is forced outward against the inner race of the synchronizing ring causing it to "grow" within the sliding sleeve. Consequently, there is an instantaneous increase of friction between the synchronizing ring and the inner race of the sliding sleeve which further increases the force exerted upon the brake band and, in turn, upon the synchronizing ring. As may be seen, the synchronizing effect is thus obtained from the self-energized thrust exerted by the brake band upon the synchronizing ring.

Fig. 2

1 Sliding sleeve   3 Clutch carrier   5 Brake band energizer   7 Brake band
2 Spider   4 Synchronizing ring   6 Brake band stop   8 Retaining ring

The gear about to be engaged is forced to assume the speed of the sliding sleeve. As long as there is a difference in speed between the sliding sleeve and the gear-coupled synchronizing ring, the energized brake band prevents a further compression of the synchronizing ring, preventing the engagement of the sliding sleeve with the teeth in the clutch carrier.

As the difference in speed between the sliding sleeve and the gear decreases, the friction between the synchronizing faces also decreases. When the speeds between the two parts equalize, the servo-thrust components relax and, now, it becomes possible to compress the synchronizing ring in its diameter and move the sliding sleeve fully onto the synchronizing ring. At this point, the synchronizing ring snaps into the groove machined in the inner race of the sliding sleeve and locks itself in that position. For this reason it is no longer necessary to incorporate a locking device in the selector shaft.

All forward speeds of the transmission are equipped with identical synchromesh components with the exception of the 1st gear which is used for starting. Care was taken to ensure that this starting gear engages with the least possible effort when the car is not in motion.

As shown in Fig. 3, the brake band energizer for 1st gear has been provided with a tab which rests in a recess machined into the clutch carrier; also, only one brake band is utilized. The engine idle speed is very low when compared with revolutions prevailing at operating speeds. When the engine clutch is disengaged prior to shifting into low speed at standstill, the clutch plate stops within a short time following disengagement. To further shorten the engine clutch stopping time and enable the driver to quickly shift into low gear without gear clash, it was necessary to provide a synchronizing device for this purpose; in this case, the synchromesh unit acts as a brake.

Fig. 3

As the gear is slowed down, the force resulting through friction at the synchronizing ring acts directly onto the gear by way of the brake band energizer and its tab. Due to its slanted tab, the brake band energizer exerts a pressure, through its longer end, against the inner face of the synchronizing ring. This small force is sufficient to ensure an easy engagement of the low gear while still preventing a gear clash.

When a shift from 2nd to 1st gear is made while the car is in motion, the 1st gear must be accelerated to match its counterpart. For this purpose, a normal brake band has been provided on the respective synchromesh side ensuring the same synchronization as on all other gears (see Fig. 4).

Fig. 4

Rear Axle and Transmission

The power is transmitted to the rear wheels through a spiral bevel gear differential with bevel spider gears, and two double-joint half-axles. Quiet operation and long service of the rear axle is contingent upon the exact adjustment of the ring and pinion gears.

The ring and pinion gear ratio is 1 : 4.428 (7 : 31)

When driving through curves, the outside wheel covers a longer distance than the inside wheel, resulting in differing axle speeds. The purpose of the differential is to make up for the varying axle speeds and ensure that driving torque is evenly distributed between both rear wheels.

Oil Capacity

The transmission oil capacity is approx. 2.5 liters (5 pints). The transmission oil should be changed at intervals indicated in the lubrication schedule using lubricants of prescribed specification. When changing transmission oil, refill with approx. 2.5 liters (5 US pints), as specified.

DISMOUNTED TRANSMISSION AND DIFFERENTIAL ASSEMBLY

Synchromesh Components

1. Sliding Sleeve

Friction contact with the synchronizing ring is made on the tapered part of the inner race of the sliding sleeve. In addition, the toothed race engages with corresponding teeth in the gear-coupled clutch carrier of the selected gear providing a firm mechanical connection.

The inside race contour, in addition to the tapered outer edges, includes a machined groove in its center which has the purpose of locking the sliding sleeve onto the synchronizing ring once the respective shift has been completed; for this reason it is no longer necessary to incorporate a locking device in the selector shaft (see Fig. 5).

Fig. 5

2. Spider

The three-pronged spider carries the sliding sleeve and transmits the engine torque; the sliding sleeve is free to move sideways to engage or disengage a given gear (see Fig. 6).

Fig. 6

3. Clutch Carrier

The gear-coupled clutch carrier is the actual gear coupler connecting the gear with the sliding sleeve. The synchronizing ring and the servo-thrust components are contained within the clutch carrier (see Fig. 7). The 1st gear clutch carrier has two slots machined into the body and located opposite one another.

The slanted slot is provided for the brake band energizer. The retaining ring tab must never be positioned within the slanted slot since it belongs into the slot of the brake band stop.

Fig. 7

4. Synchronizing Ring

The synchronizing ring is a split spring ring with two beveled outer edges. One beveled edge represents the synchronizing friction face, the other edge completes the contour to mate with the machined inner groove within the inside race of the sliding sleeve provided for locking the sliding sleeve on the synchronizing ring when the shift has been completed (see Fig. 8).

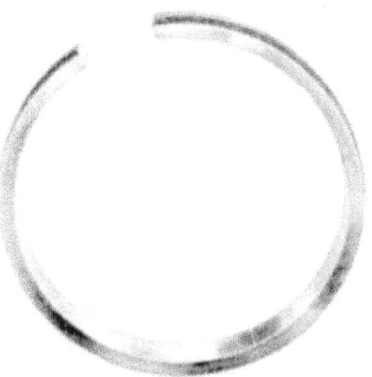

Fig. 8

5. Brake Band Energizer

One end of the synchronizing ring exerts pressure onto the brake band energizer which, in turn, transmits this pressure to the brake band (see Fig. 9).

Fig. 9

Incorporated into the 1st gear synchronization is a modified brake band energizer, i.e., one with an actuating tab (see Fig. 10).

Fig. 10

6. Brake Band Stop

The brake band stop is contained within the slot machined into the clutch carrier and is mechanically connected with the respective gear, transmitting the friction forces (moment of friction) from the synchronizing components to the clutch carrier (see Fig. 11).

Fig. 11

7. Brake Band

The brake band receives the synchronizing force, or thrust, exerted by the synchronizing ring against the brake band energizer; consequently, the brake band is forced outward against the inner face of the synchronizing ring (see Fig. 12).

Fig. 12

8. Retaining Ring

The retaining ring has the purpose of containing the synchronizing ring and the synchromesh components in the clutch carrier (see Fig. 13).

Fig. 13

CHAPTER 6 - TRANSMISSION

MANUAL TRANSMISSION
1 General description
2 Routine maintenance
3 Transmission removal
4 Dismantling transmission
5 Servicing input shaft
6 Servicing intermediate plate
7 Servicing pinion shaft
8 Overhauling and setting differential
9 Adjusting pinion shaft setting and backlash
10 Servicing front cover
11 Reassembling transmission
12 Gearshift mechanism
13 Servicing ZF differential
14 The four-speed transmission

SPORTOMATIC TRANSMISSION
15 General description
16 Routine maintenance
17 Driving hints
18 Removal and installation
19 Separating and refitting transmission
20 Servicing control valve and sensors
21 Servicing gearlever and microswitch
22 Servicing torque converter and clutch
23 Servicing clutch controls
24 Overhauling gearbox

FAULT DIAGNOSIS & TRANSMISSION CHARTS
25 Fault diagnosis (manual gearbox)
26 Fault diagnosis (Sportomatic)

1 General description

To simplify instructions, the transmission system has been divided into two sections, this chapter dealing with the gearbox and final drive gears. **Chapter 7** covers the rear axles, universal joints, rear hubs and suspension.

Servicing details will be given for fourspeed and five-speed gearboxes with synchromesh engagement of all forward gears, for the optional ZF self-locking differential unit and for the Sportomatic transmission. The instructions for the fivespeed gearbox will be given in full and most of these are applicable to the fourspeed box, any differences for the latter being given in **Section 14**. The Sportomatic transmission is described in **Section 15**.

The fivespeed transmission is shown in **FIG 1**, housing 18 being bolted to the engine to form the power unit. **This unit can be removed or installed only as an assembly.** The housing is a tunnel which contains the input shaft 11 and pinion shaft 5, the pinion engaging with the crownwheel or ring gear which is bolted to differential carrier 12. Gears A, B, C, D and E are in constant mesh with companion gears on the pinion shaft and one gear of each pair is free to revolve on needle roller bearings. When a gear is selected, synchronizing device 6 to 9 speeds up or slows down the particular gears until sliding teeth can be engaged and the freely-revolving gear can be locked to its shaft to complete the drive. Front cover 2 encloses the first-speed gears, but gear A also drives a pair of gears on a layshaft. These drive large gear 20 when it is moved to the left, to provide reverse gear.

911T models from 1968 onwards have a simplified differential unit. **It is important to check this when fitting an exchange unit, as the simplified type must be used only with LOEBRO half-axles.**

2 Routine maintenance

Just forward of the ribbed differential cover on the left-hand side of the transmission housing there are two plugs. The lower one is a drain plug and the upper one is a filler plug. Drain the oil while it is hot, doing this every 6000 miles. Clean the magnetic drain plug free from adhering steel particles and refit it. Refill to the bottom of the filler plug hole with SAE.90 Hypoid transmission oil. Approximate capacity is 2.5 litres ($4\frac{1}{2}$ Imp pints or 5 US pints). Tighten both plugs to 2 to $2\frac{1}{2}$ mkg ($14\frac{1}{2}$ to 18 lb ft) torque.

Maintenance recommendations for the Sportomatic transmission are given in **Section 16**.

3 Transmission removal

Fourspeed and fivespeed transmission:

To remove the complete power unit from the car, refer to **Chapter 1**. Note that the differential assembly may be removed without detaching the complete unit (see **Sections 4** and **8**), but if adjustment or renewal of parts is intended it is best to remove the entire power unit.

Sportomatic transmission:

Use the removal instructions in **Chapter 1** but note a few extra details. Remove the vacuum hose from the reservoir. Adjacent to the lefthand bank of carburetters is the control valve. Withdraw the rubber cap, remove the splitpin and pull off the wire connector (see **FIG 29**). Detach B+ cable from connector mounted just above coil and remove connectors from bypass switch.

After lowering the power unit a little, detach cables from temperature switch and temperature gauge sensor which are adjacent to the vacuum servo cylinder (see **FIG 30**).

FIG 1 Longitudinal section through fivespeed gearbox and differential

Key to Fig 1

1. Shift rod
2. Front cover and oil seal
3. Tachometer driven gear
4. Tachometer drive gear
5. Pinion shaft
6. Synchronizing ring
7. Spider
8. Shift fork
9. Sliding sleeve
10. Fifth-speed gear
11. Input shaft
12. Differential carrier
13. Spider gear
14. Side gearshaft
15. Oil seal
16/17. Clutch release bearing
18. Housing
19. Clutch plate splines
20. Pinion shaft gear for first-speed and reverse
21. Intermediate plate
A. First-speed fixed gear
B. Second-speed fixed gear
C. Third-speed fixed gear
D. Fourth-speed free-running gear
E. Fifth-speed free-running gear

FIG 2 Prising out caps from universal joint flanges

FIG 3 Five-speed gearbox. Arrow indicates selector fork retaining screw

Key to Fig 3

A. Pinion shaft bolt
B. Castle nut on input shaft spider wheel
C. First and reverse-speed

FIG 4 Guide fork for inner shift rod partially removed

4 Dismantling fivespeed transmission

Servicing the Porsche transmission demands a high degree of mechanical skill and the use of many special tools not normally available. The relative positions of the pinion and crownwheel (ring gear) must be set with great accuracy if the gears are to operate silently. Any error may lead to rapid tooth wear and noisy running which will call for expensive renewals.

Due to manufacturing tolerances, renewal of such parts as the housing, the differential carrier, the intermediate plate, the pinion shaft and its bearings and the crownwheel will upset the relative positions just mentioned and it will be necessary to go through the whole procedure for meshing the drive gears. It is, of course, possible to dismantle and reassemble the transmission without the need for adjustment, provided that all shims and spacers are refitted in their original positions. It is also possible to renew parts which obviously have no effect upon the meshing of the drive gears.

The following instructions are therefore given primarily to help those who have access to the necessary tools and precision measuring equipment.

1. Drain oil and remove starter. Prise up flange caps as shown in **FIG 2**. Hold input shaft splines securely and engage fifth gear. Remove bolts and withdraw flanges.
2. Remove side cover and withdraw differential assembly. Remove support from front cover 2 (see **FIG 1**). Remove front cover with care as reverse gears may fall out.
3. Remove selector fork screw (top arrow in **FIG 3**). Remove gear and fork.
4. Engage fifth-speed and lock pinion with tool P37. Remove bolt A from pinion shaft (see **FIG 3**). Drive out locking pin from nut B, remove nut and first-speed gear.
5. Select neutral. From underside of housing remove plate and guide fork shown in **FIG 4**. Pull out inner shift rod through rear acess hole. Insert screwdriver in guide fork hole and select fifth-speed. **Gears cannot be withdrawn or inserted unless transmission is in this position.**
6. Tap intermediate plate with soft-faced hammer and detach it complete with gears. **Check gasket thickness for correct reassembly.** Hold plate in a vice with soft jaws and prise off spider wheel C (see **FIG 3**). Remove first-speed gear and needle bearing from pinion shaft. Shift into neutral.
7. Remove plug and detent spring (top view in **FIG 5**). Withdraw selector shaft and detent ball for first and reverse gear (see **FIG 18**). Mark forks to avoid confusion and remove shafts, forks and detents (see lower view in **FIG 5** and also **FIG 18**).
8. Tap dowels forward and remove throttle linkage. Place intermediate plate under a press with gears downwards and press out input and pinion shafts simultaneously. Balls may fall out of input shaft bearing. Service intermediate plate as in **Section 6**. Prise out circlips from centre web as in **FIG 6**.
9. Heat housing to 120°C (248°F) and tap out bearing races one at a time using tool P254 and a soft-faced hammer.

Clean the parts and check for damage, cracks or wear. Tooth breakage and subsequent jamming may cause housing cracks and possible damage to bearing bores. Check bearings when clean and dry. Service the various assemblies according to the instructions in the following Sections.

FIG 5 Five-speed gearbox. Removing detent plug for selector shaft (top view). Arrows indicate selector fork screws (bottom view), where A is the bearing retaining plate and B is the fork for second and third gear

FIG 6 Prising out front spring retainer (circlip) for pinion shaft bearing

FIG 7 Input shaft section and components (fivespeed gearbox)

Key to Fig 7

1. Input shaft (with Gear I for 2nd speed)
2. Gear I of 3rd speed (fixed)
3. Thrust washer
4. Gear I of 4th speed (free-wheeling)
5. Sliding sleeve
6. Spider
7. Gear I of 5th speed (free-wheeling)
8. Thrust washer (5.9 mm thickness)
9. Roller bearing
10. Hex nut
11. Oil seal race
12. Splined end for clutch plate
13. Needle bearing inner race
14. Needle bearing cage
15. Brake band
16. Synchronizing ring
17. Needle bearing inner race
18. Needle bearing cage
19. Nut lock plate
20. Spigot for flywheel bearing

5 Servicing the input shaft

Details of the shaft and its components are given in **FIG 7**. These may be compared with the shaft for the fourspeed box by referring to **FIG 25**.

Removal:

It is not necessary to remove the differential assembly in order to take out the input shaft. Having pressed the shaft out of the intermediate plate as described in the preceding Section, proceed as follows:

Dismantling:

1. Unlock and remove nut 10 (see **FIG 7**) after checking runout. Press roller bearing 9 off shaft. Mark needle bearing cages for position and pull all components off shaft.
2. The inner half of the front bearing race is hard against gear 1. Drift it away a little and use a puller to remove it, taking care not to damage the gear.

Inspection:

Clean parts and check for wear or damage. Runout must be checked before shaft is dismantled because tightening nut 10 may alter it. Assemble bearings on shaft and mount in V-blocks. Check runout of pilot spigot 20.

Maximum permissible is .10 mm (.004 inch). Excessive runout up to .30 mm (.012 inch) may be corrected cold under a press, using tools VW.405 and VW.406.

Check spigot for wear. Check clutch plate splines for radial play. Oil seal race 11 must be smooth and unmarked. Running surfaces of gears and bearings must be unworn and check parts which must be a press fit on the shaft. Gear 1 is integral with the shaft. If worn, renew shaft after checking mating numbers. Also check numbers when renewing gears or bearings. Check synchromesh parts for wear and renew parts, particularly if gearchanging has been noisy.

Reassembling:

Fit all components dry. Gear 2 has its small collar facing the shaft flange. Follow up with thrust washer 3 and inner race 13. Fit cage 14, gear 4 and spider 6. **Used bearing cages must be fitted in original positions.** Fit sleeve 5 followed by bearing 17 and 18 and gear 7. Fit thrust washer 8 and roller bearing 9 with cover ring of cage facing towards the clutch plate splines. Press bearing into place using a tubular extension to avoid damaging the threads at the front end of the shaft. Fit new lockplate 19 with inner tab in the groove in the shaft and under the inner race of the bearing. Oil face and threads of nut and fit with spherical part uppermost. Tighten to 10 to 12 mkg (72 to 86 lb ft). Bend up locking tab. Check mating numbers then press inner half of front bearing race into place.

6 Servicing intermediate plate

Dismantling:

Unlock four bolt heads inside plate, remove bolts and lift off bearing retaining plate A (see **FIG 5**). Heat intermediate plate to 120°C (248°F) and press out the bearing outer races. There are bushings in the holes for the detents and springs (see **FIG 18**). These may be withdrawn with tool P.66a and new ones fitted with tool P.262.

Reassembling:

Clean the parts and check the bearings when unlubricated. Heat the plate as before and fit the bearing races as shown in **FIG 8**. Use grease to fit any loose balls. Fit the retaining plate and bolts, using new lockplates. Tighten to 2.5 mkg (18 lb ft) and bend up locktabs.

FIG 8 Correct location of flanged outer races for bearings in intermediate plate

When fitting new detent bushings, drive the long one up to the collar of tool P.262. Drive the short one to the second mark on the tool. Drive the middle-length one to the first mark. **Check that no bush protrudes into a selector shaft bore.**

FIG 9 Components of pinion shaft (fivespeed gearbox). Numbered items are to rear of intermediate plate

Key to Fig 9
1 Thrust washer (6.6 mm)
2 Needle bearing inner race
3 Needle bearing cage
4 Second-speed gear (free-running)
5 Synchronizing assembly
5a Energizer
5b Stop
5c Brake band
5d Synchronizing ring
5e Retainer
6 Spider
7 Sliding sleeve
8 Synchronizing assembly
9 Needle bearing inner race
10 Needle bearing
11 Third-speed gear (free-running)
12 Thrust washer
13 Fourth-speed gear (fixed)
14 Spacer bush
15 Fifth-speed gear (fixed)
16 Spacer
17 Shim
18 Retaining ring
19 Roller bearing
20 Pinion shaft

7 Servicing pinion shaft

FIG 9 shows the components of the shaft, the parts which are not numbered being in front of the intermediate plate.

Dismantling:

Place the shaft, pinion downwards under a press, using tool P.225 as an abutment to the roller bearing so that the shaft may be pushed through the gear and bearing assemblies. **Mark the positions of the needle bearing cages for correct reassembly and take great care of the shims 17 as they control the endwise location of the pinion.**

Inspection:

After cleaning, look for wear and damage. **Note mating numbers when renewing gears and bearings.** Check shaft for condition of splines and pinion for worn, cracked or broken teeth. Check synchromesh parts for wear, particularly if gearchanging has been noisy. Dismantle these by removing retaining plate 5e with circlip pliers. Make a note of the positions of the bands 5c, energizers 5a and stops 5b. When installed, diameter of ring 5d should be 76.30 mm ± .18 mm (3.004 inch ± .007 inch).

Reassembling:

Remember that the pinion and crownwheel (ring gear) are a matched pair and are marked as such (see **FIG 12**). If no parts are renewed which affect the endwise location of the pinion shaft, then there is no problem in reassembling, but otherwise refer to the instructions which follow after these.

1 All parts must be fitted to the pinion shaft in a dry state. Press roller bearing into place with thin coverplate of cage facing away from the pinion. Fit shims 17 as removed or as calculated under 'Pinion shaft shims'.

2 Fit spacer 16. Fit fifth-speed gear 15 with small collar facing away from pinion. Fit spacer bush 14, followed by fourth-speed gear 13 with collar against the bush.

3 Fit thrust washer 12 and needle bearing inner race 9. Fit bearing cage 10. Reassemble synchromesh parts and fit third-speed gear 11 followed by spider 6. **Always fit used needle bearing cages in their original positions.**

4 Fit inner race 2, bearing cage 3 and sliding sleeve 7. Fit gear 4. Fit bevelled thrust washer 1 with wide face against needle bearing. Follow up with the thin spacer but note that starting with transmission No. 100.407 the washer and spacer were replaced by a single washer 6.60 mm (.26 inch) thick. Using a tubular drift, press on the inner half race for the front bearing. This must be marked with the mating number without the letter X.

FIG 10 Differential carrier assembly (five-speed gearbox)

Key to Fig 10
1 Carrier
2 Side gear
3 Spider gearshaft
4 Pinion
5 Lockplate
6 Side gearshaft

FIG 11 Adjusting relative positions of pinion and crownwheel (ring gear). A-A is centreline of differential assembly, B is the pinion and E is the adjustment value, S1 and S2 are the adjustment spacers

Pinion shaft shims:

Preliminary adjustment of the meshing of the pinion with the crownwheel is necessary if parts have been renewed which affect the position of the pinion with respect to the intermediate plate. The plate controls the endwise location of the pinion because the rear roller bearing permits axial movement of the pinion shaft. Final adjustment is made by using gaskets under the intermediate plate after accurate measurement of distance E in **FIG 11** (see **Section 9**).

Refer to **FIG 12** and note that designed dimension R is 63.50 mm (2.50 inch). Manufacturing tolerances make it impossible to set every pinion face to this dimension and any variation is marked at 1 (lefthand view) as a + or − value. 2 is a mating number which must be the same as that on the crownwheel.

The deviation is in $\frac{1}{100}$ mm. Take +4 as an example and call it +.04 mm. Add this to the designed dimension R and the result is 63.54 mm, which becomes dimension E.

The makers suggest a basic approximation of 64.70 mm as a starting point. Take value E away from this and the answer is 1.16 mm, which is the thickness of shims required (see 17 in **FIG 9**). These are made .25, .30 and .40 mm thick. Do not use the earlier thickness of .10 and .15 mm. Calculate the required thickness to the nearest .05 mm, either up or down. Thus 1.16 mm becomes 1.15 mm by using three shims .30 mm thick and one .25 mm thick.

8 Overhauling and setting differential

Withdraw the differential unit as described early in **Section 4**. If this is done with the transmission in the car, first detach both rear axle halfshafts at the differential flanges. Also detach the clutch cable and the rear throttle linkage. The unit is shown in **FIG 10**. See end of **Section 1** for 911T differential details. Dismantle as follows:

1 Remove roller bearings with a puller. **Take careful note of spacers.** Inside shaft 6 is a pin which secures the spider gearshaft 3. Drive out this pin and drift out the spider shaft.

2 Remove gears from inside carrier 1. Unlock tabs of plates 5, unscrew bolts and remove crownwheel (ring gear).

Check inside of carrier for wear of gear seats. Check bearings when dry. Renew carrier if worn or if inner races of bearings are not a good fit. Renew complete bearing including outer race as a set. Check gear teeth and spherical seats. Check shafts and side gear splines as well as axle joint flanges.

Side bearings are preloaded by selection of spacers S1 and S2 in **FIG 11**, but note that diaphragm springs were used instead of spacer S2 on transmissions up to No. 100.268. **Gear backlash is adjusted by spacer S1.** For the springs to be effective the inner race of the bearing must be free to move on the carrier trunnion. Do not use the diapragm springs on replacement carriers but fit spacers S1 and S2. However, if a carrier with diaphragm springs is being modified to use spacers only, put a packing ring 5 mm (.197 inch) thick under spacer S2.

Reassembling:

Reverse the dismantling procedure, coating bearing surfaces with molybdenum disulphide compound. Make sure to set the locking pin hole in the spider gearshaft so that it lines up with the hole in the longer side gearshaft,

FIG 12 Typical pinion and crownwheel (ring gear) markings for use when adjusting relative positions of gears

Key to Fig 12

R Designed value of 63.50 mm (five-speed) and 54.50 mm (Sportomatic)
r Plus or minus deviation from R shown in $\frac{1}{100}$ mm (+4) or in mm (+.04)
1 Deviation r   2 Mating number   3 Gear backlash   4 Deviation from T-value (+ or —mm)

then drive the rollpin up to the stop using Tool No. P.257/1. Tighten crownwheel bolts to 9.5 to 10 mkg (69 to 72 lb ft). Tap new lockplates into bolt grooves, squeeze open end inwards with pliers and bend down tabs. Do not forget to fit the spacers before pressing on the bearing inner races.

If new outer races are fitted in the housing or side cover, heat the housings to 120°C or 248°F and drive in the races with a drift.

The crownwheel must be readjusted if a new carrier or a new housing is fitted.

Setting differential position:

Refer to **FIG 11**. Fit spacers under side bearings, S1 being 3.5 mm (.138 inch) thick and S2 being 3.0 mm (.118 inch) thick. Insert unit in housing and fit cover without oil seal. Use a gasket .20 mm (.008 inch) thick and just tighten two opposite nuts. Check gap under cover flange with feelers. Gap for bearing preload should be .15 mm (.006 inch). If gap is, say, .40 mm (.016 inch) when it should be .15 mm (.006 inch), spacer S1 must be replaced with one which is .25 mm (.01 inch) thinner.

Tighten side cover nuts to 2.5 mkg (18 lb ft). Insert axle flange and tighten bolt a little. Check differential drag with a rotating torque measuring device. The pinion must not be engaged and there must be no oil seal in the side cover. Torque to move differential unit must be 18 to 24 cmkg (15.6 to 20.8 lb in). If incorrect, adjust by fitting a different thickness of spacer.

Withdraw unit, remove side bearings and measure spacer thickness at four equidistant points. Determine total thickness of spacers S1 and S2 and say that it is 6.25 mm (.246 inch). To prepare for final adjustment of crownwheel and pinion meshing, spacer S1 must be .10 mm (.004 inch) thinner and spacer S2 the same amount thicker, the total thickness being unaltered. Thus, spacer S1 must be 3.025 mm (.119 inch) thick and spacer S2 must be 3.225 mm (.127 inch) thick. Spacers come in thicknesses from 2.5 to 3.5 mm (.098 to .138 inch) in steps of .10 mm (.004 inch) and there is a .25 mm (.01 inch) washer also available, so that adjustments to the nearest .05 mm (.002 inch) are possible. Round off thickness to the nearest available spacer thickness but make sure that the total thickness of S1 + S2 remains unaltered. For example, S1 + S2 = 3.025 + 3.225 = 6.25 mm. When rounded off S1 + S2 = 3.0 + 3.25 = 6.25 mm.

FIG 13 Dummy carrier P.258 for setting pinion relative to differential assembly centreline. Dial gauge is adjusted to a preload of 1 mm, using a setting plate

Permissible variation in spacer thickness (measured at four points) is .02 mm (.0008 inch). Remove all burrs from spacer edges.

9 Adjusting pinion shaft setting and backlash

Preliminary adjustments have been outlined in **Sections 7** and **8**.

Adjusting pinion shaft:

Fit intermediate plate, gears and selector shafts into housing without a paper gasket. Put spacers on four opposite studs and tighten nuts diagonally to secure plate. Tighten shaft bolt to 11 to 12 mkg (79 to 86 lb ft). Put carrier P.258 on the setting plate (see **FIG 13**) and secure the dial gauge so that small pointer is on 1 and large pointer on 0, giving a preload of 1 mm (.04 inch). Fit dummy carrier and side bearings into housing with axial preload of .10 mm (.004 inch) when cover is secured. Use differential spacers if necessary to ensure that carrier has no end play. A notch on the face of the carrier indicates the position of the gauge plunger. Turn carrier until plunger is at right angles to the face of the pinion and note highest reading. Now follows an example of the calculations.

FIG 14 Adjusting backlash of crownwheel (ring gear). Top arrow shows dial gauge holder P.259 bolted to axle flange. Bottom arrow points to tool P.259 (part of) which locks pinion shaft against turning

FIG 15 Five-speed gearbox. Reverse gearshaft installed with oil hole downwards (upper view) and reverse gears fitted, with needle bearing and thrust washer (lower view)

Side of dummy carrier is marked with dimension from centre line to surface for setting plate. Setting plate is marked with dimension from surface to recess for gauge plunger. Add together and say that result is 53.98 mm + 9.52 mm = 63.50 mm (2.5 inch). If gauge reading differs in clockwise direction, subtract the difference. For example, small pointer between 1 and 2, large one at .24 mm. Subtract .24 mm from gauge setting of 63.50 mm and answer is 63.26 mm. If value E (see **FIG 11** and **Section 7**) is 63.54 mm then pinion is too near and as difference between 63.54 mm and 63.26 mm is .28 mm, that is the thickness of gasket required under the intermediate plate.

If gauge reading differs in anticlockwise direction, add the difference. For example, small pointer between 1 and 0, large one at .08 mm. Add .08 mm to gauge setting of 63.50 mm and result is 63.58 mm. If, for example, value E is 63.68 mm, that figure minus 63.58 mm gives .10 mm, which is the thickness of gasket required.

Paper gaskets for the intermediate plate are available in thicknesses of .10, .15 and .20 mm (.004, .006 and .008 inch). Total thickness may lie between .10 and .50 mm (.004 and .02 inch). If calculations prove that gaskets must be thicker than .50 mm then pinion shaft must be dismantled and further adjustment made to shims 17 (see **FIG 9**).

When determining the thickness of gaskets, round off second figure decimal fractions as follows. Make 3 and over into 5 and 7 and over into 10. Thus .28 mm becomes .30 mm.

After the intermediate plate has been installed on the correct gaskets, check value E again. Deviations of ± .03 mm (.001 inch) are permissible.

Adjusting backlash:

Refer to **FIG 14**. Build up the transmission with the required gaskets and spacers. Secure the intermediate plate as described in the preceding instructions. Check backlash when securing the side cover on a .20 mm (.008 inch) paper gasket, as there must always be some play between the drive gears. **Jamming of the gears is not permissible.** Tighten nuts to 2.5 mkg (18 lb ft). Fit anchoring tool P.259 to the pinion shaft bolt as shown. Insert the axle flange, fit dial gauge holder P.259 to flange and tighten bolt (top arrow). Fit dial gauge so that its plunger contacts the bottom of the clutch cable bracket. Move holder from stop to stop to determine backlash. Make four checks by turning the crownwheel through 90 deg. each time. Backlash must not differ by more than .05 mm (.002 inch) between each measuring point. The correct figure is etched on the crownwheel (see 3 in **FIG 12**), but a backlash of .12 to .18 mm (.005 to .007 inch) is permissible.

Errors may be rectified by adjustment of spacers S1 and S2 (see **Section 8**) but total thickness of spacers must not be altered.

10 Servicing front cover

Remove front cover as in **Section 4** and collect the thrust washer, axial thrust needle bearing, reverse gears and bearings. Remove screw 7 and withdraw tachometer drive (see **FIG 16**). If reverse gearshaft needs renewal, drive out retaining pin, heat cover to 120°C or 248°F and drive shaft inward. Press bronze thrust washer off shaft. Check cover for cracks or damage, clean up joint faces. Check gears, shaft and bearings for wear or damage. Renew oil seal for inner shift rod if defective.

To dismantle tachometer drive, hold body 4 between soft jaws in a vice, unscrew nut 9 and pull out drive 10 and centring disc 13 (see **FIG 16**). Pull out shaft 3. Renew shaft, bushes or oil seal if defective. Check thrust stud 2 in cover. This is a press fit. Check condition of gears. If the gear which extends from the pinion shaft bolt is worn, it may be removed by driving out the cross-pin (see part 4 in **FIG 1**).

When refitting the drive in the body, orientate it so that the cable connection and the locating hole for the setscrew are pointing in the same direction. Insert assembly in cover so that hole lines up with setscrew orifice, insert screw and tighten to 2.5 mkg (18 lb ft). If pinion shaft bolt was removed, tighten to 11 to 12 mkg (79 to 86 lb ft).

Reassembling:

Check that mating numbers of gears are correct. Heat cover to 120°C or 248°F and refit shaft with oil hole pointing down (see upper view in **FIG 15**). Fit retaining pin. Heat bronze washer to same temperature and fit to shaft, pressing it firmly against cover. Fit bearing cages and spacer bush. Fit gears, thrust needle bearing and washer (see lower view in **FIG 15**).

Fitting cover:

Fit a new .20 mm (.008 inch) paper gasket. Pull reverse gear assembly and thrust washer as near to the end of the shaft as possible. Feed cover into place, making sure that curved recess in thrust washer fits over outer race of ballbearing. Tighten nuts to 2.5 mkg (18 lb ft).

11 Reassembling transmission

Reverse the dismantling procedure. Lubricate the assemblies as required. Heat the housing to 120°C or 248°F when fitting the outer races of the two roller bearings into the central web. Make sure spring rings are correctly seated. If the clutch release bearing guide was removed from the rear face of the housing for attention to the input shaft oil seal, refit it. Note that this seal may be renewed without dismantling the transmission, by prising it out with a screwdriver, taking care not to damage the bore or the running surface of the shaft. Put sealer on the outer circumference of the seal, and oil the lip. Drive seal into place with tool VW.244b.

With front bearing inner races in place, fit both shaft and gear assemblies to the intermediate plate. Use a tubular drift to fit outer halves of inner races, the one for the pinion shaft being marked X. **Make sure mating numbers match.** Insert plate and shaft assemblies into housing, fit spacers to four studs and tighten nuts lightly in diagonal sequence with fifth-speed engaged.

Fit first-speed gear and spacer washer to input shaft. Tighten nut to 6 to 6.5 mkg (43 to 47 lb ft). Secure nut with rollpin. Fit pinion shaft thrust washer with small collar facing bearing. Fit needle bearing race, followed by needle bearing and large helical gear. Make sure only one brake band is fitted to the synchronizing unit as shown in **FIG 17**. Fit spider wheel for sliding gear, oil pressure face of bolt and tighten to 11 to 12 mkg (80 to 86 lb ft) while holding input shaft at clutch end with tool P.37. Remove intermediate plate and hold in soft jaws in a vice.

Fit selector shafts and forks. Fit fork 8 (see **FIG 1**) and push shaft through until it enters plate. The shaft must be complete with shift arm secured by rollpin. Slightly tighten fork screw on spring washer. Refer to **FIG 18** for details of the selector detents and springs. Fit ball 3, stick pin 6 in spring 5 with grease and drop into bore. Fit ball 7.

FIG 16 Components of tachometer drive as fitted to gearbox front cover

Key to Fig 16

1 Front cover	5 O-ring	9 Coupling nut
2 Thrust stud	6 Spring ring	10 Elbow drive
3 Shaft and gear	7 Setscrew	11 Bushes
4 Body	8 Elbow drive sleeve	12 Oil seal
		13 Centring disc

FIG 17 Five-speed gearbox. Correct position of single brake band and brake band energizer in first-speed synchronizer

FIG 18 Section through detent components in intermediate plate

Key to Fig 18

1 Intermediate plate	6 Detent pin	11 First and reverse selector shaft
2 Fourth and fifth selector shaft	7 Ball	12 Ball
3 Ball	8 Second and third selector shaft	13 Detent bush
4 Detent bush	9 Detent bush	14 Detent spring for reverse
5 Detent spring for second and fifth-speed	10 Detent pin	15 Plug

FIG 19 Arrows in top view show where clearance of 2 to 3 mm must exist. Lower view shows tool P.260 supporting the shafts for selector fork adjustment

Fit second and third-speed fork and push its shaft into place with shaft 2 in the neutral position. Press down ball 7 when inserting the shaft in the plate. Slightly tighten fork screw on a spring washer. Push shaft into neutral. Fit detent 10 followed by first and reverse shaft 11 and fit ball 12 with spring 14. Tighten plug to 2.5 mkg (18 lb ft).

Fit gear 20 and fork (see **FIG 1**). Slightly tighten fork screw. For help in recognizing the detent springs, the short one should have a free length of 29.2 mm (1.15 inch) with a minimum length of 28.2 mm (1.11 inch). Long spring should be 38.5 mm (1.52 inch) with a minimum of 37.3 mm (1.47 inch).

Take up all free play of sliding gear for first-speed and reverse, pressing it (in neutral) in the direction of forward travel of the car. Put plasticine on gear teeth adjacent to reverse gear and push the transmission cover into place to check that there is at least 1 mm (.04 inch) clearance between the teeth of the two gears under conditions which bring them closest together. Check that selector shaft control forks for first and reverse have a side clearance of 2 to 3 mm (.08 to .12 inch) with those for second and third-speed (see lefthand arrow in top view of **FIG 19**). Tighten first and reverse selector fork screw to 2.5 mkg (18 lb ft).

It is not possible to set the remaining forks accurately without supporting the shafts with tool P.260 as shown in the lower view of **FIG 19**. Adjust the position of second and third and fourth and fifth-speed forks so that the sliding sleeves are exactly central between the synchronizing rings. After a shift test, tighten the fork screws to 2.5 mkg (18 lb ft), making sure that the control forks clear each other by 2 to 3 mm (.08 to .12 inch) as shown by righthand arrow in top view of **FIG 19**.

Take shift rod 1 (see **FIG 1**) and assemble the shift lever and pin, making sure the pin and hole tapers are correct. Fit cotterpin.

Insert shift rod into housing and install the intermediate plate and gears, fitting the correct gaskets under the plate as determined during the drive gear meshing adjustments carried out in **Sections 7, 8** and **9**. It is essential to select fifth-speed for this operation and care must be taken not to damage the input shaft oil seal. Shift back into neutral. Set shift lever between selector control forks and pushrod into rear bore. Put on a new gasket and install the guide fork (see **FIG 4**), locating the lever in the fork correctly. Fit front cover.

Starting with transmission No. 100.100 there is a breather fitted to the differential section of the transmission housing. If there is no breather pipe or ventilation labyrinth in the front cover which is being fitted as a replacement it is necessary to fit a breather. The hole in the breather must point forward at an angle of 45 deg. from the transmission centre line.

If the reversing light switch is removed, make sure, when refitting it, that the operating pin is fitted with the rounded end entering first.

12 Gearshift mechanism

This is illustrated in **FIG 20**. Early gearlever knobs were screwed on, but from 21st March 1967 they were pressed into place. The later type of knob has the gearshift pattern marked on it. To remove the pressed-on type, make a steel fork from 6 mm ($\frac{1}{4}$ inch) flat bar, the slot being 15.5 mm ($\frac{5}{8}$ inch) wide to accommodate the lever. Slip this under the knob and drive it upwards by striking the bar with a hammer.

With gearlever and heater knobs removed, lift off boot 3 and tunnel cover and release base 4. Remove tunnel cover in rear compartment (4 screws), push boot 18 forward, loosen clamp bolt 19 and drive rod 17 off coupling 23. Pull off clamp and boot. Cut locking wire, unscrew square-headed screw 16 and remove socket 15. With transmission unit removed, gearshift rod may be pulled out rearwards.

Installation:

Refit in the reverse order. Tighten screw 16 to 1.5 mkg (11 lb ft). Coat working faces of coupling 23 with lithium grease. Tighten bolts for gearlever base to 2.5 mkg (18 lb ft). Tighten bolts securing guide bracket 10 to 1.0 mkg (7 lb ft). Adjust linkage as described later.

Overhauling gearlever base:

Remove plastic socket 14 from lever. Remove retainers 13 and push one pin out halfway. Take care that spring 11 does not jump out. Put a cloth round the base and prise the free end of the spring out. Remove the second spring in the same way. Remove stop plate 8. Remove parts 5, 6 and 7. Withdraw lever and clean all parts. Renew worn or defective items.

Reassemble by coating working surfaces with lithium grease and snapping seat 5 into the spring. Insert lever in base and put one retainer on each guide pin. Fit stop plate and partly insert pins. Thread springs over pins. Grind a pilot stub on an old screwdriver so that it will enter the first coils of the spring and compress each spring until it can be inserted in the plate. Fit guide pins and retainers. Coat all parts with lithium grease and drive on ball socket 14.

Adjusting linkage:

Through aperture in tunnel, loosen bolt 19. Put gearlever in neutral and press it to the right as far as it will go. With transmission in neutral, move coupling 23 as far to the left as it will go and tighten the clamp bolt to 2.5 mkg (18 lb ft), using a serrated lockwasher under the nut.

Try all gears and check for play in the linkage. Gearlever play should be the same in all gears in every direction.

Fitting gearlever knob:

There is a locking ring inside the later type of press fit knob. This may be hooked out. Fit a new ring by driving it down until it seats in place. Mark travel depth of knob on lever, select third-speed and drive knob into place with a block of wood suitably recessed to accommodate the top face of the knob. Check that knob has reached the mark.

13 Servicing ZF differential

The components are shown in **FIG 21**. Note the additional views of friction disc assemblies for 50 per cent and 75 per cent non-slip effectiveness. These were introduced from 6th March, 1967, the 75 per cent assembly being used for sporting events.

With ordinary differential assemblies, if one wheel is held stationary the other will spin helplessly. In the ZF self-locking assembly this effect is largely eliminated so

FIG 20 Components of gearlever and linkage (manual gearchange)

Key to Fig 20

1	Gearshift knob	12	Guide pin
2	Gearshift lever	13	Retainer
3	Dust boot	14	Ball socket
4	Gearshift base	15	Shift rod joint
5	Spring seat	16	Tapered screw
6	Gearshift spring	17	Shift rod
7	Spring seat	18	Dust boot
8	Gearshift stop plate	19	Hex bolt
9	Guide bushing	20	Clamp
10	Guide bracket	21	Serrated washer
11	Stop plate thrust spring	22	Hex nut
		23	Shift rod coupling

that the greater the need the greater the torque. Examine **FIG 21** and note the squared-off ends of spider shafts 9. These engage angled recesses in side gear rings 6 which are driven by the crownwheel carrier. Driving force thus tends to press both side rings outwards so that they exert a compressive effect on the friction discs and plates. As the discs are splined to the axle shafts, the greater the compression through high torque, the more the assembly is virtually locked together, so that one-sided wheelspin is impossible.

Recommended lubricant is Shell Transmission Oil S.1747.A. In other countries the correct grades are— Australia, Shell SCL Gear Oil 90, Canada, Shell HDR Gear Oil 90 and USA, Shell HDR Gear Oil 90 EP.

Dismantling:

1 Unlock and remove bolts 12. Remove cover 10 (see **FIG 21**). Lift side gear 7 together with associated parts out of carrier 1.
2 Lift out spider gears and shafts 8 and 9. Lift out the opposite side gear and friction assembly. **In both cases, do not confuse the locations of the discs and plates 4 and 5. Clean all parts.**

Key to Fig 21

1. Differential carrier
2. Thrust washer (non-ferrous)
3. Thrust washer (ferrous)
4. Friction plate
5. Friction disc
6. Side gear ring
7. Side gear
8. Spider gear
9. Spider shaft
10. Differential cover
11. Lockplate
12. Bolt

FIG 21 Components of ZF self-locking differential with standard assembly of plates and discs in top row. Plate and disc assemblies for 50 per cent and 75 per cent anti-slip effectiveness are also shown

FIG 22 ZF self locking differential. In differentials with preloaded disc and plate assemblies, install as in top view. Under 100 kg (220 lb) pressure, check installed length of retarder assembly (lower view)

Inspecting:

Check carrier and cover thrust faces for wear and scoring. Check plate grooves for wear. Side gear rings must slide freely in carrier. The locating tabs and thrust faces must not be worn or grooved. Thrust washer faces must be smooth and unworn. Friction discs must slide freely on side gear splines. Check plates for worn tabs and spline teeth.

Check dimension indicated in **FIG 22** by assembling all internal parts between the carrier and its cover and putting them under a load of 100 kg (220 lb) in a press. Tolerance lies between a maximum of 82.3 mm (3.24 inch) and a minimum of 81.6 mm (3.213 inch). Renew worn parts which reduce overall length below the minimum.

Reassembling:

Fit non-ferrous thrust washer 2 with machined recess downwards. Fit steel washer 3, then plates and discs in order of removal, starting and finishing with a plate. Differentials fitted with pre-loaded disc and plate assemblies must have the undulated plate fitted first and last, and so arranged that a space exists between the oil groove in the carrier and the cover and the bow in the plate as shown by the insert in the illustration. Check that plates and discs are correctly assembled (see **FIGS 21** and **22**).

Continue assembling the side gear, spider shafts and gears, and second side gear and the second set of plates and discs. Fit the steel washer followed by the non-ferrous one with the groove facing upwards. Secure the cover, tightening the bolts on new lockplates to a torque of 2.5 mkg or 18 lb ft. Turn up locking tabs.

The assembled differential must turn freely under a torque of 1 to 1.5 mkg (7.2 to 10.8 lb ft) without binding.

Note that slight noises may be heard when driving through sharp curves under power. These are inherent in the design and are not the result of defects.

Note also that the ZF self-locking differential must always be used in conjunction with NADELLA halfshafts.

14 The fourspeed transmission

When servicing this transmission, follow the instructions for the five-speed type. For reference purposes it will be found that the Sportomatic fourspeed gearbox closely resembles the manual box and **FIGS 25** and **35** may be useful.

As first-speed is inside the gearbox, the front cover accommodates reverse gear only. Due to reversed action the synchronizing parts for first-speed gear must be fitted the opposite way round (see **FIG 23**). Note that there is only one brake band A. This gear occupies the position taken by gear 4 in **FIG 9**. Use the same torque values and adjustment data as those given for the five-speed transmission.

15 Sportomatic description

FIG 25 is a sectional view of the Sportomatic transmission showing the torque converter 15, 16 and 17 which is driven by the engine. The torque converter casing is filled with oil and fan blades on pump unit 15 cause a power transfer to blades on turbine 16 through the inertia of the oil. Power from the turbine is transmitted to the gearbox through a normal single-plate clutch 27, 28 and 29. This clutch is used for gearchanging, being operated by a vacuum-servo unit. This unit (6 in **FIG 26**) is connected to a control valve 11 which is electrically operated when a microswitch on the gearlever is closed.

FIG 23 Four-speed gearbox. Single brake band A and brake band energizer must be fitted as shown when assembling first-speed synchronizer. This is the opposite of the five-speed arrangement

FIG 24 Diagram showing power flow through converter and clutch in Sportomatic transmission

Key to Fig 24

F Freewheeling unit   L Stator
P Pump   T Turbine

Key to Fig 25 FIG 25 Longitudinal section through Sportomatic transmission

1 Selector shaft
2 Oil seal
3 Speedometer gearshaft
4 Speedometer drive gear
5 Input shaft
6 Pinion shaft
7 Synchronizing ring
8 Sliding sleeve
9 Selector fork
10 Spider
11 Fourth-speed gear
12 Differential case
13 Pinion gear
14 Pinion gearshaft
15 Pump
16 Turbine
17 Stator
18 Freewheeling unit
19 Turbine shaft bush
20 Oil restrictor in turbine shaft
21 Oil seal
22 Freewheeling unit support
23 Clutch pilot needle bearing
24 Oil seal
25 O-ring
26 Clutch release bearing
27 Clutch carrier & turbine shaft
28 Clutch plate
29 Clutch pressure plate
30 Oil seal

Key to Fig 26 FIG 26 How clutch is disengaged when gearlever is moved

1 Microswitch in gearlever
2 Bypass switch
3 Gear selector shaft
4 Reverse light switch & 'park' position contact
5 Shift rod P and R
6 Vacuum servo unit
7 Transmission clutch
8 Torque converter
9 Reverse light
10 Crankshaft
11 Control valve
12 Adjusting screw
13 Vacuum reservoir
14 Electric solenoid switch
15 Cam and plunger
16 Inlet manifold
17 Check valve
18 Auxiliary valve
19 Main valve
a Wire from fuse 1
b Wire from ignition switch
c Wire to starter terminal 50
d Wire to intermediate fuse 8/15 A

The switch closes as soon as the gearlever is moved for gear selection. Releasing the lever, after a gearshift, opens the switch, the control valve allows atmospheric pressure to break down the pull of the vacuum servo unit and the clutch re-engages. Rapid accelerator opening causes a still more rapid engagement of the clutch, the throttle spindle carrying a cam which operates a plunger to open an auxiliary valve in the control unit (see parts 15 and 18 in **FIG 26**).

A pump driven from the lefthand camshaft keeps the converter filled with oil and promotes cooling by oil circulation. The oil is drawn from the main oil tank, the outlet from the tank being 30 mm higher than that for engine oil circulation to ensure that a leaking converter will not cause failure of engine lubrication. To prevent excessive temperature rise under adverse conditions there is an oil temperature gauge and a red warning light on the instrument panel. When the gauge shows 145°C (295°F) the lamp will light up and the driver must drop down into a lower gear to reduce oil temperature.

16 Routine maintenance

Lubrication:

Follow the recommendations in **Section 2** for the gearbox and differential. Check the oil level in the tank by means of the dipstick. Do this with the engine running. Top-up with oil to the specification given in **Chapter 1**. Change oil at the intervals recommended in the same chapter, the quantity being 9 litres (19 US pints or 15.8 Imp pints). After an overhaul, when it is necessary to fill the torque converter and the oil pipes, fill up with 11.5 litres (24 US pints or 20¼ Imp pints). The converter must be filled with oil before checking the level by dipstick. If there is any doubt about this, detach the oil return pipe from the converter at the tank, run the engine and check that oil flows from the pipe.

Clutch free play:

Check this every 6000 miles. Raise the car and open throttle fully to depressurize vacuum servo unit. Push clutch intermediate lever 2 towards righthand rear wheel (see **FIG 27**). Free play at this point should be at least 5 mm (.20 inch). If play is less, readjust as follows:
1. Remove power unit (see **Section 3**). Remove clevis pin from fork 3.
2. Pull actuating rod of vacuum servo unit 4 right out to stop. Push intermediate lever 2 towards servo unit as far as possible.
3. The holes in the fork must be farther away from the servo unit than the hole in the intermediate lever by 10 to 12 mm (.40 to .47 inch). Refit the clevis pin, using a new splitpin. Tighten locknut on rod. Check control valve adjustment then refit power unit.

Control valve adjustment:

Do this every 6000 miles or when required as in preceding notes. Control linkage and engine idling speed must be correctly adjusted first.

Upshift on acceleration is adjusted as follows:
1. Refer to **FIG 28**. Clearance at 3 must be 1.5 mm (.06 inch) when the throttles are set for idling. Cam 6 must be fully returned.

FIG 27 Sportomatic transmission. Separating torque converter housing from transmission

Key to Fig 27
1 Mounting stud
2 Intermediate lever
3 Clevis
4 Servo unit
5 Clutch rod

FIG 28 On Sportomatic transmission there must be correct clearance between control valve plunger and drag spring

Key to Fig 28
1 Control valve plunger
2 Drag spring
3 Clearance of 1.5 mm
4 Allen bolt
5 Throttle cross-shaft
6 Cam disc
7 Intake manifold

FIG 29 Control valve for Sportomatic transmission. White arrow points to cover over adjusting screw, black arrow to splitpin securing cable connector

FIG 30 Sportomatic transmission. Cable connections for temperature switch and temperature gauge sensor

FIG 31 Details of the Sportomatic gearlever and microswitch

2 Put a 3 mm (.12 inch) shim under the lefthand idling stop screw (see **Chapter 2**). Adjust cam so that drag spring just touches control valve plunger 1.

3 Remove shim. In this position the original clearance of 1.5 mm may be different but a minimum clearance of 1.0 mm (.04 inch) must be maintained.

Downshift on deceleration is adjusted as follows:

1 Drive the car or run it on a roller stand. As a rough guide on a standing vehicle, set the handbrake, let the engine idle and engage a gear. Time lag between releasing gearlever and perceptible impact of engagement must be .30 to .50 seconds.

2 Check under driving conditions by running at 4500 rev/min in 'D'. Take foot off throttle and shift down to 'L'. Clutch should engage without time lag, but the rear wheels must not lock. If necessary, adjust time lag as follows:

3 Remove air cleaners. Remove plastic cover over control valve adjusting screw (white arrow in **FIG 29**). Turn screw in to give a softer delayed clutch engagement. Turn screw anticlockwise to give a harder and more instantaneous clutch engagement. Do not turn more than $\frac{1}{4}$ to $\frac{1}{2}$ a turn at a time. Refit cover and air cleaners.

Cleaning maintenance:

There is an air filter for the control valve at the end opposite to the electrical connections (see **FIG 29**). Clean this every 6000 miles.

Clean electrical contacts in gearlever switch and readjust if needed. Do this every 6000 miles (see **Section 21**).

17 Driving hints

Gearshift symbols are: P (Parking lock), R (Reverse), L (Low gear for steep hills), D (for city driving), D3 (for moderate highway speeds), D4 (for high-speed motorways).

Engine will not start unless gearlever is at P. Use hand throttle for idling when engine is cold. Start off in D or use L on steep hills. Shift up by taking foot off throttle, moving gearlever and taking hand away. **Do not shift down when engine rev/min are very high or engine may be overspeeded.**

If oil temperature warning light goes on, shift to a lower gear.

Gear may remain engaged for brief stops. To park, move gearlever to P when car has stopped moving. Pull on handbrake.

18 Removal and installation

Removal of the power unit is covered in **Section 3**. When refitting the assembly, make sure the heating ducts are not jammed. The best plan is to slide these into place on the heat exchanger outlets just before the power unit reaches its final position. Tighten engine and transmission support bolts to 9.5 mkg (69 lb ft). Half-axle flanges must be free from grease. Hollow side of serrated washers must face the baseplates and tighten the Allen bolts to 4.3 mkg (31 lb ft).

Key to Fig 31

1 Gearlever
2 Retaining pin
3 Stop ring
4 Microswitch
5 Ball
6 Spring
7 Gearlever-lower part
8 Position of switch when-engaged with pin
9 Parts to be lightly lubricated
10 Spring and guide pin

19 Separating and refitting transmission

Just to the rear of the vacuum servo unit is the temperature sensor (see **FIG 30**). The electrical cables have been detached. Now detach the oil hose and the pressure pipe. Loosen the oil hose clamp. Detach the vacuum hose from the servo unit.

Unhook and withdraw the rear throttle control rod. Through the large apertures in the housing, remove the angled 12-point bolts which secure the torque converter to the coupling plate. Remove bolts and nuts joining engine to transmission. As units are separated, take care that the torque converter remains in its housing. A short length of flat steel strip may be bolted to one of the housing bolt holes to keep the torque converter in place.

When refitting the engine to the transmission, use a torque of 4.7 mkg (34 lb ft) on the attaching nuts and bolts. The 12-point bolts for securing the torque converter to the coupling plate must be tightened to 2.4 to 2.6 mkg (17 to 19 lb ft). Set the clutch free play as described in **Section 16**.

20 Servicing control valve and sensors

Control valve:

A faulty valve must be renewed. To remove it, detach battery leads. Remove air cleaner assembly after detaching oil tank breather hose and small hose for breather valve. Withdraw rubber cap from valve, remove splitpin (see black arrow in **FIG 29**) and pull off wire connector.

Detach hoses from valve and release bracket from carburetter.

When fitting a control valve, coat sliding surface of cam and drag spring with molybdenum disulphide grease. Adjust valve as in **Section 16**. Make sure cable connector is well seated. Re-drill splitpin hole if necessary.

Temperature switch and gauge sensor:

These are shown in **FIG 30**. They may be removed without taking the power unit out of the car by following the instructions for removing the engine and transmission as described in **Chapter 1** and **Section 3** (this chapter) up to the point where the unit is lowered a little. The switch and sensor are then accessible from above. Pull cables off and remove.

When refitting, heat and quench the copper gaskets to anneal them. Tighten switch and sensor to 4.5 to 5.0 mkg (33 to 36 lb ft). Tighten engine mounting bolts to 9.5 mkg (69 lb ft).

21 Servicing gearlever and microswitch

Refer to **FIG 31**. Remove and refit microswitch as follows:

1 Lift rubber boot and remove tunnel covering. Release base flange from tunnel and lift slightly.
2 Detach microswitch cables in tunnel and lift away lever and base.
3 Drive off gearlever knob as described at the start of **Section 12**. Pull boot and switch off lever.

Clean dirty switch contacts or renew switch. Reassemble by pushing switch on lever with split facing forward. Push far enough to engage pin 2. Check contact gap with lever in neutral position. Gap must be .30 to .40 mm (.012 to .016 inch). Alter by bending outer contact tabs. Fit switch top and dust boot. Refit knob as described in **Section 12**. Connect cable connectors and fit assembly to tunnel. Earth lead from switch goes under front lefthand bolt. Tighten 8 mm bolts to 2.5 mkg (18 lb ft) and 6 mm bolts to 1.0 mkg (7.2 lb ft).

FIG 32 Sportomatic transmission. Removing freewheel support from clutch carrier plate

FIG 33 Clutch and torque converter components for Sportomatic transmission

Key to Fig 33
1 Torque converter   3 Clutch plate
2 Turbine shaft   4 Clutch pressure plate

Overhauling gearlever base:

Apart from the microswitch, the rest of the assembly resembles that for the manual gearbox lever, so refer to **Section 12** for instructions. Having fitted the plastic ball socket to the lever, lightly grease stop ring 3 and push onto lever. Grease spring 6 and insert in lower part 7, grease ball and lever and insert in lower part. Fit retaining pin 2. It must enter easily to prevent switch malfunctioning. Install switch and knob.

22 Servicing torque converter and clutch

Removing:

With engine detached from transmission as described in **Section 19**, withdraw torque converter. **Oil will run out.** Cover converter to keep out dirt. Remove external and internal nuts securing converter housing to transmission casing. Release front end of clutch rod 5 from intermediate lever 2 (see **FIG 27**). Part housing from casing while disengaging clutch release bearing from fork.

Remove socket-head bolts from clutch pressure plate flange, loosening them a turn at a time diagonally to prevent distortion. Withdraw pressure plate, noting that release bearing may fall out. Remove clutch driven plate. Remove socket-head bolts from freewheel support, fit two long bolts in opposite holes and drive out support with oil seal (see **FIG 32**).

Remove circlip from turbine shaft 2 in **FIG 33**. Support housing on blocks and drive out turbine shaft. Using a punch at alternating points, drive out shaft bearing and push out oil seal.

FIG 34 Details of clutch intermediate lever for Sportomatic transmission. Upper view on right shows correct assembly of pin and pivot, lower view A shows correct installation of spring

Key to Fig 34

1 Lock ring	5 Bush
2 Washer	6 Intermediate lever
3 Grommet	7 O-ring
4 Spacer	8 Thrust ring
	9 Spring

Inspecting converter and clutch:

Refer to **Chapter 5** for instructions on checking clutch condition but note that minimum thickness over linings (uncompressed) is 5.5 mm (.217 inch). Also, lateral run-out must not exceed .50 mm (.02 inch).

Torque converters cannot be repaired, so renew one which is damaged.

Check clutch face of turbine shaft and carrier assembly. Renew assembly if heavily scored. Check needle bearing and inspect hub seat and oil passage. Bearing is part 23 in **FIG 25**. If worn, needle bearing and oil seal may be extracted with a puller and a new bearing driven in with tool P361. The oil seal is fitted with tool P362. Grease bearing with molybdenum disulphide grease, using it sparingly so that clutch plate cannot be contaminated.

Check ballbearing in housing when dry after cleaning. To fit a new bearing, heat housing to 120°C or 248°F. and drive it in with tool P359. Renew the smaller oil seal by driving in with tool P359. Oil the sealing lip.

Check freewheel support and turbine shaft bushing for wear. Check oil passages. A defective support must be renewed as an assembly, complete with bushing and sealing sleeve (see 22 in **FIG 25**).

Reassembling:

Secure the freewheel support with three bolts and drive in the turbine shaft using tool P362. Remove bolts and support and fit circlip on shaft. Refit freewheel support, tightening socket-head bolts diagonally to 1.4 mkg (10 lb ft). Fit new O-rings to bolts. Refit seal and oil lip.

FIG 35 Plan view of Sportomatic gearbox and final drive, the front end being on the left

Key to Fig 35

1 Side bearing	7 Side gear	13 Gear 3 for reverse speed	19 Ring gear
2 Oil seal	8 Pinion gear	14 Retaining ring	20 Pinion shaft
3 Washer	9 Pinion gear shaft	15 Gear 2 for reverse speed	21 Transmission side cover
4 Stretchbolt	10 Reverse gear shaft	16 Caged needle bearing	22 Hex bolt
5 Axle flange	11 Thrust washer	17 Thrust needle bearing	23 Differential case
6 Threaded piece	12 Caged needle bearing	18 Thrust ring	

Centre clutch driven plate with a suitable mandrel (see **Chapter 5**). Lightly coat both sides of diaphragm spring segments with molybdenum disulphide grease and work release bearing in diagonally from inside. Fit clutch pressure plate, tightening bolts diagonally a turn at a time to 1.4 mkg (10 lb ft). Make sure plate is seating on dowels and release bearing is free.

Refitting:

Use molybdenum disulphide grease to coat contact faces of clutch release fork and bearing, also pilot at rear end of gearbox input shaft. Fit engine mounting bolt and spring washer into housing adjacent to temperature sensor body. **Vacuum servo unit prevents fitting bolt later on.** Bring mounting flanges together while guiding clutch release bearing into fork. Tighten large nuts to 4.0 mkg (29 lb ft) and smaller nuts to 2.2 mkg (16 lb ft).

Torque converter must hold a small quantity of oil during assembly. Put about .50 litres of engine oil in a new converter. The equivalent is 1 US pint and slightly less than 1 Imp pint. Slide converter on freewheel support and turbine shaft. Refit engine to transmission.

23 Servicing clutch controls

Intermediate lever:

Components of the lever are shown in **FIG 34**. To remove lever, detach clutch rod and actuating rod clevis. Remove circlip 1, washer 2, grommet 3, spacer 4 and lever 6. Lift off O-ring 7, thrust ring 8 and spring 9.

Renew pivot shaft and bush 5 if worn. Renew lever if eyes are worn. To remove and refit shaft and dowel pin, heat housing to 120°C or 248°F. Install to dimensions given on right in **FIG 34**. Coat shaft with molybdenum disulphide grease. Fit spring as shown at A. Fit thrust ring with cavity over dowel pin and end of spring. Fit O-ring, lever and remaining parts. Install circlip.

Clutch fork:

Detach rear end of clutch rod 5 from release fork lever (see **FIG 27**). Fork is carried on shaft located in transmission casing, holes being covered on outside by caps. Prise out caps with two screwdrivers. Drive out rollpin securing fork to shaft. Drift out the shaft and remove fork and washers.

If worn, renew the shaft bushes, driving them below the outer surface so that the caps may be refitted. Reassemble the fork and shaft so that the holes for the rollpin are aligned. Fit the rollpin. Use molybdenum disulphide grease on shaft and bushes.

24 Overhauling gearbox

Apart from the parking lock shown in **FIG 36**, the gearbox is much the same as the manual fourspeed box. Sectional views in **FIGS 25** and **35** will be found to be useful, and a comparison with the fivespeed manual box shown in **FIG 1** will reveal how closely the components behind the intermediate plate resemble each other. Reading **Section 14** will show how the parts in front of the intermediate plate differ.

Servicing the fourspeed gearbox and differential unit may be carried out by following the instructions in **Sections 4** to **11**, and any differences which call for changes in procedure will be covered in the rest of this section.

FIG 36 Sportomatic transmission. Parking lock and reverse gears

Key to Fig 36
1 Reverse selector fork 4 Roll pin
2 Parking lever and pawl 5 Reverse sliding gear
3 Pinion shaft bolt 6 Circlip

Initial dismantling:

1 Release clutch intermediate lever from vacuum servo clevis (see **FIG 27**). Release servo unit and bracket from transmission casing.
2 Remove transmission front support. Remove parking lock cap screw just above tachometer elbow drive. Withdraw spring and ball. Remove bypass switch.
3 Remove front cover. Refer to **FIG 36** and remove parking lockpin and ball from reverse selector fork 1. Remove circlip 6 and pull off reverse sliding gear 5 and fork. Detach springs and lift off parking lock lever and pawl 2.
4 Select fourth-speed by turning selector rod clockwise and pulling it out. Fit tool P37 to splines at rear end of input shaft to prevent turning and unscrew bolt 3. Remove splined muff.
5 Remove rollpin 4 and unscrew castle nut. Remove reversing light switch and actuating pin. Remove selector shaft guide fork and continue with removal of intermediate plate as in **Section 4**. Carry on dismantling as instructed for the fivespeed transmission.

Pinion shaft:

Note, when servicing the pinion shaft according to **Section 7**, that the dimension R (see **FIG 12**) is not 63.50 mm but 54.50 mm (2.146 inch). The method of calculating the spacer thickness remains the same.

Input shaft:

As can be seen from part 5 in **FIG 25**, the gear for first-speed is splined to the shaft and is mounted to the rear of the intermediate plate, the shaft carrying no gear in front of the plate as it does in the fivespeed box. The gear may be pressed off the shaft together with the inner race half of the ballbearing. When refitting gear, its small collar faces outward.

When identifying the gears, remember that there is one speed less, so that what is called a second-speed gear in the fivespeed transmission is the first-speed gear in the fourspeed gearbox, and so on.

Adjusting pinion shaft setting and backlash:

Follow the instructions in **Section 9** but remember that dimension R in **FIG 12** is not 63.50 mm but 54.50 mm (2.146 inch) in the Sportomatic transmission. This does not, however, affect the method of making the adjustments. In the case of backlash the dial gauge is mounted on the axle flange as shown in **FIG 14** but the gauge plunger must be fitted with an angular sensor which is offset. This is made to bear on a projecting fin on the front one of the two lowest ribs on the side cover.

Overhauling differential:

The method given in **Section 8** may be followed, but note that there is no rollpin to secure the spider shaft. Reference to part 4 in **FIG 35** will show that the shaft is secured by short projections on the flange bolts. Make sure the hole in the shaft is correctly aligned when assembling. Note the use of threaded blocks 6 and spring retainers. These must be inserted in the side gears before the spider shaft is fitted.

Servicing intermediate plate:

Follow the instructions in **Section 6** but start by drawing off the front reverse gear with a puller. This will break the retaining ring (see parts 13 and 14 in **FIG 35**). **Make sure broken ring is removed.**

When reassembling, push gear 15 into place from inside. Fit a new retaining ring in the groove in the splines on the outside of the plate. Fit gear 13 while squeezing the ring with pliers. Tap gear into place.

Servicing front cover:

Follow the instructions in **Section 10**. Refer to **FIG 35** and note that reverse gear 13 may, in some cases, touch the reverse sliding gear. Starting with transmissions 4180176 and 3180261 respectively, a spacer was fitted between the cover and the bronze washer 11. Do not forget to fit this spacer.

Before refitting cover, grease the parking lockpin and insert in selector fork bore, followed by the ball. With cover installed, refit parking lock ball and spring and tighten plug to 3.5 to 4.0 mkg (25 to 30 lb ft).

Those transmissions which are fitted with the spacer just mentioned must have the axial play of the reverse gear checked. Select reverse by turning selector rod to the left and pulling out. If reverse gear binds, fit a second gasket under the cover flange.

Reassembling transmission:

Follow the instructions in **Section 11** but remember that when they mention engaging fifth-speed gear, convert this to fourth-speed gear, and to the other gears where applicable. Note the following variations:

1 When intermediate plate is installed, put washer on input shaft with bevel outwards and tighten nut to 9.0 to 11.0 mkg (65 to 80 lb ft). Lock rear end of input shaft against turning, using tool P37. After fitting rollpin, push splined muff onto pinion shaft with inner splines facing outwards. Fit and tighten pinion shaft bolt.

2 The selector rod detent spring lengths are 38.5 mm (1.52 inch) for first and fourth-speed gears and 37.3 mm (1.47 inch) for reverse gear and parking lock.

3 Having tightened the selector fork screws and checked clearance between control forks, insert the detent pin with fork rod for gears 1 and 2 in neutral (see part 8 in **FIG 18**). Insert rod for reverse and parking lock (part 11). Make sure detent pin is still in place.

4 Grease and fit thrust bearing 17 in **FIG 35** with needles facing reverse gear 15.

5 When fitting the intermediate plate and gear assembly, pull out the selector rod for reverse and parking lock until it rests against the plate. With plate installed, push rod into housing bore (neutral position) and fit detent ball and spring, followed by screwed plug. Test-shift to check that detent pin is still in place.

6 After fitting the guide fork (see **FIG 4**), slide reverse gear fork and gear onto selector rod and pinion shaft and fit circlip to rod (see **FIG 36**). Grease and insert parking lock pin in selector rod and fork, followed by the ball. Fit parking lock lever and pawl and connect springs. Fit front cover and check reverse gear (see 'Servicing front cover').

25 Fault diagnosis
MANUAL TRANSMISSION

(a) Difficulty in changing gear

1 Bent or worn gearshift mechanism
2 Shift rod coupling wrongly set
3 Faulty or worn synchronizing mechanism
4 Faulty clutch or release bearing
5 Stiffness of clutch pedal, cable or release mechanism
6 Input shaft spigot bearing tight
7 Excessive clutch clearance
8 Faulty selector rod detent or springs

(b) Noisy gearchanging

1 Check 3 to 7 in (a)
2 Wrong grade of transmission oil

(c) Slipping out of gear

1 Check 8 in (a)
2 Excessive end float of free-running gears
3 Worn synchronizing teeth
4 Selector fork wrongly positioned
5 Gearshift mechanism worn
6 Worn bearings

(d) Noisy transmission

1 Check 2 and 6 in (c)
2 Incorrect or insufficient lubricant
3 Worn drive gears and differential
4 Insufficient preload on differential bearings
5 Drive gears incorrectly meshed

26 Fault diagnosis
SPORTOMATIC TRANSMISSION

Malfunction	Cause	Remedy
1. Clutch slipping under full throttle although not only upon completion of a shift	Oily clutch linings	Replace clutch plate, eliminate oil leak
	Defective clutch	Replace clutch
	Improperly adjusted clutch linkage	Readjust linkage (basic adjustment), check clutch free play, check clutch
2. Excessive clutch slippage under open throttle upon completion of a shift	Improperly adjusted control valve	Readjust control valve for acceleration upshift
3. Harsh or delayed clutch engagement upon completion of a downshift	Improperly adjusted control valve	Readjust control valve for deceleration downshift
4. Clutch does not disengage	Improperly adjusted clutch linkage	Check adjustment, reaccomplish basic adjustment if necessary, possibly check the clutch
	Leaks in connecting hoses or vacuum reservoir	Eliminate leaks
	Defective diaphragm in vacuum servo unit	Replace vacuum servo unit
	Defective needle bearing in pilot seat of input shaft inclutch	Replace needle bearing and oil seal in turbine shaft
	Break in electric solenoid circuit	Repair damage, possibly by replacing the fuse
	Dirty or oxidized contact points in gearshift lever switch, poor ground to chassis	Clean contacts or install new switch, as appropriate; check ground connection to chassis
	Defective solenoid in control valve	Replace control valve
	Crimped or flattened hoses (blocked air passage)	Replace defective hoses

continued

Malfunction	Cause	Remedy
5. Engine dies when a shift is made, idle speed cannot be adjusted	Leak in hose between control valve and vacuum servo unit	Replace hose
	Defective diaphragm in vacuum servo unit	Replace vacuum servo unit
	Leaking check valves in intake manifold	Replace check valves
	Loose or defective hose between control valve and vacuum reservoir	Tighten or replace hoses
	Leak in vacuum reservoir	Eliminate leak
6. Clutch does not engage upon completion of a downshift, but engages harsh when throttle is opened	Gearshift switch contacts sticking, or shorting due foreign matter in switch	Clean switch, free contacts, or replace the switch
	Short circuit in wire between switch and solenoid	Repair damage, install new wire if necessary
	Sticking solenoid in control valve	Replace control valve
7. Car leaps when gearshift lever is released while engine is idling and gear engaged (engagement jerk)	Idle speed too high	Readjust idle speed
	Improperly adjusted control valve	Readjust control valve (for deceleration shift)
8. Noisy torque converter (high-pitch whining)	Not enough oil in torque converter	Replenish oil in oil tank
	Oil pressure too low	Check oil pump
	Torque converter losing oil through pump hub	Replace oil seal in pump hub
	Oil leaking through weld seam between pump and turbine	Replace torque converter unit

continued

Malfunction	Cause	Remedy
9. Poor acceleration characteristics despite well performing engine and Sportomatic system	Defective torque converter: check stall speed by setting handbrake, depressing footbrake, shifting into D4, and opening the throttle. Engine speed should be between 2400 and 2800 rpm under the above conditions Caution: When performing the above test, watch the temperature gauge. Do not let the temperature rise to the red field on the dial	If the engine speed is higher than stated here, and possibly continues to rise, it will be necessary to replace the clutch. If the lower value (2400 rpm) cannot be attained, the torque converter will have to be replaced.

TRANSMISSION TYPE BY VEHICLE

Trans Type	Vehicle Application	Remarks	No. of Speeds	Crownwheel and Pinion Ratio	Gear Ratios				
					1st	2nd	3rd	4th	5th
902/0	Type 911		4	7:31	11:34 A	19:32 H	24:27 Q	28:24 X	
902/1	Type 911		5	7:31	11:34 A	18:34 F	22:29 M	25:26 S	28:24 X
901/0	911/2000		5	7:31	12:34 AA	18:32 GA	23:28 O	26:25 U	28:23 Y
901/02	Type 911S		5	7:31	11:34 A	18:34 F	22:29 M	25:26 S	29:23 Z
901/03	Type 911T		5	7:31	11:34 A	18:34 F	22:29 M	25:26 S	29:23 Z
901/10	Type 911T and 911S		4	7:31	11:34 A	19:31 HB	25:26 S	29:23 Z	
901/12	Types 911T 911E, 911E-USA and 911S	Effective from November 1968 Optional on types 911E and 911S	4	7:31	11:34 A	19:31 HB	25:26 S	29:23 Z	
901/13	Types 911T 911E & 911S	Effective from November 1968 Optional on Type 911T	5	7:31	11:34 A	18:34 F	22:29 M	25:26 S	29:23 Z
901/50	Types 911 and 911S	Special ratio/standard ratio	5	7:31	14:37 B	18:32 GA	22:29 M	26:26 T	28:23 Y
901/51	Types 911 and 911S	Special ratio for Hill climbs	5	7:31	12:34 AA	17:34 E	20:31 I	22:29 M	23:28 O
901/52	Types 911 and 911S	Special ratio for Airport races	5	7:31	12:34 AA	18:34 F	21:31 J	23:28 O	25:26 S

Continued

Trans Type	Vehicle Application	Remarks	No. of Speeds	Crownwheel and Pinion Ratio	Gear Ratios				
					1st	2nd	3rd	4th	5th
901/53	Types 911 and 911S	Special ratio for speed circuits	5	7:31	15:36 C	20:32 HA	23:28 O	26:26 T	28:23 Y
901/54	Types 911 and 911S	Special ratio for Nurburgring	5	7:31	14:37 B	20:32 HA	22:29 M	25:27 R	27:25 V
901/80	Types 911T 911E & 911S	Effective from November 1968 Optional on Type 911S	5	7:31	14:37 B	18:32 GA	22:29 M	26:26 T	28:23 Y
901/81	Types 911T, 911E & 911S	Effective from November 1968. Optional on Type 911S	5	7:31	12:34 AA	17:34 E	20:31 I	22:29 M	23:28 O
901/82	Types 911T 911E & 911S	Effective from November 1968 Optional on Type 911S	5	7:31	12:34 AA	18:34 F	21:31 J	23:28 O	25:26 S
901/83	Types 911T 911E & 911S	Effective from November 1968 Optional on Type 911S	5	7:31	15:36 C	20:32 HA	23:28 O	26:26 T	28:23 Y
901/84	Types 911T 911E & 911S	Effective from November 1968 Optional on Type 911S	5	7:31	14:37 B	20:32 HA	22:29 M	25:27 R	27:25 V
911/00	Type 911T	Effective from Model 70	4	7:31	11:34 A	19:31 HB	25:26 S	29:22 ZA	
911/01	Types 911E & 911S	Effective from Model 70	5	7:31	11:34 A	18:32 GA	23:28 O	27:25 V	29:22 ZA
911/80	Types 911T 911E & 911S	Effective from Model 70 Optional on Type 911S	5	7:31	14:37 B	18:32 GA	22:29 M	26:26 T	28:23 Y
911/81	Types 911T, 911E & 911S	Effective from Model 70 Optional on Type 911S	5	7:31	12:34 AA	17:34 E	20:31 I	22:29 M	23:28 O
911/82	Types 911T 911E & 911S	Effective from Model 70 Optional on Type 911S	5	7:31 7:31	12:34 AA	18:34 F	21:31 J	23:28 O	25:26 S
911/83	Types 911T 911E & 911S	Effective from Model 70 Optional on Type 911S	5	7:31	15:36 C	20:32 HA	23:28 O	26:26 T	28:23 Y
911/84	Types 911T 911E & 911S	Effective from Model 70 Optional on Type 911S	5	7:31	14:37 B	20:32 HA	22:29 M	25:27 R	27:25 V
905/00	Types 911 - USA & 911L	Sportomatic	4	7:27	15:36 C	19:31 HB	23:28 O	26:25 U	
905/01	Types 911T and 911S	Sportomatic	4	7:27	15:36 C	19:31 HB	23:28 O	27:25 V	
905/20	Types 911T and 911E	Sportomatic Effective from Model 70	4	7:27	15:36 C	20:31 I	24:27 Q	28:24 X	

NOTES

CHAPTER 7 - REAR SUSPENSION AND DRIVE AXLES

1. General description
2. Damper maintenance
3. Servicing axle halfshafts
4. Removing control arm
5. Servicing and refitting control arm
6. Removing and refitting torsion bar
7. Adjusting torsion bar
8. Modified radius arms
9. Stabilizer (anti-roll) bar
10. Rear wheel alignment
11. Height adjustment
12. Fault diagnosis

1 General description

The layout of the system is shown in **FIG 1**, each independent suspension unit consisting of a radius arm 1 bolted at the rear end to the flange of control arm 3. The front end of the radius arm is coupled to the outer splined end of torsion bar 2, the inner end of the bar being fixed.

Triangulated control of the suspension is maintained by arm 3, the inner end being pivoted in a bracket on the body. Drive from the transmission is taken through halfshaft 4, each shaft being provided with two universal joints. Telescopic hydraulic dampers 5 are fitted and each incorporates a rubber buffer which supplements the torsion bar springing. Eccentric bolts 6 and 7 permit adjustments to camber and wheel tracking.

Starting with 1968 models, 911T (Sportomatic), 911L and 911S cars had ventilated brake discs, new rear hubs with spacer rings and a wider track. Stabilizer (anti-roll) bars were standard on the 911S, and from 1968 models onwards the bar was optional on all types.

There is no routine maintenance required on the rear axle or suspension system.

2 Damper maintenance

BOGE dampers are standard on 911T, 911L and all Targa models. Koni dampers are standard on 911S cars and are optional on all other types except Targa models. From 1968 models onwards the rubber buffer has 9 rings instead of 8. A section through the standard damper is given in **FIG 2**. Adjust Koni dampers as instructed in **Chapter 8**.

Removing, testing and refitting damper:

Do this with car standing on its wheels. Alternatively, if car is jacked up, lift radius arm with special tool P.289 or lift outer end of control arm with a jack. In engine compartment, remove cap and self-locking nut from top of damper (see **FIG 3**). Damper rod may be held with spanner on flats. Release lower end of damper from control arm.

Clean damper. If heavily coated with oily dirt the damper may need renewal. Hold damper vertically in a vice and reciprocate top end several times to fill cylinder 11 with fluid (see **FIG 2**). Press top end in and out through full strokes to check resistance. If excessive free play is evident at any point, damper must be renewed. Check condition of rubber buffer 6. Fit buffer with 9 rings to 1968 models onwards. Do not try to dismantle damper further. **Adjustment or topping up is not possible.**

When reassembling top cover 8, make sure that stop disc 9 is fitted so that its grooves face downwards. Fit the rubber buffer dry.

Refit damper in reverse order, tightening lower bolt to 7.5 mkg (54 lb ft). Renew rubber grommets 3 if deteriorated and tighten nut until they are partially compressed.

From 1972 onwards all variants of the 911 models are equipped with modified dampers. Also, the lower mounting point of the damper has been moved rearwards approximately 10 mm (.40 inch) and the upper mounting point has been moved slightly forward and towards the vehicles longitudinal axis. This relocation was necessary because of the new transmission which has its axle flanges approximately 10 mm further to the rear.

The new dampers have a larger diameter and the overall length has been increased. Boge dampers are fitted as standard but Bilstein or Koni may be fitted as optionals. They are easily recognized by their colour: Boge-black, Koni-red and Bilstein-green. Koni dampers cannot be used on the Targa models.

3 Servicing axle halfshafts

'Nadella' and 'LÖBRO' halfshafts are shown in **FIG 4 & 6**. Cars with ZF self-locking differential must be fitted with 'Nadella' shafts. 911 and 911S cars are fitted with either type on an alternative basis, but after the introduction of the 1968 models, 911T cars are fitted with a simplified differential which must be assembled with 'LÖBRO' shafts.

Removing halfshafts:

1. Raise car and remove rear wheels. Remove splitpin and axle nut. Hub flange may be held against turning with tool P.36b and the nut unscrewed with tools P.296, P.44a and P.42a.
2. Remove socket-head bolts from halfshaft flanges and remove shaft.

'Nadella' halfshafts:

Check the joints for wear. If slack and worn, renew complete shaft, which is available on an exchange basis.

'LÖBRO' halfshafts:

To dismantle, remove clips from dust boots and circlips from shaft ends (see **FIG 4**). Withdraw joints from shaft.

Clean all parts and check for wear. When reassembling, fit new dust boots. Slide wire retainer and joint onto shaft and secure with circlip. Fill joint with 70 gm (2½ oz) of multipurpose molybdenum disulphide grease. Any that will not go in the joint and boot should be placed in the flange side. Clean flange and boot free from grease at large end and stick boot to flange with EC.750M.2G51 compound (Minnesota Mining and Manfg. Co). To fit clips, drill 2 mm ($\frac{3}{32}$ inch) holes at each end and draw together with pliers as shown in **FIG 5**. Bend tab over and tap down flat.

FIG 1 Layout of rear suspension system (left). Eccentric adjusters for camber and tracking (right)

Key to Fig 1

1 Radius arm
2 Torsion bar
3 Control arm
4 Halfshaft
5 Telescopic damper
6 Camber adjustment
7 Tracking adjustment

FIG 2 Section through rear damper, the top end being on the left

Key to Fig 2

1 Self-locking nut
2 Washer
3 Grommets
4 Seat in vehicle
5 Grommet bushing
6 Rubber buffer
7 Plunger rod
8 Cover tube
9 Stop disc
10 Plunger
11 Cylinder
12 Check valve
13 Grommet
14 Grommet bushing

Refitting halfshafts:

1 Refer to left hand view in **FIG 6**. Put new gasket ring 11 on halfshaft stub, lightly oil splines and insert stub in wheel hub.
Flange faces on halfshaft must be free from grease.

2 'LÖBRO' halfshafts must be secured with socket-head bolts marked either 130-140 or 12K on the head or on the side. Tighten to 4.3 mkg (31 lb ft) on Schnorr washers that have their hollow sides facing the base plate.

3 'Nadella' halfshafts must be secured with socket-head bolts tightened to 4.7 mkg (34 lb ft).

4 Tighten outer nut to 30 to 35 mkg (217 to 253 lb ft) and fit a new splitpin.

1971 and later models:

From October 1971 the 911 models have new and lighter axle shafts, almost .9 kg (2 lb) lighter. The constant velocity joints are 8 mm (.31 inch) narrower (see **FIG 4**) and consequently the shafts are increased by an equal amount to compensate. These new type drive shafts can be fitted to earlier models but only from 1969 onwards. If they are used it will be necessary to use new supporting plates and new M10 x 48 socket head bolts.

4 Removing control arm:

1 Refer to left hand view in **FIG 6**. Raise car, remove rear wheels. Remove shrouds 5 from behind brake discs.

2 Block brake pedal in slightly depressed position and remove fluid line from caliper (see **Chapter 10**). Remove caliper.

3 Remove two screws adjacent to wheel studs and pull off brake disc. Remove outer axle shaft nut (2nd paragraph in **Section 3**). Release halfshaft (see **Section 3**).

4 Use a drift to drive out hub 4 from the rear, taking care not to damage seal 9. Remove splitpin and nut from handbrake cable and pull cable out from behind (see **Chapter 10**).

5 From brake shoe side remove 4 bolts and withdraw brake carrier plate 6. Lift radius arm to relieve tension on damper and remove lower bolt. Tool P.289 engages arm and has a hook and long bolt to lift the arm against torsion bar pressure (see **FIG 8**).

6 At inner end of control arm 12, remove self-locking nut from mounting bolt and drive out bolt while tilting arm slightly so that it clears the transmission. It may be necessary to slacken the transmission carrier bolts. Remove the control arm.

5 Servicing and refitting control arm

Refer to left hand view in **FIG 6**. Remove inner race of roller bearing 8, move spacer tube 7 out of the way and drift out ball-bearing 2 (see **FIG 7**) and remove tube. Using a suitable mandrel and support tube, press out the roller bearing outer race and oil seal.

Check alignment of control arm on gauge P.295. A bent arm must be renewed. The bushes at the inner end are called Flanblocs and removal entails destruction. New Flanblocs must be pressed in up to the stop.

Check both bearings for roughness when unlubricated. Check spacer tube for wear or damage. Renew oil seals if leakage has been troublesome and check running surfaces for seal lips. These must be polished and free from scoring.

Reassemble by pressing in roller bearing up to stop. Press in oil seal 9 with lip facing inwards. Fit spacer tube so that wider face is at roller bearing end as in illustration. Pack hub and bearings with 40 gm (1½ oz) of multi-purpose lithium grease. Renew seal 3 in brake carrier plate using tool P.294.

When refitting control arm, move it about to ease insertion of mounting bolt. There is a washer under the bolt head as well as under the nut. **Do not tighten nut at this stage.** Connect radius arm to control arm and tighten retaining bolts to 9 mkg (65 lb ft). Tighten camber eccentric bolt to 6 mkg (43 lb ft) and tracking eccentric bolt to 5 mkg (36 lb ft) (see parts 6 and 7 in **FIG 1**).

Fit damper bolt and tighten to 7.5 mkg (54 lb ft). Stick a new O-ring in the groove round the outer race of the ballbearing, fit the brake carrier plate and tighten bolts to 2.5 mkg (18 lb ft).

Fit handbrake cable and tighten nut until splitpin hole is visible, then fit a new pin. Check that expander is correctly seated (see **Chapter 10**).

Put a new gasket 11 on the axle stub. With a plastic mallet, drive the hub into place. Support the hub flange and drive in the inner race for the roller bearing. Fit axle stub and halfshaft, tightening flange bolts as specified in **Section 3**. Tighten axle nut to 30 to 35 mkg (217 to 253 lb ft) and lock with a new splitpin. Tighten brake caliper bolts to 6 mkg (43 lb ft). Tighten bolts for disc shrouds to 2.5 mkg (18 lb ft).

Bleed the brake system (see **Chapter 10**). Adjust wheel tracking and camber (see **Section 10**). Tighten control arm mounting bolt to 12 mkg (86½ lb ft) when car is standing on its wheels.

6 Removing and refitting torsion bar

1. Raise car and remove rear wheel. Lift radius arm and remove lower bolt from damper mounting (see 2nd paragraph, **Section 2**).
2. Release radius arm from control arm flange. Remove cover bolts and withdraw single spacer (see **FIG 8**). Pry off cover with two screwdrivers.
3. Remove radius arm tensioner (part 'A' in **FIG 8**). Remove body plug from side and withdraw radius arm.
4. Pull out torsion bar taking care not to damage its protective coating.

A broken bar is removed by withdrawing opposite bar and pushing out parts with a steel rod. **Do not attempt to identify the bar by scratches or centre-punch marks.**

FIG 3 Undoing top fixing of damper inside engine compartment

Axle half-shafts from October 1971 models
Dimension A new drive shaft = 32 mm (1.26 inch)
Dimension A old drive shaft = 40 mm (1.58 inch)

FIG 4 The three types of halfshaft which are fitted

FIG 5 Drawing ends of clip together when securing boot on LOBRO halfshaft

FIG 6 Section through rear hub

Check rubber support for deterioration. Check torsion bar for cracks, rust or worn splines. Renew if necessary. Ends of bars are stamped 'R' for righthand side and 'L' for lefthand side. **They are pre-stressed and must not be interchanged.**

When refitting, coat bar and splines with multipurpose lithium grease. Adjust as instructed in **Section 7**. Coat rubber support with rubber grease and fit it. Refit radius arm and cover and start the three bolts which can be reached. Lift the radius arm until the fourth bolt and spacer can be fitted. Tighten bolts to 4.7 mkg (34 lb ft). Refit to control arm as in **Section 5**. Adjust wheel tracking and camber as in **Section 10**.

7 Adjusting torsion bar

The car must be standing level. Check with a spirit level on door sill. Radius arm must be hanging free and detached from the control arm. Check angle of radius arm with clinometer placed along the top edge.

Correct angle for all 911 models is 36 deg. prior to 1968 models. After introduction of 1968 models, angle was changed to 39 deg. and this angle may be used for setting earlier models. Adjustment is by vernier splines on torsion bar. There are 40 splines at the inner end and 44 at the outer end. If bar is turned one spline onwards at the inner end, change in angle is 9 deg. If radius arm is reset in the opposite direction by one spline the change is 8 deg. 10 min. The total movement of the radius arm is thus only 50 min. which is the minimum readjustment possible. Adjust to the nearest degree. After completing assembly of control arm, adjust rear wheel tracking and camber as described in **Section 10**.

8 Modified radius arm

At chassis serial numbers 305.101.S (911S) and 307.325 (911), the radius arms were fitted with rubber bushes which were vulcanized in place. As the seats in the transverse support tubes had to be enlarged to take these new arms, the modified arms cannot be fitted to cars before the quoted numbers.

9 Stabilizer (anti-roll) bar

On 911S cars the stabilizer bar is standard equipment, original diameter being 16 mm. At introduction of 1968 models diameter was reduced to 15 mm. The 15 mm bar is optional on all types, but from 1968 models onwards the optional bar may be either 15 mm or 16 mm in diameter.

The transverse bar is mounted in brackets just forward of the control arms, the outer ends being connected by shackles to ball-studs on the arms. To remove the bar, prise the upper eyes of the shackles off the ball-studs with a large screwdriver. Remove the bearing caps (4 bolts) and lift away the bar. Check the rubber bearing bushes for wear. Place the bar on a flat surface and check that the ends lie in the same plane. Look for cracks and rust which may lead to premature failure. Check shackle bushes and fit new ones dry, making sure they are the right size for the bar diameter. There are grommets in the upper eyes and these may be renewed by lightly lubricating new ones and pressing them in with a vice. When installing the shackles make sure that they are correctly angled to point as shown in **FIG 9**. Lubricate grommets with molybdenum disulphide grease.

To refit bar, reverse the dismantling procedure, pressing the upper eyes of the shackles into place with a screwdriver.

FIG 7 Driving outer ballbearing from hub on control arm

FIG 8 Removing radius arm cover. Arm is raised by special tool P.289, indicated at 'A'

FIG 9 Stabilizer bar, showing correct angle for top eyes on shackles

10 Rear wheel alignment

Checking alignment must be carried out in association with front wheel alignment, the total effect giving the best road-holding and cornering characteristics to the car. It is desirable to have the checking and setting made on accurate equipment and with the car properly prepared. The fuel tank must be full and the spare wheel fitted. All parts of the suspension must be in good mechanical condition and adjustment. Wheel rims must not runout excessively, tyres must not be unevenly worn and they must be correctly inflated. It is assumed that the rear torsion bars are correctly set as described in **Section 7**.

Refer to **FIG 1** and slacken the eccentric bolt nuts 6 and 7 and the retaining nuts, one of which can be seen to the left of the eccentric bolts. Turn the tracking and camber eccentrics until correct values are obtained on the equipment. Before 1968 models, camber was —55' to —1 deg. 35' and from 1968 models onwards it was —30' to 1 deg. 10', with a maximum deviation between left and right of 20'. Latest setting may be used for earlier models. Correct tracking is a toe-in of 0' ± 10'.

When installing camber eccentric make sure it points downwards so that there is adequate clearance for adjustment. If it is found that the eccentric binds at one end or the other of the slot, turn it round through 180 deg. After adjustment, tighten the nuts.

From the beginning of 1972 all 911 models produced have modified rear axle camber specifications. Rear wheel camber on these and subsequent models is minus 1 deg. with a tolerance of plus or minus 10 min. Toe-in is 0 deg. with a plus tolerance of 20 min per wheel.

FIG 10 Checking rear height adjustment on all models

11 Height adjustment

Refer to **FIG 10**. Have car correctly prepared as in **Section 10** and standing on level ground. Bounce car at rear several times to allow suspension to settle naturally. Note that dimension 'b' cannot be measured because torsion bar is eccentrically mounted in bush and cover. 'b1' is measured after the following calculations. Measure wheel centre height 'a' and add 12 mm (.47 inch) to give value 'b'. Subtract from this figure half the diameter of the radius arm cover (30 mm or 1.18 inch). The result is 'b1'.

Measured height 'b1' must not differ from calculated height by more than ±5 mm (.197 inch), and height difference between righthand and lefthand side must not exceed 8 mm (.315 inch). If correct setting cannot be obtained, check height adjustment of front suspension and rear torsion bar adjustment.

12 Fault diagnosis

(a) Noise from axle

1 Worn wheel bearings
2 Worn universal joints
3 Worn axle splines
4 Loose axle nut
5 Damper mountings defective
6 Broken stabilizer bar, faulty mountings
7 Loose radius arm or control arm
8 Control arm pivot mounting worn
9 Worn torsion bar splines or bushes
10 Brake backplate loose

(b) Excessive backlash

1 Check 2, 3 and 4 in (a)

(c) Poor handling, bad road-holding

1 Check 6, 7, 8 and 9 in (a)
2 Torsion bars 'settled' or broken
3 Radius arm setting incorrect
4 Incorrect wheel alignment
5 Incorrect height adjustment
6 Dampers inoperative, rubber buffers worn
7 Faulty transmission mountings

NOTES

CHAPTER 8 - FRONT SUSPENSION

1. General description
2. Routine maintenance
3. Servicing damper strut
4. Servicing and adjusting hub bearings
5. Servicing control arms (1st type)
6. Servicing crossmember (1st type)
7. Removing torsion bar (1st type)
8. The stabilizer bar
9. Modifications on 1968 models
10. Height adjustment
11. Wheel alignment
12. Fault diagnosis

1 General description

FIG 1 shows the earlier type of suspension system using torsion bar springing. Each control arm 9 houses a torsion bar in the longitudinal tube. Strut 1 incorporates a telescopic damper. At the lower end of the strut is the stub axle and a steering lever. A ball joint 3 couples the bottom end of the strut to the control arm, while the top of the strut is secured to the body. Except on standard 911 cars there is a stabilizer bar 5 to prevent excessive rolling. 1968 models have modified control arms (see **Section 9**).

Starting with 1969 models, 911E and 911T Lux cars are fitted with self-levelling suspension struts. These were optional on 911T and 911S cars. The suspension layout remains the same but there are no torsion bars. The control arms or wishbones have rubber bushes at the inner ends and a new type of ball joint. There is no stabilizer bar. **FIG 2** is a section through the strut showing the gas chambers and oil chambers which perform the suspension, damping and self-levelling functions. Gas in the high pressure chamber is isolated from the oil by a diaphragm shown as a thick black line. Oil and gas are not separated in the low pressure chamber. Gas pressure acting on the piston rod area takes 90 per cent of the weight of the empty car. Pump rod 12 forms a hydraulic pump in conjunction with piston rod 11.

Road bumps cause the pump to transfer oil through valves 7 and 9 from the low pressure cylinder to the high pressure cylinder. The pressurized gas is further compressed, which raises the car to a predetermined level. The pump action also acts as a damper. At a predetermined height, port 5 is cleared by the damping piston and normal suspension movements continue, the ports being too small to affect them. The pump rod is reduced in diameter higher up so that no pumping can take place. This prevents excessive raising of the suspension.

The struts will bring the car up to normal level within 300 to 1500 yards on smooth roads and much shorter distances on rough roads. The level remains constant if the load is not altered after parking.

Since the beginning of 1972 no model is fitted with self-levelling suspension struts unless required as an optional extra, previously the 911E and 911T Luxe cars were fitted with it as standard equipment. From 1972, only Boge dampers are fitted, but again, Bilstein or Koni suspension struts can be fitted on request. The exception is the Targa models; Koni dampers or suspension struts cannot be used on these vehicles.

The basic adjustment of these struts has been changed to attain a higher degree of passenger and driver comfort. By reducing the damping forces a softer ride is obtained but not to such a degree as to adversely effect the handling characteristics. These new struts may be used in earlier models providing the setting is the same for both sides.

Also modified in these later struts is the ball joint mounting, details of which are given in **Section 3**.

Type 911S vehicles now have 15 mm (.59 inch) diameter stabilizers as standard equipment and they may be fitted optionally to the 911T and E types.

Servicing self-levelling suspension:

It is most important to check ground clearance during servicing operations. If the car is lifted so that the wheels are clear of the ground, pressure in the struts is equalized. When the car is lowered the strut will then support only the basic load and the car will drop below the normal static load position.

As there are no height adjusters on this system, wheel alignment must be entrusted to a Porsche Service Station. The agent must also be consulted if the strut gives trouble.

2 Routine maintenance

There are no lubrication points, but the front hubs must be filled with fresh grease at major overhauls.

At every 6000 miles check tightness of wheel nuts, check tyre pressures and check wheel alignment and balance. At the same mileages check the wheelbearings for play. Adjust as described in **Section 4**.

3 Servicing damper strut

Removing:

1. Raise car and remove front wheels. Remove shroud 1 from behind brake disc 2 (see **FIG 3**). Block brake pedal in slightly depressed position and remove fluid line from caliper (see **Chapter 10**). Detach line from bracket, pull out hose and withdraw line and retaining spring.
2. Remove brake caliper. Prise cap 6 off hub. Loosen socket-head screw and remove nut 7 with washer 8. Pull off hub 3. Remove brake carrier (4 bolts and lockplates).
3. Release outer end of steering tie-rod from lever 12 using tool VW.266h. Remove bolts from outer end of control arm (2 castle nuts). Inside luggage compartment, release top end of damper strut (see **FIG 4**).

Key to Fig 1

1 Shockabsorber strut
2 Brake disc
3 Ball joint
4 Universal joint
5 Stabilizer
6 Steering tie rod
7 Adjusting screw
8 Bellows
9 Transverse control arm
10 Steering Post
11 Steering gear assembly
12 Reinforcing crossmember
13 Bearing support

FIG 1 The suspension layout prior to the introduction of the 1968 models. FIG 9 shows the control arm and cross-member details for later cars

FIG 2 Section through the self-levelling hydro-pneumatic suspension strut fitted to 1969 models onwards. Standard on 911E cars, it was optional on 911T and 911S models

Key to Fig 2

1 Low pressure chamber
2 Low pressure cylinder
3 High pressure chamber
4 High pressure cylinder
5 Relief port orifice
6 Overload valve
7 Suction valve
8 Piston ring seal
9 Pressure valve
10 Damping valve
11 Piston rod
12 Pump rod

FIG 3 Section through front hub, showing bearings and seal

Key to Fig 3

1 Cover shroud
2 Brake disc
3 Hub
4 Seal
5 Taper roller bearing
6 Cap
7 Clamping nut
8 Washer
9 Taper roller bearing
10 Distance ring
11 Damper strut
12 Steering lever
13 Ball joint

FIG 4 Releasing top end of damper strut

FIG 5 Section through the damper strut fitted to all models before the introduction of self-levelling suspension

Key to Fig 5
1 Hex nut
2 Safety plate
3 Washer
4 Bracket (on vehicle)
5 Rubber bushing
6 Rubber buffer
7 Piston rod
8 Shielding tube
9 Stop disc
10 Oil seal
11 Cylinder
12 Strut tube
13 Piston
14 Bottom valve

Dismantling:

1 Remove shield 8 and buffer (see **FIG 5**). Remove steering lever and ball joint 15. Take care of bush.
2 Release ball from lever (castle nut) and press it out. Drive distance ring off stub (see 10 in **FIG 3**).

Checking strut:

Alignment of the damper and stub axle is checked on special tool P.286. Renew the strut if the outside is covered in oily dirt. Hold strut vertically in a vice and pump it a few times. Then give long full strokes up and down and check for free play at any point. Excessive free play calls for strut renewal.

Koni adjustable dampers are standard on 911S cars and are optional on other models except Targa. To adjust outside car, mount vertically, press top end right down and turn gently to left until lugs engage inside damper and mark position. Check damper action by pumping top end up and down. If more damping is needed, press down and engage lugs at mark and then turn top tube to left for harder setting and to the right for a softer setting. Make sure both dampers have the same setting. To adjust Koni dampers when installed in car, raise front end and remove wheels. Hold up control arm with a jack and remove nut from top end of strut (inside luggage compartment). Adjust as just described. When finished, fit top nut on a new safety plate with tab upwards. Tighten nut to 8 mkg (58 lb ft).

From chassis No. 301800 damper spares kits can be installed in the struts of all 911 models. This does save a renewal of the whole strut but it does also entail the local or home manufacture of a special kind of tool to open the damper. The tool dimensions are shown in **FIG 5A**.

The 1972 models have a modified ball joint mounting which is attached to the strut by a double-wedge arrangement as shown in **FIG 5B**. The former clamping arrangement is no longer used. A special adaptor tool with four lugs spaced at 90 deg. is necessary to remove the nut 6 shown in the illustration, if it is possible to obtain it the part number is P2806. To remove the ball joint refer to **FIG 5B**.

1 Take-off the nut 1, remove the washer 2 and drive out the double-wedge bolt 3.
2 Extract the splitpin 4, remove the lockplate 5 and with the special adaptor tool and a wrench unscrew the nut 6.
3 Reassemble in the reverse order of dismantling and coat the double-wedge bolt with multi-purpose grease before assembling. Install it so that the retaining nut 1 is forward and the notch on the face of the double-wedge and the wedge contour are directed towards the stub axle. Renew the splitpin 4, but renew the lockwasher 5 only if it is incapable of carrying out its function.
4 Tap the double-wedge bolt with a hammer before finally tightening the nut to a torque of 2.2 kgm (15 lb ft).

Checking steering lever and ball joint:

Check the lever on special tool P.284. **Never try to straighten a bent lever.** Renew the ball joint if it moves freely and if play can be felt. There must be slight drag when the stud is moved. Renew the rubber boot if defective.

Assembling and refitting strut:

Do this in the reverse order. Fit O-ring R32-2.5 on axle when installing ring 10 (see **FIG 3**). Heat ring to 150°C (300°F) and push into place.

Fill rubber boots on new ball joints with 6.5g (.20 oz) of multipurpose molybdenum disulphide grease. **Taper of ball stud must be grease-free.** Tighten stud nut to 4.5 mkg (32½ lb ft). Use new lockplates and tighten steering lever bolts to 4.7 mkg (34 lb ft). Fit rubber buffer dry. Fit top nut of strut on a new safety plate with tab upwards. Tighten nut to 8 mkg (58 lb ft).

Use following torques on fixings:
Ball joint to control arm nuts 7.5 mkg (54 lb ft). Use washers and new splitpins. Tie rod ball joint nut 4.5 mkg (32½ lb ft) using new splitpin. Brake carrier plate bolts on new lockplates 4.7 mkg (34 lb ft). Caliper bolts on spring washers 7 mkg (50½ lb ft). Gland nut for brake pipe at caliper 2 mkg (14½ lb ft). Shroud bolts 2.5 mkg (18 lb ft).

Adjust wheel bearings as in **Section 4**. Bleed brakes as in **Chapter 10**. Check wheel alignment as in **Section 11**.

For BOGE shockabsorber strut   For KONI shockabsorber strut

FIG 5A Sketches for the manufacture of a special tool to open the damper for servicing. All dimensions are in millimetres

4 Servicing and adjusting hub bearings

Removing:

Do first two operations in **Section 3** but do not remove carrier. Press out outer races of bearings and inner oil seal using appropriate tools and spacer tube. If the brake disc is in the way, remove it after marking position. Removal of bearings is easier if hub is heated to 120° to 150°C or 250° to 300°F.

Checking:

Clean out old grease from hub and check flange for cracks, distortion or loose studs. Clean bearings and check in dry state. Renew if rough, but note that renewed parts must be of same make if mixed with original parts. Various makes of bearing have been fitted, such as SKF, FAG or Timken. **Do not mix parts of one make with those of another.**

Reassembling:

Heat hub to 120° to 150°C (250° to 300°F) and press in outer race of inner bearing. Insert inner race and press in oil seal until flush with hub. Fit outer race of outer bearing.

Refit brake disc with marks aligned and fit bolts from inside. Tighten nuts on spring washers to 2.3 mkg (16½ lb ft). Fill hub with 50cc or 43g (3 cu in or 1½ oz) of multipurpose lithium grease, pressing it well into bearings. Smear grease on both lips of oil seal. Refit hub to axle stub.

Tighten clamping nut to about 1.5 mkg (10.8 lb ft) while turning hub to seat the rollers in their races. Slacken nut until it is possible to turn the washer 8 in **FIG 3** with a screwdriver (see **FIG 6**). There must be no free play in the bearings. Lock nut by tightening socket-head screw to 2.5 mkg (18 lb ft). Check that adjustment is still correct.

FIG 5B Front axle ball joint, 1972 models

Key to Fig 5B		
1 Nut, M8	3 Double wedge bolt	6 Nut
2 Washer	4 Splitpin	7 Ball joint
	5 Lockplate	8 Strut

Coat nut and washer with lithium grease. Fit cap without filling with grease. Fit caliper, tightening bolts on spring washers to 7 mkg (50½ lb ft). Tighten gland nut of brake pipe at caliper to 2 mkg (14½ lb ft). Bleed the brakes.

FIG 6 Checking adjustment of front hub bearings by turning thrust washer with a screwdriver

FIG 7 Adjust crossmember braces so that they fit body location without strain. Bolt has been removed from body fixing point

5 Servicing control arms (1st type)

These are part 9 (see **FIG 1**). Remove as follows:
1 Remove undershield below crossmember 12. Slacken torsion bar adjusting screw 7.
2 Release ball joint 3 from end of control arm (two bolts). Remove bearing support and cap 13 (3 bolts). Torsion bar lies inside control arm tube.
3 At front end, remove dust cap and circlip and drive torsion bar forward and out. Loosen socket-head bolt just forward of adjusting screw 7 and pull and turn control arm until it is free. The adjusting lever may be driven out with a punch, taking care not to damage the splines.

Checking:

Note that the bearing block at the rear end cannot be removed without damaging the arm. Renew the parts as a pair. Check arm for distortion on fixture P.288. Check rubber bush for deterioration. Check torsion bar for cracks, worn splines or rust. **Rust pitting may lead to premature failure.**

Reassembling:

A new bearing block (Flanbloc) may be pressed onto a new control arm. Apply grease to mating surfaces, fit Flanbloc spacer to smaller journal of control arm, chamfered side first, and press Flanbloc into place. Refit rear end of control arm into crossmember. Set control arm so that it hangs down at 10 deg. to the horizontal and tighten the Flanbloc socket-head bolt to 4.7 mkg (34 lb ft). **This is important to prevent unequal torsion on the Flanbloc during suspension movements.**

Coat torsion bar and splines with lithium grease and insert at front end of control arm tube. Fit circlip and dust cap. End of torsion bar is marked 'R' for righthand side and 'L' for lefthand side. **Do not transpose.**

Coat front bush with rubber grease and fit to control arm with flange against face of arm. Install bracket and cap with radiused faces coinciding. Fit front bolt finger tight, check that bush is not trapped between the bracket and cap and fit remaining two bolts. Tighten to 4.7 mkg (34 lb ft).

Fit ball joint arm to outer end of control arm. Tighten nuts to 7.5 mkg (54 lb ft). Use washers and new splitpins.

To fit torsion bar adjusting lever at rear end, turn the adjusting screw right back. Smear lever with graphite grease. With damper strut attached, hook a long bar over the control arm and press it down to the full extent of the damper strut. Push lever into place on torsion bar, leaving minimum clearance at the adjusting point. Fit circlip and dust cover. Adjust front height as in **Section 10** and check wheel alignment as in **Section 11**.

6 Servicing crossmember (1st type)
Removing:

Crossmember is part 12 in **FIG 1**. To remove after control arms have been taken off, release rear ends of braces from body (see **FIG 7**). Release steering gearbox from both brackets on crossmember. Loosen bolts, tap crossmember off studs, remove bolts and crossmember.

Checking:

Make up two steel tubes as in **FIG 8** (upper view). Fit into crossmember housings as in central view and tighten Flanbloc clamping bolts. Check dimensions 'A' and 'B'. Maximum deviation from parallel must not be more than 2 mm (.08 inch). Place assembly on flat plate as in **FIG 8** lower view and check for twist. With one tube in full contact with plate, other tube must not be clear of plate at either end by more than 2 mm (.08 inch).

Check steering gearbox mounting brackets for cracks and distortion.

Refitting:

Ensure that crossmember is correctly seated on the aligning studs, then tighten fixing bolts to 9 mkg (65 lb ft). Fit braces so that they are not strained (see **FIG 7**).

Tighten nuts to 6.5 mkg (47 lb ft) and bolts to 4.7 mkg (34 lb ft).

7 Removing torsion bar (1st type)

Follow the instructions in operations 1, 2 and 3 in **Section 5** but do not detach the strut ball joint from the control arm or disturb the control arm mounting beyond removing the front bearing bracket and cap (see 13 in **FIG 1**). Refit torsion bars as described under 'Reassembling' in **Section 5**.

NOTE: all dimensions are in mm

FIG 8 Methods of checking crossmember, showing dimensions of tubes (top). Check dimensions 'A' and 'B' to test for parallelism (centre). Check for twist on a flat plate (bottom)

FIG 9 The modified control arm and crossmember introduced on 1968 models. The arm has integral rubber mountings

Key to Fig 9

1 Cover bracket
2 Transverse control arm (left)
3 Crossmember
3a Crossmember bolt
4 OWA-seal
5 Adjusting screw
6 Adjusting lever
7 End cap
8 Torsion bar

8 The stabilizer bar

Removing:

The bar is part 5 in **FIG 1**. At outer ends of bar, loosen lever clamp bolts and pull levers off squared ends of bar. Release support flanges from body (3 bolts), apply penetrating oil to support and rubber bush on one side and prise off with screwdrivers. Pull out stabilizer bar from other end. Press off rubber bush. Remove tie rods. Check all rubber bushes and renew if necessary. Check bar for rust, cracks or distortion. Squared ends must lie in same plane.

Refitting:

During installation, treat the bushes with rubber grease. Lightly attach support flanges and centre the bar. Tighten bolts to 2.5 mkg (18 lb ft). Fit levers so that about 1 mm (.04 inch) of squared end of bar protrudes. Fit tie rods, tightening bolts to 2.5 mkg (18 lb ft).

Stabilizer bars:

These are not fitted to 911 cars. Until the 1968 models were introduced, the standard bar for 911L models was 13 mm (.512 inch) diameter and for 911S models it was 14 mm (.55 inch) diameter. For 1968 models onwards these diameters were changed to 11 mm (.433 inch) and 15 mm (.59 inch) respectively. Optional diameters for models up to 1968 are 11, 14 and 15 mm (.435, .55 and .59 inch). For 1968 models onwards, optional diameters are 13, 14 and 15 mm (.512, .55 and .59 inch).

9 Modifications on 1968 models

The redesigned control arm and crossmember are shown in **FIG 9**, the arm having integral rubber mountings. The track was increased to 1367 mm (53.82 inch) with modified hubs having grease caps without expansion slots to prevent loss of grease. Standard stabilizer bar diameter on 911L cars (except USA) is 11 mm (.433 inch) and for 911L (USA) and 911S cars it is 15 mm (.59 inch). **It is essential to make sure that the mounting rubbers are the correct size for the stabilizer bar.**

Servicing control arm:

1 Unscrew torsion bar adjusting screw 5 in **FIG 9**. Release damper strut from outer end of control arm 2 (2 bolts and castle nuts).
2 Pull off lever 6 and remove OWA seal 4. Remove crossmember bolt 3a.
3 Remove bracket 1. Press control arm 2 and torsion bar 8 out of the crossmember 3. If both control arms are to be removed, first remove one arm and replace the crossmember bolt to keep the member in place.

Check control arm rubber mountings for wear or deterioration. Defects call for renewal of the complete control arm. Check torsion bar for damaged splines, chipped paint, rust or cracks. **Deep rust pitting may lead to premature failure.** Have control arm checked for distortion on fixture P.288, first driving out the plug at the splined end. To fit a new plug, insert with bulge outwards and partially flatten with a punch.

Refitting control arm:

1 Torsion bars are marked on the end 'L' for lefthand and 'R' for righthand. **Do not interchange.** Coat bar lightly with lithium grease and insert into control arm.
2 Insert arm and bar assembly into crossmember and tighten front mounting bracket bolts to 4.7 mkg (34 lb ft). Tighten crossmember bolt to 9 mkg (65 lb ft).
3 Fit damper strut ball joint arm into control arm and tighten castle nuts to 7.5 mkg (54 lb ft). Fit new split-pins.
4 Fit OWA seal on torsion bar and into outer recess in crossmember. See that the end cap is fitted to the adjusting lever. Press the control arm down as far as possible, using a long lever, and fit the adjusting lever. Engage the splines to give the maximum clearance for adjustment, coat the adjusting screw with molybdenum disulphide grease and fit it without tightening. Fit cover bracket and tighten bolts to 4.7 mkg (34 lb ft).
5 Adjust front height as described in **Section 10** and have the wheel alignment checked on optical equipment.

FIG 10 Dimensional checks on the crossmember for 1968 models

FIG 11 Checking steering angles for wheel alignment (left and centre). Method of height adjustment (right) where 'A' is wheel centre height and 'B' the height of the torsion bar centre at the adjusting lever end

Servicing torsion bar:

To remove a bar, remove the adjusting screw 5 in **FIG 9**. Pull lever off bar and remove seal 4. Remove cover bracket 1. Taking care not to damage splines, drive torsion bar forwards and out. Refit bar as described in the preceding instructions for the control arm.

The crossmember:

Checking points for correct alignment are shown in **FIG 10**. To remove the crossmember, remove control arm as described earlier. Detach undershield and steering gearbox, remove crossmember bolts and withdraw it. Check crossmember against dimensions given, placing it on a flat surface to test for distortion. Check for cracks and damage.

When refitting, make sure crossmember seats properly on body studs. Tighten steering gearbox bolts to 4.7 mkg (34 lb ft) using new spring washers. Refit the control arm.

10 Height adjustment
(for vehicles with self-levelling suspension)

1 Distribute a load of 100 kg (220 lb) in the luggage compartment so that both front wheels are evenly weighted.
2 Drive the car onto a level surface and, referring to the extreme right silhouette shown in **FIG 11** accurately measure the distance 'A' from the ground to the front wheel centre. Distance 'B' should be equal to 'A' minus 124 mm (5 inch), that is, the distance between wheel centre and the mounting point centre of the traverse control arm. Special cone-shaped plugs (P301b) are used by the service agents which fit into the box section as shown in **FIG 11A** to provide an accurate datum point. Work on both sides of the vehicle.
3 Raise the car with a jack under the front centre until distance 'B' is attained. Now measure, and make a note of the reading, the distance between ground and the bottom edge of the front fender on both sides. To eliminate tyre deflection when the jack is lowered measure also the distance between the wheel flange and ground; measure again when the jack has been lowered and deduct the difference from that obtained between ground and fender.
4 Remove the ballast from the boot, load the car with passengers and drive the vehicle on a straight but rough road for a distance of 2 km (1¼ miles), without hard braking.
5 The driver and passengers must stay in the car, which is also parked on a level surface, and by previous arrangement obtain the help of another person to measure the distance between lower edge of fender and ground. The values should not have differed by more than 10 mm (13/32 inch) either way.

(for vehicles with standard suspension)

Prepare the car as described in **Section 10** of the preceding chapter. Mark the centre of the hub caps. Bounce the front end of the car several times and allow it to rise by itself on the rebound from the last depression. Measure height 'A' from level ground to wheel centre (see righthand view in **FIG 11**). Measure height 'B' from ground to torsion bar centre. The centre will be visible if the dust cover is removed from the adjusting lever. Turn the torsion bar adjusting screw (see part 7 in **FIG 1**) until the value 'B' is 108 ± 5 mm (4.25 ± .20 inch) less than 'A'. Check both sides and bounce car again for a further check on dimensions. Although permissible deviation is given as ± 5 mm (.20 inch) the difference between the heights of both sides must not exceed 5 mm.

FIG 11A Using cone-shaped plugs (arrowed) to measure centre point to ground

FIG 12 Releasing top end of damper strut to adjust camber and castor angles

11 Wheel alignment

Refer to **Chapter 9** for details of toe-in adjustment.

Camber angle and steering axis inclination are shown in the lefthand view of **FIG 11**. Camber is the angle the wheel makes to the vertical. Steering axis inclination is the angle of the damper strut to the vertical.

Castor angle is shown by the central view in **FIG 11**. The centre line of the damper strut meets the ground ahead of the point of tyre contact to give a self-centring effect.

Note that the 1972 models have a slightly different camber angle to previous models. The front camber should be 0 deg.±10 mins with a maximum camber difference, left to right, of 10 mins. The castor angle is virtually the same, that is, 6 deg. 5 mins±15 mins.

Adjusting camber:

Note that castor and camber cannot be adjusted on cars up to chassis No. 302.694, on chassis No. 302.736 or on chassis No. 302.805. Any errors on these cars must be corrected by checking the suspension parts and damper strut mountings for distortion and renewing faulty components.

To adjust camber (see lefthand view in **FIG 11**), pull away the carpet in the luggage compartment to reveal the three retaining screws which permit damper strut adjustment (see **FIG 12**). Remove sealing compound from pressure plates and dished ring and then mark round the plates to register their positions. Loosen the socket-head screws. Re-position the dished ring sideways to alter the camber angle. Moving it 1 mm (.04 inch) makes an alteration of 6' to the angle of the damper strut. Correct angle is 0±20' with a permissible deviation between left and right of 20'.

Adjusting castor:

Read the comments on certain cars at the start of 'Adjusting camber'. Follow the instructions for loosening the top fixing of the damper strut but instead of moving the dished ring sideways for adjustment, move it fore and aft. Correct castor angle is 6 deg. 45'±45' with a maximum deviation between left and right of 30'. Tighten retaining screws to 4.7 mkg (34 lb ft). Apply a non-hardening sealer and stick the carpet back into place.

12 Fault diagnosis

(a) Wheel wobble

1 Unbalanced wheels and tyres
2 Worn steering ball joints
3 Incorrect steering angles
4 Weak or incorrectly set torsion bar
5 Worn hub bearings

(b) Erratic steering

1 Check (a)
2 Bent suspension components
3 Worn ball joints and control arm mountings
4 Uneven tyre wear or pressures
5 Defective damper strut

(c) Excessive pitching, rolling or 'bottoming'

1 Check 4 in (a) and 5 in (b)
2 Buffer rubbers missing or faulty
3 Broken stabilizer bar or tie rod

(d) Rattles

1 Check 3 in (b) and 3 in (c)
2 Loose damper strut mountings
3 Loose crossmember or control arm mountings

NOTES

CHAPTER 9 - STEERING

1. General description
2. Routine maintenance
3. Removing and refitting steering wheel
4. Servicing switch and steering shafts
5. The intermediate shaft and universal joints
6. The steering coupling
7. Servicing the steering gearbox
8. Adjusting toe-in
9. Steering and wheel alignment
10. Fault diagnosis

FIG 1 Support ring and spring correctly located on steering wheel hub

1 General description

Reference to **FIG 1** in the preceding Chapter shows that the steering gearbox assembly 11 is mounted on two brackets forming part of crossmember 12. The steering pinion shaft is connected by universal joint 4 to a relay shaft which is connected by another universal joint to the steering wheel shaft at the top of post 10. The pinion engages a rack in the steering gear housing (as shown in **FIG 15**). The outer ends of the rack are coupled by tie rods and joints 6 to the steering levers attached to damper struts 1. A modified rack and pinion assembly was introduced at the same time as the self-levelling suspension fitted to some 1969 models.

2 Routine maintenance

As the steering gearbox is packed with a special grease at the time of manufacture, or after a complete overhaul, there is no provision for subsequent extra lubrication. The same applies to the universal joints and ball joints in the steering system. There is no need for routine adjustment at any point.

3 Removing and refitting steering wheel

Removal:

1. Disconnect battery. Release horn button by turning anticlockwise and then pull out the contact pin.
2. Unscrew wheel retaining nut. Mark relative positions of wheel and shaft and withdraw wheel, taking care of the bearing support ring and spring (see **FIG 1**).

Refitting:

1. Fit spring and support ring on wheel hub. Set road wheels straightahead and install steering wheel, aligning marks made before dismantling. In the correct position the return striker must point towards the flasher switch and the wheel spokes must be horizontal.
2. Tighten wheel nut to 8 mkg (58 lb ft) using a spring washer under nut. Check flasher return striker for correct operation.
3. Lightly grease the horn contact ring, insert the contact pin and fit the horn button, turning it clockwise until it is locked.

FIG 2 Prising up prong of spring clip when removing intermediate shaft cover (top). Removing heater pump bolts (bottom)

4 Servicing switch and steering shafts

Removal:

1. Disconnect battery. Remove luggage compartment carpet and lift access flap. If fitted, detach auxiliary heater duct from steering column post.
2. Refer to top view in **FIG 2** and pry up a prong of the spring clip as shown. Remove clips and cover over intermediate shaft.
3. Remove heater pump bolts (lower view in **FIG 2**). Lay pump to one side.
4. Release the lower clamping bolts in each of the two universal joints. One joint is shown as part 4 in **FIG 1** in preceding chapter. Note large bush just below it. Release cap from this bush as shown in **FIG 3** and pull the lower universal joint off the shaft. Withdraw the intermediate shaft and lower joint out of the upper universal joint.
5. Remove the steering wheel (see **Section 3**). If car is fitted with a steering lock, remove cover, drill out the bolts indicated by the arrows in **FIG 4** and remove the lock and spacer without disconnecting the cables. Remove the light switch alongside and let it hang on the cables.
6. Loosen socket-head bolt in clamp which secures the switch assembly (see **FIG 5**). Turn clamp lugs downwards and pull out locking pin with pointed-nosed pliers (see **FIG 10**). Detach cable connectors, marking the cables for correct reassembly.
7. Switch assembly is now free and may be pulled away, complete with upper shaft and universal joint. Feed cables through instrument panel. Inside luggage compartment, unlock and remove two bolts securing lower end of steering post. Squirt glycerine under the grommet and twist the post to remove it.

FIG 3 Removing cap from bush on lower steering shaft

FIG 4 Arrows show position of shearing bolts for steering lock. Light switch is to left of lock

FIG 5 Slackening bolt in clamp which retains switch assembly

FIG 6 Removing universal joint from upper shaft

Inspection:

Check cables and connections. Check condition of grommet. Test universal joints for play and renew them if worn. If it is necessary to remove the upper shaft proceed as follows:

Servicing upper shaft:

1 Remove universal joint (see **FIG 6**). From same end of post extension prise out spring ring and remove washer, seal and second seal retainer.
2 Remove socket-head bolts and drive post extension out of switch assembly (see **FIG 7**). From lower end of shaft remove bearing circlip and drive out shaft.
3 Remove bearing circlip and drive out bearing at lower end. At top end, tap out column bearing with a blunt screwdriver, working from side to side to keep it square.

Inspecting upper shaft and bearings:

Check both bearings and renew if worn or rough in action. Check shaft splines.

Reassembling:

Fit top bearing as shown in **FIG 8**. Pack both bearings with multipurpose lithium-based grease before installation. Refit shaft after fitting and securing lower bearing. Push post extension into switch assembly and align it so that the hole for the steering lock is central (see **FIG 9**). Set relative positions so that post extension is 7 mm (.28 inch) below face of switch assembly (see **FIG 8**). Tighten socket-head bolts to 2.5 mkg (18 lb ft). Fit universal joint using a new bolt. Fit a 'Schnorr' lockwasher under the nut, tighten to 3.5 mkg (25 lb ft) and fit a new splitpin.

FIG 8 Correct relative positions of steering post extension and top face of switch assembly

FIG 9 Hole for steering lock must be centrally aligned with switch assembly

FIG 7 Releasing steering post extension from switch assembly

Refit steering post, lightly tightening bolts at lower end on washers and a lockplate. Fit retaining clamp so that the threaded lug is on the right. Coat sealing ring on steering post extension with assembly paste such as Conti-Fix and push the switch assembly into place, at the same time guiding the cables through the instrument panel. Fit the steering lock, insert the protecting plate and lightly tighten the new shear bolts.

Refit locking pin between lugs of clamp (see **FIG 10**). Turn clamp anticlockwise, fit socket-head bolt and spring washer and tighten to 2.5 mkg (18 lb ft). At this point, check clearance between switch assembly and instrument panel. It should be about 2 mm (.08 inch). If necessary, move steering post. Tighten bolts at lower end of steering post to 2.5 mkg (18 lb ft). Turn up tabs on lockplate.

Tighten steering lock bolts until heads break off. Refit intermediate shaft and universal joints using new bolts and 'Schnorr' lockwashers under the nuts. Tighten to 3.5 mkg (25 lb ft) and fit new splitpins. Refit cap over bush on lower shaft, put spring washers on socket-head bolts and tighten to 2.5 mkg (18 lb ft).

FIG 10 Removing or replacing locking pin between lugs of switch assembly clamp

FIG 11 Engaging dowel pin with slot when driving universal joint onto intermediate shaft

FIG 12 Releasing coupling from flange on pinion shaft

FIG 13 Recessed holes in coupling must engage flanges of pinion shaft and lower shaft

5 The intermediate shaft and universal joints

This is the angled shaft which connects the lower shaft to the steering wheel shaft by means of two universal joints. When dismantled, check shaft and splines for damage. Joints must have no play.

If necessary, fit new dowel pins. Install the ring seal and then drive in the dowels with the grooves entering first. Tap the universal joint into place so that the dowel engages the slot in the joint as shown in **FIG 11**. Always fit a new bolt, place a 'Schnorr' lockwasher under the nut and tighten to 3.5 mkg (25 lb ft). Fit a new splitpin.

Modified universal joints:

Early joints were fitted to their respective shafts without splines. Starting with chassis Nos. 305.101, 354.001 and 458.101, the internally-splined universal joints mate with splined shafts. These are not interchangeable with joints and shafts without splines. When fitting splined joints it is also necessary to fit splined shafts.

When installing splined joints, push them onto the shafts to the point where the bolts will enter freely. Tighten to 2.5 mkg (18 lb ft).

6 The steering coupling

This joins the lower steering shaft to the pinion shaft flange next to the steering gearbox as can be seen in **FIG 12**. Remove the coupling and lower shaft by unlocking and unscrewing the bolts as shown. The flexible part of the coupling is provided with recessed holes (see **FIG 13**). **Make sure, when fitting the coupling, that it is the recessed holes which contact the pinion and lower shaft flanges.**

7 Servicing the steering gearbox

Removal:

Do operations 1, 2 and 3 in **Section 4**. Remove bolt securing lower universal joint to lower steering shaft and pull joint off shaft. Remove socket-head bolts from cap over bush (see **FIG 3**). Pull off bush and rubber boot. Unlock and remove coupling bolts (see **FIG 12**).

Working underneath car, remove undershield which covers crossmember. Release outer ball joints from steering levers. Tie rods are part 6 in **FIG 1** in preceding chapter. Do not hammer taper pins of joints out of steering levers but use an extracting tool like VW.266h. Unscrew bolts holding steering gearbox to crossmember 12 see **FIG 1** in preceding chapter. Remove the right-hand crossmember brace (see **FIG 7** in preceding chapter). Pulling it out to the right, remove the steering gearbox assembly.

Dismantling: (See next section for 1970 & later models)

1 Release tie rods from eyebolts at ends of rack and remove damper (see **FIG 14**). Unlock and slacken the eyebolt locknuts, holding rack housing in a vice between soft jaws. **Do not overtighten.** Unscrew eyebolts and remove the stop plates and bellows.
2 Refer to **FIGS 15** and **16** for details of the construction of the rack and pinion steering gearbox. Rack is carried in housing 2 in bushes 8 (see **FIG 15**). Engaging with it is pinion 5 which is connected by shafts and couplings to the steering wheel. The pinion bearings are mounted in a floating carrier so that a spring-loaded pressure block 4 can maintain the rack and pinion teeth in close contact to give freedom from backlash. The amount of pressure is adjustable through nut 3.

Key to Fig 14
1 Face of mounting boss
2 Pinion flange
3 Damper
4 Eyebolt with Silentbloc

FIG 14 Correct positioning of rack eyebolts relative to centre line and mounting bosses

FIG 15 Sectional view of steering gearbox

Key to Fig 15
1 Thread for eyebolt
2 Housing
3 Adjusting nut
4 Pressure block
5 Steering pinion
6 Steering rack
7 Rubber bellows
8 Bush

3 To dismantle, remove base plate 14 (see **FIG 16**). Unscrew adjusting nut 13, using the base plate as a spanner. Remove pressure block 6 and spring 7.

4 Unlock and remove the pinion shaft nut and use a puller to withdraw the flange 8. Prise out oil seal 9 with a screwdriver. Remove circlip 12 and possible spacers.

5 Using a puller such as P.282 which has an extracting bolt that screws on the pinion shaft thread, extract the pinion and ballbearing. Remove key 10 and press off the bearing.

6 Mark rack 5 for correct reassembly and then withdraw it from the housing. Pull out pinion carrier 2 and press out the second ballbearing.

7 To extract bushes 8, prise out the spring rings from the housing (see **FIG 15**). Push a thin punch into the small hole in the bevelled end of the housing to lift the ring. Remove supporting ring and then drive out the bush with a drift and supporting tube. Do not remove bushes unless worn.

FIG 16 Section through steering pinion mounting and pressure block

Key to Fig 16
1 Housing
2 Pinion carrier
3 Pinion
4 Ballbearing
5 Rack
6 Pressure block
7 Spring
8 Flange
9 Oil seal
10 Key
11 Washer
12 Circlip
13 Adjusting nut
14 Base plate

Inspection:

Clean all the parts and check the rack and pinion for wear and damaged teeth. Check the ballbearings when clean and dry and discard if rough in action or if slack. Check housing bushes and renew if worn. Renew oil seal.

FIG 17 Using torque meter on pinion flange nut to check steering drag

Reassembling: (See next section for 1970 & later models)

1. To fit new bushes in the housing, insert the wide supporting rings first. Grease the outer surface of each bush and press into place with recessed face outwards. Fit the narrow ring and spring ring so that the gap in the latter is at right angles to the carrier bore.
2. Coat pinion carrier and inner bearing with multipurpose molybdenum disulphide grease such as Liqui-Moly LM-KFZ3 or LM-47L. Insert into housing. 40 g (1.3 oz) of this grease will be needed during reassembly.
3. Coat the rack with grease and fit into housing, checking the assembly marks made during dismantling. Press the remaining grease into the housing and insert the pinion with ballbearing and key. Press pinion right home, fit spacers and circlip and check axial play of pinion. There must be no play and correction is made by using spacers which are available in thicknesses of .10, .12, .15 and .30 mm (.004, .005, .006 and .012 inch).
4. Fit oil seal with sealing lip outwards. Fit pinion flange, checking that key is properly seated. Coat washer with jointing compound and tighten nut to 2.5 mkg (18 lb ft). Secure with a new splitpin.
5. Fit pressure block, spring and adjusting nut. Adjust gear as follows:
6. Adjustment varies with the type of pressure block. If the block is steel with a plastic contact face, the steering housing will have a large flange to accept the dust boot as in **FIG 17**. Adjust this type by tightening the nut until it is fully seated. The base plate may be used as a spanner to do this. Back the nut off three teeth. Use torque meter P.261 on the pinion nut to check the drag of the assembly over the full working length of the rack (see **FIG 17**). The correct drag is 8 cmkg (7 lb in). If higher than this, slacken the nut a little and recheck. After the initial slackening by three teeth it is possible that the drag may be less than the required figure. If the drag is not less than 4 cmkg (3.5 lb in), do not retighten the nut.
7. If the pressure block is all plastic, there will be no large bevelled flange to take the lower end of the rubber dust boot. In this case simply tighten the adjusting nut until the torque meter registers the correct drag of 8 cmkg (7 lb in).
8. With drag correctly set, refit base plate and paper gasket, tightening the bolts to 2.2 mkg (16 lb ft). Move the adjusting nut slightly if the pins in the plate do not engage the teeth easily. Surplus grease may be injected in the bolt hole opposite the base plate. Coat bolt threads with jointing compound when refitting.
9. Check the eyebolts for faulty Silentbloc bushes and look for cracks and deterioration of the bellows. **FIG 14** shows the correct settings for the eyebolts, and although this may be done by measurement it is better to use the setting fixture P.285. The angles are important to ensure free movement of the tie rods.
10. Fit the bellows to the housing. Put gasket compound on the eyebolt threads, the end faces of the rack and on both faces of the stop plate and lockwasher. Fit eyebolts, set them correctly and tighten nuts to 6.5 mkg (47 lb ft), locking them when secure. Refit the damper, leaving one end disconnected.

Servicing the steering gearbox for 1970 and later models

A modified version of the ZF rack and pinion steering is fitted to the models 911T and S as follows:

Type 911T from May 25th 1970

Coupe from Chassis No. 9110101699 and 9110123497
Targa from Chassis No. 9110112140

Type 911S from August 26th 1970

Coupe from Chassis No. 9111300043
Targa from Chassis No. 9111310043

The rack and pinion details are shown in **FIG 17A** and the dismantling procedure is as follows:

1. Refer to **FIG 17A**, dismantle by following the numerical sequence shown; 1 to 20 is fairly straightforward.
2. Use a puller to extract the rack bushing 21. Withdraw the bearing 17 off the pinion 18 by removing the snapring 15 and thrustwasher 16 and forcing the pinion through the bearing with a flypress or any other small press.
3. Drive the needle bearing 22 out of the housing with a special drift P362 or any other suitable drift.

Reassembling:

4. Fill the steering and rack housing with multipurpose grease and drive in the needle bearing until the top edge of the bearing is 3 mm (.12 inch) below the top edge of the housing. (See **FIG 17B**).
5. Fit the pinion 18 complete with bearing 17 thrustwasher and snapring and measure the distance between ball bearing and contact face of housing (see **FIG 17C**). This clearance must be taken up by the shims 14. Free play between the cover 13 and bearing should be not more than .05 mm (.002 inch).
6. Continue the reassembly and measure the distance between pressure block 6 and the housing flange face (see **FIG 17D**). This clearance must be taken up by the shims 4 but allow for a maximum free play between the block and cover 3 of .20 mm (.008 inch).

Key to Fig 17A

1. Bolts M8
2. Spring washer
3. Cover
4. Shims
5. Spring
6. Pressure block
7. Self-locking nut M10
8. Coupling flange
9. Washer
10. O-ring
11. Bolt M8 x 18
12. Spring washer
13. Cover
14. Shims
15. Snapring
16. Thrust washer
17. Ball bearing
18. Pinion
19. Rack
20. Lockring
21. Rack bushing
22. Needle bearing
23. Steering housing

FIG 17A Modified ZF rack and pinion steering (1970 models onwards)

7 Temporarily fit the shims and covers and check the gear drag over the entire working length of the steering rack (see **FIG 17**). A drag of 6 to 8 kgcm (5 to 7 lb inch) must be attained. If the drag cannot be attained renew the spring 5 (see **FIG 17A**).

8 Remove the covers and smear the contact surfaces with gasket compound. Tighten the bolts 1 and 11 to a torque of 1.5 kgm (10 lb ft).

9 Lubricate O-ring 10 when fitting and fit a new self-locking nut 7 (size M10), tighten to a torque of 4.7 kgm (33 lb ft). Ensure the lockring 20 seats correctly when refitting.

Installing:

Reverse the order of dismantling but do not reconnect the tie rods to the steering levers. At this stage, check the drag at the steering wheel as shown in **FIG 18**. A drag of 10 cmkg (8¾ lb in) must be recorded with tie rods and damper disconnected. If check is satisfactory, connect damper and tie rods to complete the installation. If a major overhaul is in progress, check the tie rods and ball joints before fitting. Tie rods must not be bent and ball joints must have slight drag when the ballpin is articulated. Free movement or play calls for renewal of the joint. When connecting the inner ends of the rods, coat the bolts with molybdenum disulphide paste and tighten to 4.7 mkg (34 lb ft). Fit ball joint pins dry.

Fit the crossmember brace without strain and tighten nut to 6.5 mkg (47 lb ft) and bolt to 4.7 mkg (34 lb ft) see **FIG 7** in preceding chapter. Tighten steering gear mounting bolts on new lockwashers to 4.7 mkg (34 lb ft). Tighten ball joint castle nuts to 4.5 mkg (32½ lb ft) and fit new splitpins. Tighten socket-head screws for bush cap to 2.5 mkg (18 lb ft) as in **FIG 3**. Put new lockwashers on the coupling bolts and tighten to 2.5 mkg (18 lb ft) as in **FIG 12**.

FIG 17B Measure distance from top of bearing to top of housing to determine correct position of bearing

FIG 17C Measure distance from top of ball bearing to contact surface of housing to determine shim pack

FIG 17D Measure distance from top of pressure block to contact surface of housing to determine shim thickness. This measurement minus .20 mm (.008 inch) will give correct end float

FIG 18 Checking steering drag at steering wheel nut, using a torque meter

FIG 19 When front wheels toe-in, dimension 1 is less than 2 (left). Right-hand view shows 'A' parallel to 'A1', 'B' the wheel centre line and 'C' the angle differential with wheels locked over at 20 deg.

8 Adjusting toe-in

Toe-in is shown in the left view of **FIG 19**. Note that the distance between the wheel rims at centre height is less at the front than the back. The front wheels are set parallel on 1968 models onwards.

When the wheels are on either lock at 20 deg. there may be an angle differential as shown in the right-hand view. 'A1' is parallel to 'A', and 'B' is the centre line of the wheel. The differential angle is thus 'C'. Before the 1968 models the deviation could be 40' to 1 deg. From 1968 models onwards it should lie between 0' and 30'. Excessive error may be due to bent steering arms, tie rods or the steering knuckle at the damper strut. **Corrections cannot be made at the steering tie rods.**

Adjustment:

Accurate equipment must be used for checking. Methods will vary, but the basic test is as follows:

Move steering wheel fully to the stop in one direction and note the angle of one particular spoke to any datum such as the instrument panel edge. Turn the wheel on the opposite lock and note the angle of the partner spoke on the other side. If the angles are not the same, the wheel must be removed and replaced in the correct position (see **Section 3**).

Now set the steering wheel in the mid-position and adjust the righthand and lefthand tie rods so that, on models prior to 1968, each road wheel has a toe-in of 20', while pressing the wheels together with a preload of 15 kg (33 lb). The yoke and ball joint are screwed into the tie rod and secured by clamps. Make sure the ends are set in the correct plane before tightening the clamps.

9 Steering and wheel alignment

It must be appreciated that incorrect wheel alignment will have an effect on steering. The correct settings of camber and castor angles for the front wheels are given in **Section 11** of the preceding chapter. It is also possible for errors in rear wheel alignment to affect steering qualities, so that it is always advisable to make a complete check of all height adjustment, suspension and steering angles on precision equipment.

10 Fault diagnosis

(a) Wheel wobble
1 Unbalanced wheels and tyres, uneven pressures
2 Free play in steering gear and connections
3 Front end damaged, incorrect steering angles
4 Incorrect toe-in adjustment
5 Worn or slack hub bearings
6 Faulty damper strut
7 Insufficient drag in steering gear

(b) Steering wander
1 Check 2, 3, 5 and 7 in (a) and 6 in (c)
2 Smooth front tyres, pressures too high or too low

(c) Heavy steering
1 Check 3 in (a)
2 Low or uneven tyre pressures
3 Too much drag in steering gear
4 Insufficient lubricant
5 Steering gearbox mountings out of line
6 Faulty steering damper
7 Weak or broken torsion bars
8 Faulty steering shafts and joints
9 Defective bearing assembly in post extension

(d) Lost motion
1 Check 2 in (a)
2 Loose steering wheel
3 Worn ball joints
4 Steering gearbox loose on mountings
5 Worn steering gearbox, ineffective pressure block
6 Universal joints loose on steering shafts

(e) Steering pulls to one side
1 Check 3 in (a) and 2 in (c)
2 One front brake binding
3 Broken or sagging front or rear suspension

NOTES

NOTES

CHAPTER 10 - BRAKES

1. General description
2. Routine maintenance
3. Renewing brake pads
4. Servicing front brakes
5. Servicing rear brakes
6. Handbrake carrier plate
7. Servicing brake discs
8. Servicing single master cylinder
9. Servicing dual master cylinder
10. Bleeding the brake system
11. Servicing the handbrake
12. Fault diagnosis

1 General description

Every model has front and rear disc brakes which are hydraulically operated, but the handbrake is cable-operated and expands shoes inside a drum which is integral with each rear disc. A diagrammatic layout of the system is given in **FIG 1,** early models having the single master cylinder 2. 1968 models onwards have the dual master cylinder shown in **FIG 18**. This has the advantage that failure in one set of brakes, either front or rear, leaves the remaining set in full working order.

Fluid reservoir 3 ensures that the system is always full. When pedal 1 is depressed it pushes on a piston in master cylinder 2, forcing fluid along metal pipes 4 and flexible pipes 5 to the brake cylinders in calipers 6 and 8. The pressure on the pistons in these cylinders forces them to press pads lined with friction material into braking contact with the discs 7 and 9 secured to the hubs. Because each disc is nipped between a pair of pads, the resultant braking is both smooth and powerful. The rubber seals round the pistons are slightly deformed when the brakes are applied. Releasing the brakes causes these seals to resume their original shape and this action slightly retracts the pistons, leaving the discs free to revolve. In consequence the footbrakes are self-adjusting.

Although early discs were solid and were the type always fitted to 911T models with manual gearboxes, ventilated discs were fitted to 911S cars, to 911T models with Sportomatic transmission, to later 911, to 911L and 911E models. These reduced operating temperatures to give improved braking. Later models with self-levelling suspension were also fitted with light alloy wheels. The handbrake housing was modified to incorporate the heater and hand throttle controls.

FIG 1 Diagrammatic layout of braking system using a single master cylinder

Key to Fig 1
1 Brake pedal
2 Master cylinder
3 Fluid reservoir
4 Metal pipes
5 Flexible hoses
6 Front caliper
7 Disc
8 Rear caliper
9 Disc
10 Handbrake lever
11 Handbrake cables

FIG 2 Location of fluid reservoir in luggage compartment

FIG 3 Slackening handbrake cable adjuster behind rear brake (top). Using screwdriver to turn brake shoe adjuster for handbrake (bottom)

2 Routine maintenance

Every 6000 miles the whole system must be checked for fluid leakage, for damaged hoses and pipes and for condition and thickness of braking pads.

Cars in America that have dual-circuit brakes must have the warning device checked every 6000 miles.

Fluid level:

At regular intervals the fluid level in the reservoir must be checked and fluid added if required. The reservoir is below the luggage compartment (see **FIG 2**). Correct fluid level is approximately 2 cm (.80 inch) below the top ridge of the reservoir. If topping up is needed, use only genuine ATE Blue Fluid. **Be careful not to let the fluid drip on the body paintwork as it is a solvent.**

Handbrake adjustment:

When lever movement is excessive, adjust the handbrake as follows:

1 Raise car and remove rear wheels. Release handbrake. Push back the pads of the rear disc brakes so that the discs rotate freely.
2 Behind shrouds, loosen cable adjusting nuts to relieve cable tension (see upper view, **FIG 3**). Insert screwdriver as in lower view and turn adjusting sprocket until shoes lock inside drum and disc is immovable. Sprocket can be seen in **FIG 11**. Repeat adjustment on opposite wheel.
3 Remove cable slack at adjusting nuts (see **FIG 3**, top). Pull back cover from handbrake lever mounting and note two holes in flange near rear bolt. Looking vertically downwards, the ends of the cable crossbeam should be visible. The beam should be at right angles to the car centre line. If not, adjust at nuts behind shrouds. Tighten adjusting nut locknuts.
4 Now back off the two sprockets by about 4 or 5 teeth so that the discs can be turned freely. Check that handbrake is applied when pulled up about 4 teeth but is quite free when lever is released. Finally, depress brake pedal several times to set the pads and then check fluid level in reservoir.

3 Renewing brake pads

Check the thickness of pad linings at regular intervals. Wear limit is reached when plate touches cross-spring or when pad lining is worn down to 2 mm (.08 inch) thickness. Arrows in **FIG 4** show minimum desirable thickness.

When new, total thickness of lining and plate is approximately 15 mm (.60 inch). Touring and competition pads are available, the latter being marked TE.10. Front pads differ in size from rear ones, so pads are not interchangeable. Mark used pads before removal to ensure correct replacement. It is not permissible to change their positions. Front pads and rear pads must always be complete sets of one particular type. Although it is possible to renew one pad only, it is best to renew all the pads of an axle pair, either front or rear.

Changing pads:

1 Jack up car and remove wheels. Extract pins 7 and push out retaining pins 8 (see **FIG 5**), pressing down on the cross-spring 6 and pushing pins inwards.
2 If pads are still usable, mark their positions. Withdraw pads.

3 The next operation may cause overflowing of the fluid reservoir (see **FIG 2**) so drain it. Press both pistons into their bores, either with tool P.83 (see **FIG 9**) or with a strip of hardwood. Do not use steel tools which may damage disc or pistons.

4 Clean out the pad cavities with methylated spirits and a soft-edged tool. **Do not use other solvents.** Check condition of dust cover and clamping ring. Renew hardened or cracked covers.

5 Polish the brake discs with fine emerycloth and smooth out any inner and outer ridges on each face.

6 Fit pads and check that they are free to move in the cavities. Reassemble in the reverse order, fitting new spring pins in the retaining pins if the original pins are distorted or worn. Put clean fluid in the reservoir and depress the brake pedal several times to set the pistons in the correct positions. Recheck the fluid level in the reservoir.

Do not use the brakes heavily during the first 200 km (125 miles) if new pads are fitted. Condition the pads by moderate pedal pressure, with intervals for cooling, unless an emergency occurs. The pads, with careful bedding-in, will then give effective braking without fade.

4 Servicing front brakes

Removal:

1 Remove pads (operations 1 and 2 in preceding instructions). Block brake pedal in slightly depressed position, then detach fluid pipe at banjo connection behind caliper (see **FIG 6**).

2 Remove bolts to release caliper and shroud. Prise off hub cap

3 Slacken socket-head screw in clamping nut on end of axle, unscrew nut and remove thrust washer. Parts are shown in **FIG 3** in 'Front Suspension' chapter. Pull off disc and hub. If tight, do not hammer on disc but use a puller.

4 From behind axle, remove disc shroud. Unlock and remove bolts and lift off brake carrier (see **FIG 7**).

Dismantling:

1 If necessary, separate disc from hub after marking for correct reassembly.

2 Do not part the caliper halves unless there has been leakage. Loosen bleed screw arrowed in **FIG 9** and use gentle air pressure (1 atm or 14 lb/sq in) to eject any fluid in the caliper.

3 Remove clamping ring and dust cover (see **FIG 8**). Depress one piston with tool P.83 (see **FIG 9**) or use a clamp. Place a block of wood in the slot as shown and blow out the opposite piston with air pressure of 2 atm or 29 lb/sq in, raising pressure if necessary. **Serious injury may result if fingers are not kept out of slot during this operation.**

4 Remove piston seal from inside cylinder bore with a plastic or wooden tool so that the groove and bore are not damaged. Restore removed piston and seal and clamp in order to remove opposite piston. Clean all the parts in methylated spirit (industrial alcohol). **Do not use any other type of solvent or the rubber seals will be damaged.** Check cylinder bores and pistons for wear, scoring or pitting and renew faulty parts. Renew all seals as a matter of course. It is dangerous to refit any doubtful parts. The components of the automatic pad adjustment cannot be renewed. Always fit a new piston if the automatic device is defective.

FIG 4 Arrows indicate minimum pad thickness, showing ample clearance from cross-spring

FIG 5 Details of front disc brake

Key to Fig 5

1 Brake disc
2 Caliper cover
3 Disc shroud
4 Caliper base housing
5 Brake pad segment
6 Cross-spring
7 Pin retainer
8 Retaining pin

FIG 6 Arrow indicates metal fluid pipe to caliper on front brake

FIG 7 Removing bolts that secure brake carrier to front axle

FIG 8 Prising out spring ring that secures caliper piston dust cover

Reassembling caliper:

1 Use ATE brake cylinder paste to coat the cylinder and piston parts. Insert seals in cylinder grooves.
2 Note cutaway step on piston pressure face. Use aligning tool P.84 or make up a thin sheet-metal gauge with an included angle of 20 deg. as shown in **FIG 10** to set piston correctly. Insert piston carefully so that it does not tilt or jam and align it so that the stepped-down part faces the disc rotation as shown. Use clamp to press piston into place. The aligning tool must rest against the upper edge of the brake pad slot. If caliper is installed, a piston may be turned by clamping the opposite piston and ejecting the required piston until it may be turned by hand.
3 Wipe off assembly grease and fit dust covers dry.
4 If caliper was separated into halves because of O-ring leakage, clean faces with methylated spirit (industrial alcohol), fit new rings and assemble with new bolts, nuts and spring washers, using genuine Porsche spares. Tighten to half the required torque and then fully tighten. Torque for front calipers is 3.4 mkg (24½ lb ft). Do not forget packing plate 7.3 mm (.287 inch) thick between halves when ventilated discs are fitted.
5 Fit disc to hub with marks aligned and tighten nuts to 2.3 mkg (16½ lb ft). Refit hub as described in **Chapter 8** and adjust bearings. Use a dial gauge to check the lateral runout of the disc faces as described in **Section 7**.
6 Fit caliper using new spring washers and tighten bolts to 7 mkg (50½ lb ft). Fit brake pads in original positions (see **Section 3**). Bleed the hydraulic system (see **Section 10**).

5 Servicing rear brakes

Removing:

1 Jack up car and remove rear wheels after chocking front wheels and releasing handbrake.
2 Remove brake pads (see **Section 3**). From behind, remove disc shrouds. Block brake pedal in slightly depressed position and detach fluid pipe from caliper, then detach caliper.
3 Remove two countersunk screws adjacent to wheel studs and pull off disc.
4 Refer to **FIG 11** and remove castle nut 1 and washer. From behind, pull out handbrake cable. Remove expander 2 and spring.
5 Turn retainer 3 to release it from pin, remove spring and pull out pin from rear. Lift upper shoe with screwdriver, withdraw adjuster 4 and unhook spring between shoes.
6 Release retainer from lower shoe. Remove both shoes in forward direction and unhook second return spring.

Servicing caliper:

For this operation, follow the instructions for front brake calipers in **Section 4**. There is a packing plate 10.6 mm (.417 inch) thick between the caliper halves when ventilated discs are fitted to car. Bolt torque for caliper halves is 1.8 mkg (13 lb ft).

Checking parts:

Clean and examine mechanical parts for wear. Renew broken or distorted springs and check that adjuster works freely. Discard oily brake linings as it is not possible to clean them satisfactorily. Worn linings must be replaced by Porsche-approved makes.

Reassembling:

1. Insert handbrake cable and fit washer against spacer tube. Fit inner expander struts. Fit special return spring 5 to both shoes with coils pointing inwards (see **FIG 11**).
2. Slide shoes rearwards onto brake carrier plate and fit the retaining pins, springs and retainers 3. Fit inner expander of handbrake into seats in shoes.
3. Lift upper shoe with screwdriver and fit adjuster 4. Sprocket faces down in righthand brake and up in lefthand brake. Fit return spring at adjuster end of shoes.
4. Slacken adjusting nut on handbrake cable right back. Fit expander spring, second half of expander 2 and tighten castle nut until one of its slots clears the splitpin hole. Fit a new splitpin. Make sure expander struts are correctly seated in shoes.
5. Refit disc and check for runout (see **Section 7**). With ventilated discs, fit intermediate plate between caliper and rear axle control arm. Fit caliper and tighten bolts to 6 mkg (43½ lb ft). Fit pads in original positions. Bleed hydraulic system (see **Section 10**) and adjust handbrake (see **Section 2**).

6 The handbrake carrier plate

This is part 6 in **FIG 6** in **Chapter 7** (Rear Suspension) and the instructions in **Section 4** of that same chapter cover the removal of the carrier plate and the correct procedure for reassembly.

FIG 10 Using 20 deg. plate to set piston step correctly in relation to caliper and to disc rotation

FIG 9 Using clamp to press piston back into cylinder. Arrow points to bleed screw

FIG 11 Handbrake assembly with drum removed. Dotted lines show correct alignment of coils of righthand spring

Key to Fig 11
1 Nut for cable
2 Brake shoe expander
3 Shoe retainer
4 Shoe adjuster
5 Interrupted return spring

7 Servicing brake discs

Solid type:

Front discs are 12.5 to 12.7 mm (.492 to .500 inch) thick when new and rear discs are 9.8 to 10.0 mm (.386 to .394 inch) thick, or alternatively, rear ones may be 10.3 to 10.5 mm (.406 to .413 inch). Wear limit, if symmetrical, is 11 mm (.43 inch) front, and 8.5 mm (.33 inch) rear.

Concentric scoring of discs is normal, but if it is excessive, with possible pitting or cracking, the disc must be reground or renewed. Remove up to .50 mm (.02 inch) equally from each side, the surface finish being within .006 mm (.00024 inch). Thickness must not vary more than .03 mm (.0012 inch). Reground discs must not runout more than .05 mm (.002 inch).

To check front disc runout when installed, remove the brake pads (see **Section 3**) and adjust the front wheel bearings. Set up a dial gauge so that its plunger bears on the disc face about 10 to 15 mm (.40 to .60 inch) below the outer edge. It is advisable to check both faces. Maximum permissible runout when mounted is .20 mm (.008 inch), and discs with excessive runout must be reground or renewed.

To check rear discs, remove pads and set up dial gauge as before. Brake disc must be fully tightened onto hub by refitting the wheel nuts on steel spacers so that the nuts may be tightened to 10 mkg (72¼ lb ft). To avoid warping, tighten evenly and diagonally. Runout must not exceed figure given for front discs.

Ventilated discs:

A brake with ventilated disc is shown in **FIG 12**. Note plate 2 between caliper halves. Disc thickness is 19.8 to 20 mm (.780 to .787 inch) both front and rear.

Smooth, rounded concentric scoring is normal, but sharp ridges, cracking and pitting call for disc renewal or regrinding. This is also the remedy for excessive runout or variation in thickness.

When regrinding, remove no more than .70 mm (.028 inch) equally from each side, the minimum disc thickness being 18.6 mm (.732 inch). Surface finish must be within .006 mm (.0002 inch). Deviation in thickness .03 mm (.001 inch) maximum. Runout up to .05 mm (.002 inch) measured on faces 10 mm (.4 inch) inside the outer edge.

Wear limit of disc thickness is 1 mm (.04 inch) from each face. If worn symmetrically, lowest limit of disc thickness is 18 mm (.71 inch).

Check runout of mounted discs as described for solid discs, noting the extra tolerance allowed when discs are fitted to hubs.

FIG 13 Arrows point to datum surfaces used when regrinding discs. Front disc (left) and rear disc (right). Dimension 'a' must be maintained (see text)

Regrinding of solid discs:

When regrinding discs it is most important to preserve the original symmetry, which is the reason for taking an equal amount off each side. To ensure that this may be checked by the operator, the following dimensions are given. Measurement 'a' in **FIG 13** is listed together with the original disc thickness, and a simple calculation will enable the check to be made.

When thickness of new front disc is 12.5 to 12.7 mm (.492 to .500 inch), dimension 'a' is 35±.10 mm (1.378 ±.004 inch).

When thickness of new rear disc is 9.8 to 10.0 mm (.386 to .394 inch), dimension 'a' is 62±.10 mm (2.441 ±.004 inch).

When thickness of new rear disc is 10.3 to 10.5 mm (.406 to .413 inch), dimension 'a' is 62.25±.10 mm (2.451 ±.004 inch).

FIG 12 A ventilated disc brake, showing disc 1 and packing or intermediate plate 2 (between caliper halves)

Regrinding of ventilated discs:

The same symmetry must be maintained as stated for solid discs. Check against the following specification when regrinding.

When thickness of new front disc is 19.8 to 20.0 mm (.780 to .787 inch), dimension 'a' is $35 \pm .10$ mm ($1.378 \pm .004$ inch).

With same thickness of new rear disc, dimension 'a' is $65 \pm .10$ mm ($2.559 \pm .004$ inch).

Pad thickness:

All the preceding limits for wear and regrinding apply only if the pad thickness is not allowed to fall below 2.0 mm (.08 inch). **This is important if the brakes are to function correctly.**

Disc balance:

Ventilated discs are balanced at the factory by inserting spring clips into the ventilating slots. Do not remove these clips.

Ventilated disc cleanliness:

Using the car on dirty roads may lead to clogging of the ventilating slots. When washing the car, use a hose to clear the slots to ensure adequate cooling.

8 Servicing single master cylinder

Removing:

1 Jack up car. Detach accelerator pedal from rod by pulling pedal back. Remove mat and floorboard. From behind brake pedal, pull rubber boot off master cylinder (see part 11 in **FIG 15**).

2 Drain brake fluid reservoir (see **FIG 2**). Underneath car, remove shield from suspension crossmember. Detach pipes and switch wires from cylinder (see **FIG 14**).

3 Loosen clamp and withdraw hose connecting reservoir to cylinder. Release cylinder flange from body (2 nuts) and withdraw cylinder.

FIG 14 View under car showing pipes being detached from master cylinder

FIG 15 Components of single master cylinder

Key to Fig 15
1 Housing
2 Special check valve
3 Spring
4 Primary piston cup
5 Piston with washer
6 Secondary piston cup
7 Piston stop plate
8 Lock ring
9 Washer
10 Rubber grommet
11 Rubber boot

FIG 16 Correct clearance between master cylinder piston and pedal pushrod is 1 mm (.04 inch)

FIG 17 Adjusting length of brake pedal pushrod

Key to Fig 18
1 Fluid reservoir
2 Dual master cylinder
3 Brake pedal
4 Mechanical stoplight switch

FIG 18 Diagram showing layout of dual master cylinder braking system

Dismantling:

Refer to **FIG 15**. Hold cylinder lightly between soft jaws in a vice.
1 Prise out ring 8. Withdraw stop plate 7.
2 Tap out piston and washer 5 with secondary cup 6.
3 With gentle air pressure of 1 atm (15 lb/sq in) at outlet port, blow out primary cup 4 and remove spring 3 and valve 2.

Cleaning and inspection:

Clean all parts in methylated spirit (industrial alcohol). **Use no other solvents as they may cause rapid deterioration of the rubber seals.** Always renew the seals or cups, which are available in kit form. Check the cylinder bore and piston surfaces for wear, scoring or corrosion, and discard if not smooth and polished. Check all ports and valve passages for obstruction. When clean and dry, the piston must produce suction drag when moved either way in the cylinder.

Reassembling:

Observe absolute cleanliness: Lightly coat cylinder bore, piston and cups with ATE brake cylinder paste. Do not allow mineral oil or grease to contact any internal parts. Reassemble in reverse order of dismantling, making sure that cups are carefully inserted in bore so that lips are not turned back. Remember to install the washer 5 in correct position. Make sure that the lock ring is firmly seated.

Installation:

Apply sealer to cylinder mounting flange and check that pushrod enters cylinder, then attach flange to body, using new spring washers. Tighten nuts to 2.5 mkg (18 lb ft). Inside car, check pushrod clearance shown in **FIG 16**. To adjust to 1 mm (.04 inch), loosen locknut and turn pushrod as shown in **FIG 17**. Connect pipes and wires.

Check that vent hole in reservoir cap is clear. Fill reservoir (see **Section 2**). Bleed brake system (see **Section 10**). Check operation of brakes, check for leaks with pedal depressed firmly and check stoplights. Refit undershield, tightening nuts to 6.5 mkg (47 lb ft) and bolts to 4.7 mkg (34 lb ft).

9 Servicing the dual master cylinder

Starting with the 1968 models, 911(USA), 911T and 911S cars are fitted with dual-circuit braking systems. The difference can be seen by comparing **FIG 18** with **FIG 1**. Note the twin-tank reservoir 1 and dual outlets from the master cylinder 2. Failure of one circuit still leaves the other circuit in operative condition. USA cars have an additional brake failure indicator actuated by the master cylinder. A mechanical stoplight switch 4 is operated by a disc on the pushrod.

Removing:

Refer to **Section 8,** the sequence being the same apart from the need to detach the additional pipelines.

Dismantling:

Refer to **FIG 19**. Hold cylinder lightly in a vice fitted with soft jaws.
1 Prise out ring 14. Remove stop plate 13 and piston 11 complete with all cups, washers, spring and stop 9.
2 Remove stroke limiting bolt 24 of secondary piston 7 and use gentle air pressure of 1 atm (15 lb/sq in) to blow out piston and cups. Cover any holes in cylinder which allow air to escape. Remove spring 2 and washers.
3 Hold neck of primary piston 11 between soft jaws in a vice and unscrew stroke limiting bolt 8, keeping the spring compressed to reduce the load on the threads. Separate the parts.
4 On USA cars, remove warning sender 25 and cap screw 16 and blow out parts 19 and 20 with gentle air pressure, blocking any escape holes for air.

Cleaning and inspection:

Wash all parts in methylated spirit (industrial alcohol). **Use no other solvents as they may lead to rapid deterioration of the rubber parts.** Dry the housing and clear all ports with compressed air. Renew all rubber parts at every overhaul. They are available in kit form.

Check piston and cylinder bore surfaces for wear, scoring or corrosion. Renew if not smooth and highly polished.

Key to Fig 19

1. Housing
2. Secondary piston return spring
3. Spring seat
4. Supporting washer
5. Primary cup
6. Filler disc
7. Secondary piston
8. Stroke limiting bolt
9. Travel stop
10. Primary piston return spring
11. Primary piston
12. Secondary cup
13. Stop plate
14. Lock ring
15. Dust boot
16. Bolt
17. O-ring
18. Spring
19. Piston
20. Piston cup
21. Grommet
22. Washer
23. Gasket
24. Stop bolt
25. Circuit failure sender

FIG 19 Components of dual master cylinder

Reassembling:

Do not let mineral oil contact any internal parts. Observe absolute cleanliness at all times. Reassemble in the reverse order, lightly coating the bore, the piston and the cups with ATE brake cylinder paste. When inserting the cups, take care not to turn back the sealing lips. Make sure cups face correctly with lips entering first.

Insert secondary piston with filler disc, primary cup, supporting washer, spring seat and spring, with large coil of spring entering first. Using a piece of clean plastic rod, push the piston down the bore until it clears the hole for the stop bolt. Fit the bolt and washer, tightening to 1 to 1.2 mkg (7.2 to 8.7 lb ft). Check that bolt is properly seated ahead of the piston and that the piston moves freely to the bottom of the bore.

Fit filler disc, primary cup and supporting washer to primary piston. Use stroke limiting bolt to secure spring, spring seat and stop sleeve to piston. Insert in bore and fit lock ring, making sure it is well-seated.

On USA models, coat warning system plungers with ATE brake cylinder paste and install as shown in **FIG 19**. Use a new O-ring under the cap screw and tighten to 1.5 mkg (11 lb ft). Fit new O-ring to sender unit and tighten to the same torque.

Installation:

This operation is similar to the one described for the single master cylinder (see **Section 8**). Check the failure warning system on USA cars as follows:

Test the warning system every 6000 miles and whenever the hydraulic system has been under repair. Switch on the ignition. Apply handbrake and check that control lamp lights up. This will test the bulb.

Depress brake pedal to brake actuation point. A second operator must now simulate failure of one brake circuit by slackening a bleed screw on one of the brake calipers. Further depression of the brake pedal to actuation point for the other brake circuit should cause the control lamp to light up. Tighten the bleed screw and release pedal.

Repeat the operation but select a bleed screw in the second circuit. If the lamp does not light up during one of the tests, check the sender unit on the master cylinder and renew if necessary.

Stoplight switch:

This is mounted on a bracket to one side of the brake pedal and pushrod. Remove the two screws and detach the wires to release the switch.

To adjust the switch, place a packing piece 4 mm (.157 inch) thick under the pedal stop. This will be equivalent to a pedal pad travel of 21 mm (.827 inch). Adjacent to the cable connections on the switch is a screw and locknut. Slacken the nut and turn the screw to the point where the stoplights just go on. Tighten the locknut and check action.

10 Bleeding the brake system

Air being compressible, it follows that any air which is present in the fluid of the hydraulic brake system will lead to excessive pedal travel and a 'spongy' feel. The object of bleeding the system is to get rid of this air. With the exception of the pipe connecting the reservoir to the master cylinder, any other disconnection of pipes will allow air to enter and make bleeding necessary.

When the piston in the master cylinder is fully retracted, it uncovers a port which allows fluid from the reservoir to top up the system if any fluid has been lost by leakage. If any pipe is disconnected it means that this action will lead to complete draining of the reservoir. To prevent this, block the brake pedal in a slightly depressed position so that the supply port is covered.

Two operators are needed for the operation. For cars with lefthand drive, start at the outer bleed screw of the lefthand rear wheel, follow with the inner bleed screw, repeat on the other rear wheel, then do the righthand front wheel followed by the left. **At all times during the operation, make sure that there is plenty of fluid in the reservoir.** If the supply becomes exhausted, air will enter the master cylinder and the procedure must then be restarted. Proceed as follows:

1 Remove dust cover from bleed screw and fit bleed hose as shown in **FIG 20**. Immerse the free end of the tube in some clean brake fluid in a clean glass container. Top up the supply reservoir with ATE Blue brake fluid.
2 Pump the brake pedal until pressure can be felt, hold the pressure while the second operator opens the bleed screw about $\frac{1}{2}$ to $\frac{3}{4}$ of a turn and press the pedal to the floor. Air which is present in the fluid will emerge as bubbles from the immersed tube. Close the screw and let the pedal return slowly.
3 Repeat this until no more air bubbles can be seen.
4 Follow the correct sequence and do the rest of the system, keeping an eye on the level in the supply reservoir. **Do not make use of any fluid which has been drained from the system.** Be careful to keep brake fluid off the paintwork of the car as it will attack it. Spilled fluid must be washed off immediately with water.
5 When finished, top up the fluid in the reservoir to the correct level and apply strong pressure to the pedal while another operator checks all parts of the system for leaks. Test car on road and check that pedal travel does not increase after use. If pedal feels 'spongy' or if brakes pull to one side, repeat the operation of bleeding. It is always advisable to repeat operation when the whole system has been drained during a complete overhaul.

For competition work it may be necessary to use a fluid with a higher boiling point, and Castrol Girling Brake Fluid Amber is recommended. For best results, use fresh fluid throughout the system before each event.

Bleeding dual-circuit brakes:

The procedure is the same as that just outlined, the rear brakes being bled first, followed by the front.

11 Servicing handbrake

Adjusting the handbrake cables has been covered in **Section 2**. Note that there are two types of handbrake installation, the second and later type having the heater and hand throttle control levers mounted on the support housing as shown in **FIG 21**. The following instructions will deal with this type, but such details as removing and refitting the brake cables will do for both types.

Removing handbrake:

1 Remove tunnel cover and lever dust boot. Unscrew knob off heater control lever 1. Release support housing from tunnel (3 bolts).

2 Remove nut 5 and withdraw cup spring 4, pressure disc 3, friction disc 8 and heater control lever 1. Note that numbered parts are actually at the opposite end, so work on the end closest to the heater lever.

3 Lift the housing a little. The cables and equalizer beam can be seen attached to a clevis, the clevis pin being secured by a spring clip. Release the clip and pull out the pin.

4 Remove wire from control lamp switch and lift away handbrake assembly.

Dismantling:

1 Remove locking ring and withdraw drag link and washer from lower end of hand throttle lever. Remove nut from pivot shaft 6 and lift off hand throttle lever and friction assembly. Pull out pivot shaft.

2 Remove screw to rear of pivot and withdraw control switch. Push handbrake lever slightly to rear and out of the housing to remove the ratchet plate.

3 Grind the rivet head off the ratchet pawl stud, drive out the stud and remove the pawl. If it is necessary to remove the handbrake lever, pull off the hand grip, which is glued on. This will release the button and rod, the ring and the spring.

Reassembling:

1 After fitting the handbrake control button, glue the grip in place, making sure that no surplus glue interferes with the action of the button.

2 Grease the ratchet plate pawl and pivot shaft with multipurpose lithium grease and insert into place.

3 Fit hand throttle friction discs dry. All friction assembly surfaces must be free from grease. Tighten self-locking nut until flush with end of pivot shaft.

Installation:

Do this in the reverse order of dismantling. Do not forget to attach the wire to the control lamp switch. Fit the heater control lever in the housing. Install the cable beam and check that the cables are correctly seated. Fit the housing to the tunnel and tighten the bolts to 2.5 mkg (18 lb ft). Reassemble the friction parts for the heater lever in the manner described for the hand throttle lever.

FIG 20 When bleeding brakes, tube is attached to bleed screw and free end is immersed in fluid in glass jar

Tighten the self-locking nut until the lever does not feel too stiff to move but does not slip back when heater is fully on. Check adjustment of heater flaps as in **Chapter 4**. Check adjustment of hand throttle control as in **Chapter 2**. Check handbrake adjustment (see **Section 2**).

Adjusting control lamp switch:

On some models the contact block for the switch is secured to the handbrake housing by a screw to the rear of the handbrake lever pivot. There is a slot for adjustment. Pull on the handbrake by one notch, loosen the screw and move the contact block by means of the screw until the control lamp lights up. Tighten the screw and check action again.

Key to Fig 21

1 Heater control lever
2 Hand throttle lever
3 Pressure disc
4 Cup spring
5 Self-locking nut
6 Pivot
7 Spacer sleeve
8 Friction disc

a Friction limit of heater lever is 10 kg (22 lb)
b Friction limit of hand throttle lever is 6 kg (13 lb)
c Hand throttle lever knob is pressed on
d Heater lever knob is screwed on

FIG 21 Details of mounting for handbrake and control levers

Servicing handbrake cables:

Removing:

1 Chock front wheels, release handbrake and raise rear of car. Remove rear wheels.
2 Remove handbrake housing from tunnel (3 bolts). Detach cables from equalizer beam (see 'Removing handbrake').
3 Block brake pedal in slightly depressed position to prevent draining of fluid from system and remove pipeline from rear caliper. Detach caliper from mounting.
4 Remove countersunk screws and pull off brake disc and spacer. Release cable from expander (see **Section 5**). Pull cable out from rear of brake. Pull other end out of conduit tube in tunnel.

Refitting:

1 Feed cable into conduit tube while coating it with multipurpose lithium grease. Refit cable end to brake expander as described in **Section 5**.
2 Refit caliper, tightening bolts to 6 mkg (43 lb ft) on new spring washers. Refit handbrake housing to tunnel. Bleed brake system (see **Section 10**). Adjust handbrake (see **Section 2**).

12 Fault diagnosis

(a) 'Spongy' pedal action

1 Leak in hydraulic system
2 Worn master cylinder
3 Leaking caliper cylinders
4 Air in the fluid
5 Insufficient fluid in reservoir

(b) Excessive pedal movement

1 Check 1, 4 and 5 in (a)
2 Excessive pad wear
3 Too much free movement in pedal pushrod
4 Defective cups and valve in master cylinder
5 Wheel bearings slack
6 Disc or caliper mountings loose
7 Excessive runout or thickness variation of discs

(c) Brakes grab or pull to one side

1 Check 5, 6 and 7 in (b)
2 Oily pads or mixed grades
3 Worn suspension or steering connections
4 Uneven tyre pressures
5 Dirt in pad slots, dust covers defective
6 20 deg. piston step wrongly set
7 Seized piston in caliper cylinder

(d) Pedal must be pumped to get braking

1 Check 2, 4 and 5 in (a) and 4 in (b)

(e) Brakes get hot when not used

1 Check 4 and 5 in (b); 5 and 7 in (c)
2 Reservoir supply port in master cylinder blocked by piston cup
3 Insufficient free play in pedal pushrod
4 Rubber cups swollen due to wrong fluid
5 Handbrake adjusted too tightly, cables seized (rear)
6 Handbrake shoe return springs weak or broken (rear)

(f) Frequent topping up of fluid required

1 Check pipes, connections and cylinders for leaks

NOTES

CHAPTER 11 - ELECTRICAL

1. General description
2. Routine maintenance
3. Battery maintenance
4. Servicing Bosch alternator
5. Servicing Motorola alternator
6. Servicing starter motor
7. The voltage regulator and relay switches
8. Servicing the lights
9. Fuses
10. Steering column switches
11. Flasher unit
12. Wiper and washer units
13. Reversing light switch
14. Safety belt warning system
15. Fault diagnosis
16. Wiring diagrams

1 General description

The 12-volt system has the negative battery terminal earthed. A belt-driven alternator provides alternating current which is rectified to give DC current for battery charging. The single-unit regulator controls alternator voltage to 14V. There is no current control as output does not rise after reaching the rated figure. There is no cut-out unit and the rectifier output is connected directly to the battery. Some owners will be unfamiliar with the alternator so that it is strongly recommended that they read the recommendations at the start of **Section 4** and **5** before carrying out tests. A Bosch alternator is fitted to all models except 911T which has a Motorola.

The starter motor is mounted on the transmission casing. The sliding pinion is meshed with the flywheel ring gear by a solenoid which is actuated when the ignition is switched on. When the pinion is engaged, contacts in the solenoid complete the circuit and the starter motor turns the engine. When the engine fires, an overrunning clutch prevents the pinion from being driven, and it is disengaged by a spring.

Headlamps may have renewable bulbs or sealed-beam units. Flasher and reversing lights are fitted. Instrument lights may be dimmed by turning the switch knob. The revolution indicator is transistorized and is driven by electrical impulses from the ignition system. Electrical sender units operate the fuel, oil temperature and, in the case of 911S cars, the oil pressure gauges.

Electrical tests entail the use of accurate meters, but many mechanical faults may be cured by a reasonably skilled owner. It is recommended that serious wear and major electrical faults are best cured by using the Exchange service of the manufacturers. Wiring diagrams will be found at the end of this chapter. **Always use wire for repairs which is the same cross-section as the original.**

2 Routine maintenance

Every 6000 miles, check the tension of the driving belt see **Section 2** in **Chapter 4** (Cooling). At the same mileage check the whole electrical system for correct functioning and check the condition of the battery. Once a year, check the alternator and starter brushes (see **Sections 4, 5** and **6**) and grease the alternator bearings.

FIG 1 Checking the specific gravity of the battery electrolyte with a hydrometer

General lubrication of the alternator and starter may be left until the engine is due for a major overhaul.

At regular intervals, check the electrolyte level in the battery and top up as described in **Section 3**.

3 Battery maintenance

The battery is mounted in the luggage compartment. See that the mountings are secure and if the terminals are coated with white powder, brush this off, using a solution of baking soda to neutralize it. Check that the terminal connections are clean and bright and coat them with vaseline or grease. **Difficult starting is often due to dirty or loose connections.**

Check the electrolyte level at regular intervals. Correct level is about 10 mm ($\frac{1}{2}$ inch) above the plates. **Top up with distilled water only. Do not use rain water or tap water.** The electrolyte is a solution of sulphuric acid in distilled water made to a particular specific gravity. **If the electrolyte is being prepared, do not add water to the acid as this is highly dangerous.** Add the acid very slowly to the water.

The specific gravity of the electrolyte is a guide to the state of charge of the battery. Use a hydrometer as shown in **FIG 1**, sucking up enough electrolyte to float the graduated indicator. In a fully-charged battery the specific gravity will be 1.285 (32 deg. Beaume). In a half-charged battery it will be 1.230 (27 deg. Beaume). When battery is discharged it will be 1.142 (18 deg. Beaume).

Any electrical test of a battery must be made with a voltmeter which permits a high-discharge rate. During a test of 10 to 15 seconds the voltage of each cell must not drop below 1.6. If it does, the cell is faulty. Normal voltage without load is 2. Voltage of individual cells must not vary by more than .20.

Do not leave the battery in a discharged state or it will be ruined. If it is to be left unused for long periods, give it a freshening charge every month.

FIG 2 Blower housing released from strap and pulled rearwards for access to the alternator cables

Alternator Connections

FIG 3 Removing brush plate and brushes (Bosch)

FIG 4 Separating rotor and end frame from stator housing (Bosch alternator)

4 Servicing Bosch alternator

Before carrying out alternator tests it is important to understand that it must not be run without connection to the battery, neither must the cables be removed during a running test. Be careful not to reverse the battery connections. Entrust major repairs to a Bosch service station.

Testing system:

Control lamp should light up with ignition switched on. If it does not, bulb may be broken or wire disconnected. If lamp stays on with ignition switched off it indicates a defective rectifier. Disconnect battery at once to prevent damage to alternator and battery.

Start the engine. If control lamp does not go out with increasing engine speed or lights up at certain speeds, the rectifier is defective.

For a quick test with the alternator installed, run the engine at a steady 3000 rev/min. Switch on lamps and accessories to bring the load to 28 to 30 amp. Voltage between terminals B+ and D— should lie between 13.5 and 14.5 volts.

Removing alternator:

Remove the air cleaner. Release the fuel pipe clips from the upper shroud as in **FIG 2**. Remove alternator pulley nut and take off belt (see **Chapter 4, Section 2**). Release blower housing strap, pull assembly to rear and detach wires.

Dismantling:

Remove pulley, pulley hub and key. Mark location of alternator in blower housing and remove.

Brushes:

Removing the brush plate is shown in **FIG 3**, but first check the brushes for freedom in their housings. Hook up the springs and check brush length if no further dismantling is required. Minimum length is 14 mm (.55 inch). Unsolder brush leads to renew brushes. Check that brushes slide freely, rubbing sides on a smooth file if necessary. Resolder leads with resin-cored solder, taking taking care not to let solder run up the stranded flexible connector.

Rotor:

To continue dismantling, remove brush plate complete. Remove the six long screws and part the rotor from the stator housing (see **FIG 4**). The rotor may be pressed out of the end frame for attention to the bearings and slip rings. It is not advisable to attempt repairs to the rectifier diodes which are mounted on plates at the same end as the brushes.

If the stationary windings are removed from the housing the coils may be tested as shown in **FIG 5**. Use 40V AC and a pair of probes and check for continuity and earthing. Also check for resistance using an ohmmeter. Correct resistance is .26 ohm + 10 per cent.

Using the same test voltage, check the rotor coils for earthing, putting one probe on a slip ring and the other on the polepiece. Connect an ohmmeter across the slip rings to check rotor coil resistance. It must be 4 ohm + 10 per cent. If the slip rings are worn and pitted, skim them in a lathe, taking off the minimum amount of metal. When finished, check that runout does not exceed .03 mm (.001 inch). Minimum slip ring diameter is 31.5 mm (1.24 inch) and maximum vertical runout of the rotor is .05 mm (.002 inch).

Bearings:

Renew bearings which are rough when spun without lubricant. In any case, renew bearings which have seen 60,000 miles of service. Adequately support end frame and rotor when pressing bearings into place. Coat one side of bearing with Bosche FT1v33 grease and fit to end frame with closed side entering first. Fit retaining plate.

Cleaning:

Parts must not be soaked in solvents. Momentary exposure to solvents is permissible for cleaning purposes. Always relubricate bearings after cleaning.

Reassembling:

Do this in the reverse order of dismantling. Check that the rotor turns freely after fitting the brushes.

Installation:

Fit alternator to blower housing with marks aligned. Seat blower housing on dowel in crankcase after connecting wires correctly. The red/white lead goes to terminal 1 (B+), the black lead goes to terminal 2 (DF), the brown lead goes to terminal 3 (D—) and the red lead goes to terminal 4 (D+). After fitting the pulley and belt, tighten the nut to 4 mkg (29 lb ft).

FIG 5 Using test probes to check the stator windings for shorts (Bosch alternator)

FIG 6 Component parts of Motorola alternator

Key to Fig 6

1 Isolation diode heat sink
2 Brush cover plate
3 Brush holder
4 Rear housing, supporting bearing and rotor
5 Front housing, supporting bearing and rotor
6 Positive diode heat sink
7 Negative diode heat sink
8 Stator
9 Ball bearing
10 Rotor
11 Bearing cover plate
12 Ball bearing

FIG 7 Circuit diagram of Motorola alternator, regulator and battery

Key to Fig 7

1 Battery
2 Regulator
3 Slip rings
4 Brushes
5 Rotor
6 Stator
7 Isolation diode
8 Generator control lamp
9 Ignition/starter switch
10 To accessories
11 To starter
12 Diodes

FIG 8 Removing brush holder on Motorola alternator

FIG 9 Checking rotor for shorts to D— by connecting one ohmmeter probe to a slip ring and the other to the D— terminal (Motorola alternator)

FIG 10 Using ohmmeter probes to test diodes. Illustration shows negative diode being checked by connecting one probe to D— and the other to the diode terminal (Motorola alternator)

5 Servicing the Motorola alternator

The component parts are shown in **FIG 6**. An alternator is not self-exciting so that the necessary field current has to reach the unit by way of the generator control lamp 8 (see **FIG 7**) and the voltage regulator. For this reason it is important that the lamp is not burned out or of the wrong wattage. The field current is only about 2 amp and is conducted to the field coils by brushes 4 and slip rings 3. An isolation diode 7 protects the alternator against overloading and also allows current to flow to the control lamp. The rectifier consists of three positive and three negative diodes 12. These pass current from the alternator to the battery or load but not in the reverse direction, so that there is no need for a cut-out.

Precautions:

Observe the following:
1 Do not earth the field exciter terminals DF of the alternator, regulator or the connecting wire.
2 Do not wrongly connect the voltage regulator and do not disconnect the regulator or the battery when the alternator is running.
3 Disconnect the battery before removing the alternator.
4 The voltage regulator must always be connected to alternator earth.
5 For alternator tests the battery must be in good condition and fully charged. When running alternator in car, battery must always be connected.
6 Disconnect battery before arc welding on car.
7 Heat damages diodes. Use pliers as heat sink when unsoldering or soldering. Wrong connections will cause damage to diodes.
8 Detach battery leads when charging battery in car.

Maintenance:

Apart from checking belt tension (see **Chapter 4, Section 2**) there is no need for routine maintenance of the alternator or the voltage regulator. Bearings are lubricated for life.

Testing alternator:

Make sure alternator connections are as given in 'Installation' for the Bosch alternator. Connect voltage regulator leads so that blue and red go to D+, black goes to DF and brown goes to D—. The regulator is mounted on a bracket near the ignition coil (see **FIG 16**).

For a quick test with alternator installed, run the engine at 2500 ± 150 rev/min with lamps and accessories switched on to give a load of 28 to 30 amp. Voltage between terminals B+ and D— must lie between 13.4 and 14.6 volts.

Removing alternator:

Do this according to the instructions under the same heading in **Section 4**.

Checking brushgear:

Remove brush holder (2 bolts, see **FIG 8**). Use ohmmeter and probes to check brushes for continuity, the insulated brush with the DF terminal and the earthed brush with the holder. Resistance should be nil. Resistance should be infinitely high when probes are touching brushes only.

Checking rotor:

Test for shorting to D— by connecting one ohmmeter probe to D— and the other to one of the slip rings as in **FIG 9**. Resistance should be infinite.

Test rotor coil for continuity by connecting one ohmmeter probe to each slip ring. The circuit resistance should be 4.5 to 6.5 ohm. Renew rotor if faulty.

Testing isolation diode:

First test the heat sink for earthing by connecting one ohmmeter probe to D+61 and the other to D— on the alternator and then in reverse. Resistance should be infinite in one direction and less than 50 ohm in the other. If readings differ from these, check heat sink insulation behind housing.

Test the diode by connecting one ohmmeter probe to terminal B+ and the other to D+61 and then reversing them. Resistance should be infinite in one direction and less than 50 ohm in the other.

Testing rectifier diodes:

Positive diodes are marked red and negative black. Test negative diodes by connecting ohmmeter as shown in **FIG 10**. Reverse connections and note result, which should be the same as described for the isolation diode. For positive diodes connect ohmmeter to D+61 and diode and then reverse connections to get same results as for the isolation diode.

Testing stator coil:

This is done as in **FIG 11**, the stator dismantling sequence being given later. Visually, a shortcircuit may be seen as burnt insulation at one spot. To test electrically, connect one ohmmeter probe to one end of coil and the other to the stator frame. Resistance must be infinite. Check all coil ends and renew stator if any test shows lower resistance.

Dismantling alternator:

1 Remove brush assembly (see **FIG 8**). Remove isolation diode assembly 1 in **FIG 6** (2 outer nuts).
2 Remove through-bolts and separate front housing 5 and rotor 10 from stator and rear housing 4.
3 Rotor may be pressed out of front housing and the ballbearing pulled off the rear end. To remove the bearing in the front cover, remove the bearing cover (3 screws) and press out the bearing.
4 Release diode assembly 6 and 7 from the rear housing and withdraw together with the stator 8. Mark the negative and positive diode leads if the diodes are to be removed. It would be best to leave servicing the diodes to a service station but the method is as follows:
5 Hold each lead with a pair of pliers on the diode side so that heat cannot travel into diode, and quickly unsolder the connections.

Reassembling:

1 If stator leads were unsoldered from diodes, pull them through the clips so that they lie correctly and will not need bending after soldering. Make sure connections are correct, noting that positive diodes are marked red and negative black.

FIG 11 Connect ohmmeter to a coil end and the stator. Resistance must be infinite. Repeat on all coil ends

FIG 12 Soldering stator leads to diodes, using pliers as heat sink to avoid damage (Motorola alternator)

2 Hold diode leads with pliers as in **FIG 12**. Use a hot iron and solder lead as quickly as possible.
3 Fit stator and diode assemblies into housing after placing an insulating washer and sleeve on each fixing stud of the positive diode assembly.
4 After fitting stator and diode assemblies, put insulating washers on the two positive diode studs and secure both assemblies with nuts. Make sure the stator leads are properly arranged.
5 Press rotor into front bearing in housing. Press other ballbearing into place up to the stop on the rear end of rotor shaft.
6 Make sure that the bore in the rear housing is clear and that the O-ring is in good condition. Joint the two housings together and tighten the six bolts evenly and diagonally.
7 Secure the isolation diode assembly in position and then attach the brush assembly. Install the alternator as described in **Section 4**.

FIG 13 Section through starter motor showing solenoid and actuating lever for engaging pinion with flywheel gear

6 Servicing starter motor

Details of the starter motor are shown in **FIG 13**. When the ignition and starter key is turned for starting, the solenoid is energized, the plunger is drawn in and the actuating lever starts to move the actuating sleeve to the left. When the associated locking ring has moved about 2 or 3 mm ($\frac{1}{8}$ inch) the balls round a groove in the shaft are freed and allow the pinion to move into engagement with the flywheel ring gear. The solenoid plunger has simultaneously closed a switch which passes current to the motor. If the engine fires, it may run up to a speed which would drive the motor by way of the pinion. To prevent this, a one-way or overrunning clutch is provided which allows the pinion to drive the ring gear but stops it being driven. When the switch is released the solenoid return spring starts to retract the pinion and pressure from the engagement spring pushes the locking ring over the balls and a braking disc comes into action to slow down the armature. The overrunning clutch consists of five spring-loaded rollers confined by cam-shaped recesses which allow rotation in one direction and jam in the other.

With the exception of the 911TV models with Sportomatic gearbox all other models from 1972 on are fitted with a starter motor of increased horse power. The power output is increased from .8 hp to 1.5 hp and apart from this both starters are basically of the same design. Refer to Technical Data for specifications.

Removal:

1 Disconnect battery earth cable. Detach cables from terminal 30 on starter solenoid.
2 Detach ignition switch control wire from starter terminal 50.
3 Remove flange bolts and lift starter away.

Removing and refitting solenoid:

1 Remove wire connector from terminal next to motor body. Release solenoid from drive housing.
2 Pull pinion out a little and withdraw the solenoid while disconnecting the plunger from the actuating lever.

Solenoids are not adjustable and a defective one must be renewed. It is a good plan to renew the solenoid at major engine overhauls.

Install solenoid in the reverse order. Hold the cable terminals when tightening the nuts so that the studs cannot turn and possibly cause internal twisting. Tighten nuts moderately. If solenoid is new, adjust the plunger so that distance from the centre of the hole in the clevis to the mounting flange is $32.4 \pm .10$ mm ($1.276 \pm .004$ inch) when the plunger is in position.

When the solenoid is energized the travel of the plunger must be $10 \pm .20$ mm ($.394 \pm .008$ inch), of which 3 mm ($.118$ inch) is engagement reserve.

Checking brushes and commutator:

1 Remove cover from end of starter opposite to pinion.
2 Lift brush springs and pull brushes out of holders by flexible leads. If length of brush allows lead to touch holder then it is too worn for further use and must be renewed.
3 Clean commutator with a stick wrapped in petrol-soaked cloth. Keep dirt and excess petrol out of the end bearing.

Check brush springs for tension. Renew brushes if worn, oil-soaked or if leads are loose or frayed. Always renew brushes in sets.

If commutator is badly scored or burned, remove the armature and skim the commutator in a lathe. Use fine sandpaper for polishing. Do not use emerycloth. Undercut as explained in 'Inspection and Testing'.

When refitting the brushes make sure that they are free in their holders and check that the flexible leads are out of the way.

Dismantling starter:

1 Remove dust cap from end opposite to the pinion. Remove the O-rings, the lock ring on the shaft and the spacers.
2 Detach cable from inner terminal of solenoid. Remove solenoid mounting screws, withdraw solenoid while unhooking plunger from actuating lever (see **FIG 13**).
3 Remove the two long through-bolts and the end cover or armature support. Withdraw brushes, making a note of their locations. Positive brushes have leads which are soldered to the field windings, negative brush leads go to the brush holders.
4 Remove the brush carrier plate and the metal and insulating washers from the armature shaft (see **FIG 15**). Pull complete field frame off the drive housing, taking care of the rubber seal and metal plate.
5 Remove the actuating lever pivot bolt and withdraw the armature and lever. Hold armature in a vice with soft jaws. Refer to **FIG 14** and press actuating sleeve 1 towards the overrunning clutch 4 and catch the locking balls 3 as they fall out. Release the sleeve and spring.
6 When cleaning the parts, do not put the armature or the overrunning clutch in solvent and keep solvent away from the self-lubricating bearing bushes. Normally, during a major overhaul it is advisable to renew these bushes. Clean off all carbon dust from the armature and from the brush carrier.

Inspecting and testing:

Check action of actuating lever, sleeve and overrunning clutch. Renew parts if sleeve and lever do not move freely, or if lever is bent. If necessary renew the brake disc. Renew pinion and shaft if teeth are worn.

Check the field windings for signs of excessive heat or melted solder. They must not protrude beyond the polepieces. Check coil for continuity and shorting to earth, using a 40V AC test lamp.

Test armature and brush carrier plate for short to earth in the same way. The insulated brush holders must not be shorting to earth. Apply test prods to cylindrical body of armature and to each commutator segment in turn. The test lamp should not light.

Check condition of commutator. Minimum diameter is 33.5 mm (1.319 inch) and maximum runout should not exceed .05 mm (.002 inch). Clean out excessive wear and pitting by skimming the commutator in a lathe, providing the diameter is not reduced below the stipulated figure. The mica insulation between the commutator segments must be removed to a depth of about .80 mm (.03 inch) using a piece of fine hacksaw blade ground on the sides to the correct width. Take care not to damage the segments or the soldered joints.

Brushes which are worn, broken or which have defective leads must be renewed. Always fit a complete set. Unsolder the leads one at a time to avoid confusion, and when soldering the new leads into place do not let the solder run too far up the flexible part.

Armature shaft bushes are of the self-lubricating type, so make sure that new bushes are well-impregnated with oil. At the pinion end, drill out the rivets to release the seal and press out the bush. Press a new bush into place with a shouldered mandrel having a pilot the same diameter as the shaft until it is flush on the inside. Do not reamer this type of bush after fitting. Centre a new seal with a suitable mandrel and secure the retainer with small screws, nuts and spring washers, peening the screw ends to prevent loss of the nuts.

FIG 14 Components of the starter pinion assembly

Key to Fig 14 2 Spring 4 Overrunning clutch
1 Actuating sleeve 3 Locking balls 5 Pinion

FIG 15 Starter motor with brush carrier plate removed, showing commutator and metal and insulating washers on shaft

Reassembling:

Hold armature in vice and stick balls into locking ring with grease such as Bosch Ft2v3. Fit actuating sleeve, brake disc and spring to overrunning clutch and locking ring and push assembly onto shaft until balls engage the groove in the shaft. Check that pinion and clutch are properly seated and that the mechanical engagement parts move freely when released. Grease all parts.

Fit actuating lever to sleeve and push armature and lever into drive housing. Grease and fit lever pivot stud. Fit rubber seal between solenoid and field recesses so that its tab seats correctly in the cutout provided. Push field frame over armature. Fit greased metal and insulating washers to shaft as shown in **FIG 15**. Fit brush carrier plate, aligning the notch which prevents turning, in the correct position. When the brushes and springs are fitted the spring pressure can be checked with a sensitive spring balance. Hook balance under end of spring and check moment of lifting. Recorded pressure should be 1150 to 1350 g (40.6 to 47.6 oz).

Seat rubber grommet for field lead correctly and refit end cover. Earthing points between brush carrier plate and cover and between cover and field housing must be clean and bright. Secure the two through-bolts. Fit spacer washers and locking ring to end of shaft and check that end float lies between .10 and .15 mm (.004 to .006 inch). Secure flange of end cap. Fit solenoid and connect field lead to inner terminal.

FIG 16 The voltage regulator is indicated by the arrow

FIG 16A Engine compartment console

Key to Fig 16A
1 Console
2 Relay switch for single stage rear window defroster (not used with two stage)
3 Rev/min sensor
4 Relay switch for start enrichment (not used in carburetter engines)
5 Rev/min transducer (not used in carburetter engines except 911T USA model)
6 Control relay for two stage rear window defroster (not used for single stage)
7 Radio noise suppression
8 Regulator
9 Ignition trigger unit
10 Fuse box 3

FIG 16B Headlamp dimmer, windshield defogger and turn signal relays

Key to Fig 16B
1 Headlight dimmer switch relay
2 Windshield defogger relay (not valid for USA)
3 Turn signal relay

7 The voltage regulator

The voltage regulator is mounted in the position shown in **FIG 16**. It is a single unit controlling the field circuit of the alternator and there is no current regulator or cut-out. As there is no provision for servicing, it is important to consult a Service Station if the regulator gives trouble. Renewal is the best cure for a defective unit.

Great care must be taken to ensure that the connections to the regulator are correctly fitted. The blue and red leads go to D+, the black lead to DF and the brown lead to D−.

Symptoms of regulator trouble may be no charge, or too low or too high an output from the alternator.

Relay switches

With the introduction of the CDS ignition system a repositioning of some switches and fuses was necessary. Referring to **FIG 16A**, which lists and identifies the various switch units, the console is accommodated in the engine compartment on the lefthand side.

The headlamp dimmer, windshield defogger and turn signal relays are accommodated in the luggage compartment floor on the lefthand side (see **FIG 16B**). It may be of interest to know that this relay is an electrically controlled switch. Referring to the diagram (**FIG 16C**), when the coil (2) windings are energised, through terminals 85 and 86, the electromagnetic force actuates the switch contacts (1) which breaks the circuit between terminals 30 to 87a and connects terminals 30 to 87. In this way it is possible to use low current (control current) for switching a main power circuit.

The location of standard relay switches, depending upon the optional equipment fitted, are also accommodated in the luggage compartment on the lefthand side but towards the front and alongside the fuse battery. To identify the relays refer to **FIG 16D**.

FIG 16C Diagram of relay switch circuit
Key to Fig 16C 1 Switch contacts 2 Coil

④	Air conditioner
③	Auxiliary driving lights
②	Fog lights
①	Horn

○	
③	Auxiliary driving lights/air conditioner
②	Fog lights/auxiliary driving lights
①	Horn

○	
○	
②	Fog lights/auxiliary driving lights/air conditioner
①	Horn

○	
○	
○	
①	Horn

FIG 16D Depending upon the optional equipment fitted the illustration shows the four examples of positioning standard relays (5 Fuse box 1, 6 Fuse box 2)

FIG 17 To set headlamp beam vertically, turn screw 'a' to right to lower and to left to raise it. Turn screw 'b' for horizontal setting, turning to right sets beam to left, turning to left sets beam to right. Screw 'c' secures rim

FIG 18 Removing retainer and headlamp bulb from back of reflector

8 Servicing the lights

Bulb-type headlamps:

When working on the headlamps avoid touching the reflecting surface or the bulb with the fingers.

To renew a bulb, remove screw 'c' in **FIG 17** and withdraw lamp assembly. Pull cable connector off tabs. Press retaining ring inwards and turn to the left to release the bayonet catch. Withdraw bulb (see **FIG 18**). Insert a new bulb, holding it with clean cloth or soft paper to avoid touching with the fingers. Aligning tab in base of bulb must fit into cut-out. Press retainer in and turn to right and then fit the connector. Refit lamp unit and check beam setting.

Sealed-beam headlamps:

Remove unit as just described and pull connector off tabs. Remove spring clips from lamp rim by pressing down and in with a thumb. Do not try to prise out with a screwdriver or the springs will fly. Pull out inner retaining ring and sealed-beam unit. Refit in the reverse order and check beam setting.

H4 Headlamps

The 1972 911 models are equipped with H4 headlamps and twin-filament Halogen bulbs, except on those models exported to countries which prohibit such systems.

The H4 bulb base is totally different to the type used in previous models and cannot be substituted by any other type. The lamp design provides a different light distribution from that of previous lamps, brought about by a changed reflector and lens pattern. The lens carries the identification 'H4' on its front side.

The H4 bulb is rated at 60 watts for high beam and 55 watts for low beam, the higher wattage and larger reflector area are significant in improving greatly the high beam projection.

The H4 lamp units can be installed in previous models without difficulty but they must be fitted in pairs only.

Renewing H4 bulb:

1 Unscrew and remove the cross-head screw in the lamp unit base and lift the head lamp out with an upward movement.
2 At the rear of the reflection pull off the wire connection, depress and unhook the spring retainer and take out the bulb.
3 The bulb socket is so designed that it cannot be inserted in the lamp the wrong way. Avoid touching the bulb glass and under no circumstances fit it with the glass smeared with grease.

FIG 19 Arrangement for headlamp beam setting. 'a' is width of headlamp centres, 'b' is height of centres from ground, 'c' is 1 per cent of distance 'd' from lamps to board or wall

FIG 20 Fuses are mounted under luggage compartment mat. Numbers indicate circuits protected (see wiring diagrams)

4 When reinstalling the headlamp unit the best method is to first secure the lamp with one or two threads of the cross-head screw and then seat the lamp in its upper retainer. Tighten the cross-head screw and check beam setting.

Beam setting:

This is best done on proper equipment and in accordance with the regulations of the country concerned. If it must be done by the owner, select a piece of level ground and mount a board as shown in **FIG 19**, distance 'd' being about 5 m (16½ feet). Tyres must be properly inflated and car bounced to normalize suspension. Board must be central on car axis.

Mark height of headlamp centres on board as at 'b'. Mark line 'c' on board at 1 per cent of distance 'd'. If 5 m or 16½ feet, 'c' will be 50 mm or 2 inches. Mark width between headlamp centres (value 'a') on line 'c' centrally about axis. Make a cross at the intersection. From now on, remember that the example is for a lefthand drive car, so reverse the setting for a righthand drive one.

Cover one headlamp while setting the other. First adjust horizontally to bring the point of the angle between the dark and light areas onto the cross on the board. Make adjustments by turning screw 'a' in **FIG 17**.

Adjust vertically by turning screw 'b' until the horizontal plane of the dark and bright areas lies on the line marked at 'c' (see **FIG 19**). After setting vertically, check the horizontal setting again.

Dim headlamps:

Connect a voltmeter to terminals yellow and brown or white and brown behind the light unit. Switch on lights and run engine at 2000 rev/min. Meter reading should be 12 to 12.5V. If below this, check battery terminals for dirty contact or loose fixing, check regulator and lighting switch terminals, fuse contacts and connections to light unit. If no improvement, try a new bulb. If reading remains low the fault probably lies with the battery, the alternator or the regulator.

Renewing bulbs in other lights:

Access to fog lamp bulbs is by removing retaining ring, withdrawing lamp unit and pulling snap-fit socket out of unit. Bulb is of bayonet fixing type. After removing other light units, use a screwdriver to lift the plastic holder at the cut-off corner and withdraw holder and bayonet fixing bulb. Holder will snap into place when refitting. To reach the festoon bulb in the interior light, gently prise out the lamp base with a screwdriver, working along the rear edge. Make sure bulb contacts hold bulb firmly. Luggage compartment and number plate lamps also have festoon bulbs.

Control and instrument lamps are accessible after pulling luggage compartment mat forward. The lamp sockets are a push fit.

9 Fuses

These will be found under the luggage compartment mat as shown in **FIG 20**. Note that the circuits protected by individual fuses may be identified by referring the numbers to those listed in the wiring diagrams found at the end of this chapter. If a fuse blows it is essential to find the reason why before fitting a new one. Spare 8/15 and 25/40 amp fuses should be carried in the car.

Key to Fig 21

1. Fillister screw
2. Serrated lock washer
3. Contact ring
4. Hex nut
5. Lock washer
6. Fillister screw
7. Round head countersunk screw
8. Upper housing assembly
9. Combination switch
10. Spring
11. Spring
12. Fillister screw
13. Clamp
14. Steering post extension
15. Wiper and washer switch
16. Allen bolt
17. Lower housing assembly
18. Lever knob

FIG 21 Components of combination switches fitted to steering column

10 Steering column switches

The combination switch assembly is shown in **FIG 21**. To remove it, first remove the steering wheel (see **Chapter 9**). Separate all wiring connections. Remove horn contact ring 3. Remove nuts and pull upper housing assembly 8 upwards, pushing the leads and connectors through the holes provided. Remove combination switch 9 (3 screws).

Faulty switch units are best renewed as an assembly, but a broken flasher return spring may be renewed separately. Check all electrical contacts for firm seating and cleanliness. Refit the parts in the reverse order, making sure the connections are correctly made. There is a relay for the headlamp flasher switch under the left floorboard.

11 Flasher unit

This is located under the luggage compartment mat adjacent to the steering column. It is a push fit in a three-pronged connector. There is an indicator lamp to show when a flasher bulb has failed, a magnetic switch breaking the earth connection to the lamp. The flasher unit cannot be repaired and it must be renewed in the event of failure.

12 The wiper and washer units

Removing wiper motor and linkage:

Pull luggage compartment mat forward and remove the front ventilating case after releasing the clip and air duct. These are located just below the grille in front of the wiper blades. Pull off the five cables from the wiper motor. Remove the wiper arms and the rubber grommets, unscrew the large nuts to release the spindles and withdraw the motor and linkage downwards. The linkage joints are service-free.

When refitting the assembly, make sure the wire connections are correctly made. Check that the linkage moves freely. Fit the wiper blades so that they wipe a symmetrical arc.

Windscreen washer:

Up to chassis No. 302.695 the washer reservoir fitted into a recess along the side of the luggage compartment floor. To service this type, pump reservoir completely dry, remove cap and hose and turn reservoir to remove it. To remove the pump, detach the cables and suction and pressure hoses. Loosen plastic straps and lift out pump.

To service the later type, remove the two screws securing the reservoir and remove it. Remove the pump as just described.

13 The reversing light switch

This is screwed into the side of the transmission housing and is actuated by a pushrod when reverse gear is engaged. It may be removed by pulling off the rubber cap, detaching the cable connectors and unscrewing it. Make sure the pushrod is properly installed with the rounded end entering first.

14 Safety belt warning system

From the beginning of 1972 onwards all vehicles exported to the U.S.A. are equipped with a safety belt warning system. The fitment is obligatory to conform with the federal laws on safety.

The system comprises, two inertia reel safety belts with automatic locking retractions; a control lamp with the inscription 'Fasten Seat Belt'; a built-in passenger seat contact switch; a new parking brake switch and a modified warning buzzer. The modified buzzer is a three-pole type which can be used, if necessary, to replace the existing two-pole type.

A switch is built into each safety belt buckle, it remains closed when the belts are not worn and provides an earth contact for terminal 'G' in the control lamp. The handbrake switch provides an earth connection to terminal 50 a when the handbrake lever is fully released. The buzzer terminal 86 is energized when the ignition is switched on. To avoid activating the system when there is no passenger in the front seat a two-pole connector is located under the seat which breaks the independent earth contact when the seat is unoccupied.

The control lamp lights up and a simultaneous warning from the buzzer will operate when:

1 The ignition is switched on.
2 The driver (and passenger) have not put on their seat belts.
3 The parking brake is not fully released.

15 Fault diagnosis

(a) Battery discharged

1 Terminals loose or dirty
2 Battery internally faulty
3 Shortcircuits in system
4 Alternator not charging
5 Regulator defective

(b) Insufficient charging current

1 Check 1, 4 and 5 in (a)
2 Driving belt slipping

(c) Battery will not hold charge

1 Low level of electrolyte
2 Battery plates sulphated
3 Electrolyte leakage from cracked case or top seal
4 Plate separators ineffective

(d) Battery overcharged

1 Check 5 in (a)
2 Poor connections between regulator and alternator

(e) Alternator output low or nil

1 Check 3 and 5 in (a) and 2 in (b)
2 Faulty brushes, rotor coil or isolation diode

(f) Noisy alternator

1 Worn belt, loose pulley
2 Defective bearings

(g) Control lamp not lighting with ignition on

1 Defective bulb or broken connection

(h) Control lamp stays on with ignition switched off

1 Defective diodes in alternator (disconnect battery at once)

(i) Control lamp stays on

1 Check 1 in (h)

(j) Starter motor lacks power or will not operate

1 Battery discharged, loose connections
2 Solenoid switch contacts worn or dirty
3 Brushes worn or sticking, springs weak or broken
4 Commutator, armature or field coils defective
5 Engine abnormally stiff

(k) Starter motor runs but does not turn engine

1 Pinion or flywheel gear defective

(l) Starter pinion stays in mesh

1 Bent armature shaft, dirty or defective pinion
2 Solenoid switch faulty

(m) Lamps inoperative or erratic

1 Battery low, bulbs burned out
2 Switch faulty, poor earthing, loose connections, broken wires

---

NOTES

Wiring Diagram Type 911

Key to wiring diagram

1. Starter motor
2. Alternator
3. Control box
4. Ignition distributor
5. Ignition coil
6. Spark plugs
7. Fuel pump
8. Resistor
9. Battery
11. Headlamps
12. Fog lamps
13. Blink/parking lights
14. Tail/stop/blink/back-up lights
15. License plate light
19. Interior light
20. Trunk light
24. Small combination instrument
25. Large combination instrument
26. Transistorized tachometer
27. Speedometer
28. Clock
32. Blink/dimmer/signal/wiper/washer switch with signal knob on steering wheel
33. Starter/ignition switch
34. Light switch
36. Fog lamp switch with control light
37. Handbrake control light switch
38. Door post contact switch
39. Brake light switch
40. Trunk light switch
41. Back-up light switch
42. Signal horn relay
43. Relay for light signal
44. Blink light unit
45. Control light unit
46. Control light relay
47. Oil temperature transmitter
48. Fuel tank unit
49. Oil pressure transmitter
50. Oil level transmitter
51. Resistor relay
52. Windshield wiper motor
53. Windshield washer pump
54. Signal horn
55. Cigarette lighter
56. Control light switch
57. Control light fuse
61. Fuse box

Fuses

1. Stop light, blinkers, back-up lights
2. Interior light, cigarette lighter, clock
3. Auxiliary heater
4. Windshield wipers and washer
5. Fog lamps
6. License plate light, trunk light
7. Parking light, RH
8. Parking light, LH
9. Low beam, RH
10. Low beam, LH
11. High beam, RH, high beam control light
12. High beam, LH

IMPORTANT

Disconnecting of battery with running engine results in immediate destruction of alternator.

Wiring Diagram Type 911 S

Key to wiring diagram

① Starter motor
② Alternator
③ Control box
④ Ignition distributor
⑤ Ignition coil
⑥ Spark plugs
⑦ Fuel pump
⑧ Resistor
⑨ Battery
⑪ Headlamps
⑫ Fog lamps
⑬ Blink/parking lights
⑭ Tail/stop/blink/back-up lights
⑮ License plate light
⑲ Interior light
⑳ Trunk light
㉔ Small combination instrument
㉕ Large combination instrument
㉖ Transistorized tachometer
㉗ Speedometer
㉘ Clock
㉚ Blink/dimmer/signal/wiper/washer switch with signal knob on steering wheel
㉝ Starter/ignition switch
㉞ Light switch
㊱ Fog lamp switch with control light
㊲ Handbrake control light switch
㊳ Door post contact switch
㊴ Brake light switch
㊵ Trunk light switch
㊶ Back-up light switch
㊷ Signal horn relay
㊸ Relay for light signal
㊹ Blink light unit
㊺ Control light unit
㊻ Control light relay
㊼ Oil temperature transmitter
㊽ Fuel tank unit
㊾ Oil pressure transmitter
㊿ Oil level transmitter
51 Resistor relay
52 Windshield wiper motor
53 Windshield washer pump
54 Signal horn
55 Cigarette lighter
56 Control light switch
57 Control light fuse
60 Fuse box

Earth leads or cables:

a) battery – body
b) transmission – chassis
c) steering column control switch – body
d) fuel spout – body
e) windshield wipers – body
f) instruments – body
g) heater – body

Fuses

1. Stop light, blinkers, back-up lights
2. Interior light, cigarette lighter, clock
3. Auxiliary heater
4. Windshield wipers and washer
5. Fog lamps
6. License plate light, trunk light
7. Parking light, RH
8. Parking light, LH
9. Low beam, RH
10. Low beam, LH
11. High beam, RH, high beam control light
12. High beam, LH

IMPORTANT

Disconnecting of battery with running engine results in immediate destruction of alternator.

Wiring Diagram 1970
Type 911T, 911E, 911S

1. Battery
2. Starter
3. Alternator
4. Governor
5. Ignition distributor
6. Ignition transformer
7. Spark plugs
8. Gasoline pump
9. BHKZ unit
10. Intermediate unit
11. Speed switch (only E and S)
12. Electromagnetic control valve
13. Lifting magnet (stop) (only E and S; on 911 T USA solenoid valve)
14. Temperature time switch
15. Microswitch (E and S only)
17. Headlamps
18. Blinker, clearance and side marker lamps (side marker lamps USA only)
19. Tail, brake, blinker, side marker and backup lamps (side marker lamps USA only)
20. Fog lamp (optional)
21. License plate lamp
22. Trunk lamp
23. Interior lamp
24. Glovebox lamp
25. Ashtray lamp
30. Blinker, dimming, headlamp flasher, wiper-washer switch with signal button in steering wheel
31. Steering ignition starter switch
32. Light switch
33. Warning light switch (not applicable in Italy)
34. Fan and separate heater switch
35. Rear window heater switch
36. Door contact switch
37. Switch for trunk room light
38. Hand brake contact
39. Brake light switch
40. Brake warning switch (USA only)
41. Backup light switch
42. Switch for glovebox light
43. Interval switch
44. Wiper follow-up switch
45. Buzzer contact (USA only)
48. Direction warning blinker indicator
49. Horn relay
50. Headlight flasher changeover relay
51. Rear window heater relay
52. Auxiliary starting relay
53. Buzzer (USA only)
56. Oil temperature indicator
57. Oil pressure indicator
58. Oil level indicator
59. Indicator for fuel gauge
65. Small combination instrument
66. Large combination instrument
67. Transistor revolution counter
68. Speedometer
69. Electric time clock
73. Wiper motor
74. Washer pump
75. Fanfare horn
77. Cigarette lighter
78. Fuse box I 10-pole
79. Fuse box II 8-pole
80. Fuse box III 3-pole
81. Fan motor
82. Heated pane
84. Plug connection 14-pole
85. Plug-connection 6-pole
86. Plug-connection 4-pole
87. Plug-connection 1-pole
89. Ground connection – body

FUSES:

Fusebox I
1. Interior light, time clock, trunk light
2. Warning light
3. (Window lifter)
4. Cigarette lighter
5. (Slide roof)
6. Windshield wiper, washer pump
7. Fresh air fan
8. Brake, blinker, backup lights
9. Blinker light front left
10. Blinker light front right

Fusebox II
1. High beam left
2. High beam right
3. Dimmer left
4. Dimmer right
5. Clearance light left
6. Clearance light right
7. License plate light
8. (Fog lights)

Fusebox III
1. (Sportomatic)
2. Stop magnet, solenoid valve, starting valve
3. Rear window heater

CAUTION!
Disconnection of battery with the engine running will result in immediate destruction of alternator.

NOTE: IMAGES OVERLAP AT ARROWS

Wiring Diagram (Part 1) 1971 Type 911T, 911E, 911S

1 Battery
17 Headlamps
18 Blinker, clearance and side marker lamps (side marker lamps USA only)
19 Tail, brake, blinker, side marker and backup lamps (side marker lamps USA only)
20 Fog lamps (optional)
21 License plate lamp
22 Trunk lamp
23 Interior lamp
24 Glovebox lamp
25 Ashtray lamp
30 Blinker, dimming, headlamp flasher, wiper-washer switch with signal button in steering wheel
31 Steering ignition starter switch
32 Light switch
33 Warning light switch (not applicable in Italy)
36 Door contact switch
37 Switch for trunk room light
39 Brake light switch
41 Backup light switch
42 Switch for glovebox light
48 Direction warning blinker indicator
50 Headlight flasher changeover relay
67 Transistor revolution counter
68 Speedometer
69 Electric time clock
78 Fuse box I 10-pole
79 Fuse box II 8-pole
84 Plug connection 14-pole
85 Plug connection 6-pole
87 Plug connection 1-pole
89 Ground connection – body
91 Switch for fog lamps (optional)
93 Fog tail light (optional)

FUSES:

Fusebox I:
1 Interior light, time clock, trunk light
2 Warning light
7 Fresh air fan
8 Brake, blinker, backup lights
9 Blinker light front left
10 Blinker light front right

Fusebox II:
1 High beam left
2 High beam right
3 Dimmer left
4 Dimmer right
5 Clearance light left
6 Clearance light right
7 License plate light
8 (Fog lights)

CAUTION!

Disconnection of battery with the engine running will result in immediate destruction of alternator.

Wiring Diagram (Part 2) 1971 Type 911T, 911E, 911S

1 Battery
2 Starter
3 Alternator
4 Governor
5 Ignition distributor
6 Ignition transformer
7 Spark plugs
8 Gasoline pump
9 BHKZ unit
11 Speed switch (E, S and 911 T USA only)
12 Electromagnetic control valve (E and S only)
13 Lifting magnet (stop) (E and S only; on 911 T USA solenoid valve)
14 Temperature time switch
15 Microswitch (E, S and 911 T USA only)
30 Blinker, dimming, headlamp flasher, wiper-washer switch with signal button in steering wheel
31 Steering ignition starter switch
34 Fan and separate heater switch
35 Rear window heater switch
38 Hand brake contact
40 Brake warning switch (USA only)
45 Buzzer contact (USA only)
49 Horn relay
51 Rear window heater relay
52 Auxiliary starting relay (E and S only)
53 Buzzer (USA only)
54 Diode (USA only or optional)
56 Oil temperature indicator
57 Oil pressure indicator
58 Oil level indicator
59 Indicator for fuel gauge
65 Small combination instrument
66 Large combination instrument
69 Electric time clock
73 Wiper motor
74 Washer pump
75 Fanfare horn
77 Cigarette lighter
78 Fuse box I 10-pole
80 Fuse box III 3-pole
81 Fan motor
82 Heated pane
84 Plug connection 14-pole
85 Plug connection 6-pole
86 Plug connection 4-pole
87 Plug connection 1-pole
89 Ground connection – body
90 Extra fanfare horn (optional)
92 Separate heater (optional)
94 Radio (optional)
95 Oil temperature switch for SPM (optional)

FUSES:

Fusebox I:
1 Interior light, time clock, trunk light
2 Warning light
3 (Window lifter)
4 Cigarette lighter
5 (Slide roof)
6 Windshield wiper, washer pump
7 Fresh air fan
8 Brake, blinker, backup lights
9 Blinker light front left
10 Blinker light front right

Fusebox II:
1 (Sportomatic)
2 Stop magnet, solenoid valve, starting valve
3 Rear window heater

CAUTION!

Disconnection of battery with the engine running will result in immediate destruction of alternator.

Wiring Diagram (Part 1) 1972 Type 911T, 911E, 911S

1 Battery
17 Headlights
18 Turn signal, parking and side marker lights (side marker lights USA only)
19 Tail, stop, turn, back-up and side marker lights (side marker lights USA only)
20 Fog lights (optional)
21 License plate light
22 Luggage compartment light
23 Interior light
24 Glove compartment light
25 Ashtray light
30 Flasher, dimmer, wiper/washer switch with horn ring on steering column
31 Ignition starter switch and steering lock
32 Light switch
33 Emergency flasher switch (not applicable in Italy and France)
36 Door contact switch
37 Switch for luggage compartment light
39 Stop light switch
41 Back-up light switch
42 Switch for glove compartment light
48 Turn signal/emergency flasher unit
50 Headlight relay
67 Tachometer
68 Speedometer
69 Electric clock
78 Fuse box I (10 terminal)
79 Fuse box II (8 terminal)
84 Multi-connector (14 terminal)
85 Multi-connector (6 terminal)
87 Connector (single contact)
89 Ground connection-body
93 Rear fog light (optional)

FUSES:

Fuse box I:
1 Interior light, clock, luggage compartment light
2 Emergency flasher
7 Fresh air fan
8 Stop, turn and back-up lights
9 Left front turn signal light
10 Right front turn signal light

Fuse box II:
1 High beam, left
2 High beam, right
3 Low beam, left
4 Low beam, right
5 Side marker, left
6 Side marker, right
7 License plate light
8 (Fog lights)

CAUTION!
Do not disconnect battery while the engine is running as this will damage the alternator.

176

Wiring Diagram (Part 2) 1972 Type 911T, 911E, 911S

1 Battery
2 Starter
3 Alternator
4 Governor
5 Distributor
6 Ignition transformer
7 Spark plugs
8 Fuel pump
9 High tension ignition unit
11 Speed switch
12 Cold start solenoid (except 911 TV)
13 Shut-off solenoid (911 TV: solenoid valve)
14 Thermo-time switch (except 911 TV)
15 Micro switch
30 Flasher, dimmer, wiper/washer switch with horn ring on steering column
31 Ignition starter switch and steering lock
34 Switch for fan and auxiliary heater
35 Rear window defogger switch
38 Parking brake contact
40 Brake warning light switch (USA only)

43 Safety belt contact, driver side (USA only)
44 Safety belt contact, passenger side (USA only)
45 Buzzer contact (USA only)
46 Seat contact, passenger side (USA only)
49 Horn relay
51 Rear window defogger relay
52 Auxiliary starting relay (except 911 TV)
53 Buzzer (USA only)
56 Oil temperature indicator
57 Oil pressure indicator
58 Oil level indicator
59 Indicator for fuel gauge
60 Safety belt warning light (USA only)
65 Fuel gauge dial
66 Oil temperature gauge dial
69 Electric clock
73 Wiper motor
74 Washer pump
75 Horns

77 Cigarette lighter
78 Fuse box I (10 terminal)
80 Fuse box III (3 terminal)
81 Fan motor
82 Rear window defogger element
84 Multi-connector (14 terminal)
85 Multi-connector (6 terminal)
86 Multi-connector (4 terminal)
87 Connector (single contact)
89 Ground connection-body
90 Optional horn
92 Auxiliary combustion heater (optional)
94 Radio (optional)
95 Oil temperature switch sportomatic (optional)

FUSES:

Fuse box I:
1 Interior light, clock, luggage compartment light
2 Emergency flasher
3 (Electric windows)
4 Cigarette lighter
5 (Sliding roof)
6 Windshield wiper, washer pump
7 Fresh air fan
8 Stop, turn and back-up lights
9 Left front turn signal light
10 Right front turn signal light

Fuse box III:
1 (Sportomatic)
2 Shut-off solenoid, solenoid valve, solenoid for cold starting unit
3 Rear window defogger

CAUTION!
Do not disconnect battery while the engine is running as this will damage the alternator.

CHAPTER 12 - BODY

1 Paintwork
2 Servicing doors
3 Luggage compartment lid
4 The rear lid
5 Fitting bumpers
6 Fitting front wings
7 Fitting side panel windows
8 Paint codes
9 Door hardware interchange

1 Paintwork

Porsche body finish is of the oven-baked synthetic enamel type and major re-finishing must be entrusted to experts with the necessary facilities. Small areas which need re-painting may be done with air-drying synthetic enamel. It is not recommended to use cellulose lacquers for this purpose because there will be a change in colour, baked enamels lightening and cellulose enamels darkening with age. In the case of metallic finishes, small areas cannot be successfully retouched and a complete part such as a wing or door must be resprayed.

Before spraying, the existing damage must be rectified and any finish that is to take new paint must be prepared by careful cleaning, particularly if it has been protected with wax polish or polish containing silicones. Wash with a detergent solution and use a silicone remover. Do not remove grease with petrol and do not wipe clean with a dry cloth. A pad wetted with white spirit is the best way of removing lint or dust.

Prime all bare patches and use body putty for deep blemishes. Rub smooth with grade 320 Wet-or-Dry paper, using plenty of water. Finish with 400 grade paper and abrade all glossy surfaces which are to be re-painted. Give a light spray with a pre-matching colour and again get the highest degree of surface finish with the 400 paper and water. Dry thoroughly and give at least two coats of thinned enamel, letting each coat dry before applying the next. Give an extra coat of metallic paint, holding the gun farther away to prevent flotation of the metallic particles. Leave to dry several days and then polish. (Paint color codes are listed at the end of this chapter)

2 Servicing doors

Door hardware interchange is listed at the end of this chapter.

Removing:

If this is to be done by extracting the hinge pins, use an impact tool such as P.290 which is hooked under each pin and the pin driven out upwards.

Refitting:

Check the hinges for alignment as shown in **FIG 1**. Grease pins well to prevent squeaks and fit door. Check gap all round. If door must be raised so that gap between lower edge and sill is 3.5 to 4.5 mm ($\frac{9}{64}$ to $\frac{11}{64}$ inch), slacken bolts fixing hinges to pillar and lift and re-tighten. Now check door gap down edge. To increase gap set hinges with hammer as shown in **FIG 2**. The door may be set outward with the hand-made tool shown in **FIG 3**, the operation being shown in **FIG 4**.

FIG 1 Using a straightedge to check the alignment of the door hinges

FIG 2 Setting hinge with a block of wood and a hammer

179

FIG 3 Door can be reset outwards with the tool on the left (see FIG 4). Check gap between door and door flange with center gauge (see FIG 5). Use gauge on right to check gap round door edge. All items are made from mild steel

The distance between the door and the flange should be 9 mm (.35 inch) and the simple gauge shown in the centre of **FIG 3** will enable the gap to be checked as shown in **FIG 5**. The righthand gauge is used to check the gap between the door and the body aperture.

Note that a new door shell is not welded at one point so that it may be twisted to make it fit the body. When satisfactory, the door is made rigid by welding and end pieces cut and fitted to the front and rear upper door edges.

Dismantling door:

1 Remove window winder and ring. Remove safety lock button. Remove ornamental strip from window frame (screw at front, screw and snap nut at rear).
2 Press remote control push button at armrest out of nipple. Remove handgrip from passenger's side (2 bolts under ornamental strip). Remove two socket-head bolts from armrest and pivot it upwards about the single bolt. Remove bolt and armrest.
3 Release door panel by removing self-tapping screws and prising the clips out of the rubber grommets. Note the two screws, one at each end of the pocket.
4 Remove waterproofing from access holes in door. Remove window well covering rail (clips) and rubber strip. Remove door travel limiter.
5 Remove outside door handle. Remove window frame, which is secured by bolts at the places marked in **FIG 7**. Pull frame out in an upwards direction. Remove window winding mechanism and extract from window elevating rail. Remove door lock.

FIG 4 Using tool (see FIG 3) to reset door outwards

Door lock variations:

New and old versions are shown in **FIG 6**. Note the long through-pin on the left compared with the two short pins on the right. The early two-pin lock could jam if an attempt was made to open the door from the inside and the outside simultaneously. It is therefore advisable to fit the later version. This, however, entails a change in the outside handle door button. The door button actuating lever must be replaced by one with a longer pin, the new part being No. 901.531.919.20 for the left side (Lefthand drive) and 901.531.920.20 for the righthand side. When fitting the new parts make sure that the longer pin does not rest on the lock or the door may burst open on very rough roads.

Reassembling door:

Grease all moving parts of lock and winder mechanisms. Note that there are two types of winder, one with rollers and the other with plastic sliders. These are not readily interchangeable.

1. Fit winder and lightly tighten bolts, using washers and lockwashers. Turn mechanism into the up position and push the window glass and caulked elevating rail into the mechanism forward from the rear. The new type of winder will eliminate rattles on older installations.
2. Crank window to half-open and push window frame into place. Adjust frame and tighten bolts in sequence shown in **FIG 7**, noting that the short bolt is used in the upper position at the rear of the door. Gap for weatherstrip depends on age of car. Early 911 models had a hollow type of strip which may be replaced by a thicker type needing a gap of 12 mm (.47 inch). New-type strips need a gap of 9 mm (.35 inch). Use cement to secure the strip.
3. Fit outside handle and door travel limiter. Fit rubber strip in window well covering rail and cut to size. Fasten rail with clips.
4. Put a strip of pliable rubber putty under the edges of the chrome trim in the upper edge of the door and fix trim. Putty prevents wind roar.
5. Wind window fully up and tighten mechanism. Cement into place the travel stops for the cranking mechanism. On early types of cranking mechanism, cement a 50 mm (2 inch) square piece of foam rubber 8 mm (.3 inch) thick between the glass-elevating rail and the cranking mechanism to prevent friction.
6. Cement felt liners 6 mm (.24 inch) thick to the sheet metal under the remote control rods for the lock. Cement waterproof material over the access holes inside the door. Fasten door panel by sliding clips into rubber grommets. Insert self-tapping screws, putting one in each corner of door pocket.
7. Set armrest vertically and fit single bolt at rear end. Turn rest horizontally and fit remaining two bolts. Fix handgrip with two bolts under ornamental strip.
8. Guide pushbutton of remote control at armrest forward from the rear and press it into the centre of the nipple. If the button binds, enlarge the hole with a file. Secure the ornamental strip and velvet liner. There is a nut and self-tapping screw at the rear and one screw at the front. Fit the safety lock button.
9. Fit the window winder handle and ring with the handle down when the window is up. Close all apertures in the door with rubber caps. When door is refitted and correctly aligned, check action of lock and lockplate.

FIG 5 Using center gauge in FIG 3 to check gap between door and door flange

FIG 6 Latest door lock with long through-pin on left. Lock on right is earlier version with two short pins

FIG 7 Sequence for tightening bolts which secure the window frame

3 Luggage compartment lid

A gas-cushioned prop keeps the lid steady at any raised position. For opening the lid there is a control knob in the passenger's compartment. There is also a safety latch. If the control cable breaks the lid opens automatically but the latch prevents it rising too far.

When removing a lid, scribe round the hinge brackets where they are bolted so that the lid may be refitted in the same place. If a new lid is being fitted, attach the hinge brackets and the gas prop. The piston of the prop must face down. Install the lock and roughly adjust it. Tension the lock spring with a piece of wire. Check fit of lid in body aperture.

Gap between top edge of lid and centre piece of windscreen should be 4 to 5 mm (.16 to .20 inch). Check that there is a gap of 1 to 1.5 mm (.04 to .06 inch) round the edges. Adjust lid height by inserting washers where the hinge brackets are bolted to the lid. Washers placed at the front end will lower the lid, and when placed at the rear will raise it.

4 The rear lid

This is also controlled by a knob inside the car and is also fitted with a gas prop. Mark the hinge positions before removing them if the same lid is to be refitted. When installing the lid, fit the hinges and the gas prop so that the piston of the prop is attached to the lid frame.

Check the gap round the lid when it is closed. Gap at top edge should be 3.5 to 4.5 mm (.14 to .18 inch). At sides gap should be 2.5 to 3.5 mm (.10 to .14 inch). Bottom gap depends on height of wings. Lower edge must be flush with wing edges.

Fit lid lock and control cable and check that lock bolt catches properly when slammed.

5 Fitting bumpers

Front:

Straighten surface below front edge of lid to get an even gap between bumper and lid. Fit bumper without rubber strip and check distance to flasher housing and adjust if necessary. Fit flasher lens.

Adjust the bumper brackets so that there will be considerable tension during reassembly. Bend rear bracket forward for this purpose. Fit bumper reinforcement to models 911 and 911S by coating thickly with epoxy resin cement and sliding into place in the bumper.

Secure bumper braces so that there will be as much preload tension on the bumpers as possible. Cement the sealing rubber to the body and install the bumper.

Rear:

Fit bumper side pieces and straighten the attaching tabs. Fit the bumper centre piece, insert the bumper horns and adjust to equal height. File gap between bumper and horn if necessary. Remove the fitted parts.

Cement sealing rubber strip and cut off edges. Fit bumper parts and horns and cover holes with plastic caps.

6 Fitting front wings

Before fitting the lefthand wing, install the fuel filler cover. Apply body sealer strip to the mounting flange of the wing and then fit the snap nuts. Fit wing, and screw in bolts finger tight. While guiding the wing into place make sure the cable conduit for the filler cover release is correctly positioned. Do not, at this stage, install the sealing strip as it may be necessary to apply body solder in places. As a result, the gap between the wing and the door may be wider at the top edge by 1 mm (.04 inch).

Tighten the second bolt in from the rear end first and lightly tighten one at the front. Do the rearmost top bolt followed by the lowest one by the door sill, then tighten the remaining bolts on the vertical flange starting at the top. Finally, work along the top flange, starting at the rear.

When satisfied with the fit, drill two 4 mm (.16 inch) holes through the attaching flanges at front and rear locations, insert steel rivets in the holes and weld the heads to the body panel. These will act as dowels so that when the wing is removed for painting and then refitted it can be restored to its correct position and be properly aligned.

7 Fitting side panel windows

Fit the cover strip at the bottom, enlarging the holes with a file if necessary. Put body sealing strip under the cover strip and secure cover with Quicklock nuts. Put sealing strip under the vertical mounts for the window. Insert the window and tighten securely.

8 Paint codes

COLOR CODES FOR 1964 TO 1968 MODELS

Example: synthetic resin paint 6402

The two figures 64 denote the 1964 color range.

The figures 02 denote ruby red in this color range.

The figures 01 - 09 are standard production colors in the range concerned.

On the other hand 6413 is black and thus a special color in this catalog.

The new color coding has additionally two prefix numbers and a suffix letter after the coding,

e.g. 97 - 6802 - L.

The number 97 is an index number of the paint manufacturer concerned and here signifies $140^\circ C$ ($284^\circ F$)

paint from Messers. Lesonal, who are denoted by the suffix letter L.

Paint manufacturer's identification: L = LESONAL
G = GLASURIT
H = HERBERTS

For the 1964/65 models the following were standard colors:

Slate gray	6401
Ruby red	6402
Enamel blue	6403
Light ivory	6404
Champagne yellow	6405
Irish green	6406
Signal red	6407

special color.

Dolphin gray	6410
Togo brown	6411
Bali blue	6412
Black	6413

For the 1966 models the following were standard colors:

Slate gray	6601
Polo red	6602
Gulf blue	6603
Light ivory	6604
Bahama yellow	6605
Irish green	6606
Sand beige	6607
Aga blue	6608
Black	6609

plus 22 special colors.

The 1967/68 color range consists of the following standard colors:

Slate gray	6801
Polo red	6802
Ossi blue	6803
Light ivory	6804
Bahama yellow	6805
Irish green	6806
Sand beige	6807
Burgundy red	6808
Tangerine	6809

In addition the following 22 special colors are available:

Ivory	17657
Champagne yellow	16153
Signal yellow	R 1007
Lemon yellow	R 1012
Dark red metallic	30847
Crystal blue	52254
Pastel blue	R 5012
Blue metallic	52300
Ultra blue	R 5013
Lime green	62165
Signal green	R 6001
Bush green	62163
Dark green metallic	62109
Turkey green	R 6016
Grey white	75742
Fortuna gray	R 7030
Beige gray	70192
Olive	62166
Sepia brown	R 8007
Coffee brown	80342
Black	95043
Silver metallic	96024

R = Ral, is obtainable from all manufacturers under this number.

COLOR CODES FOR 1970 AND 1971 MODELS

The formerly used numerical color code on the paint nomenclature plate has been replaced with a new four-digit numerical code with letter identification of the paint manufacturer.

Paint manufacturer's identification: L = LESONAL
G = GLASURIT
H = HERBERTS
HL = HERBOL

Standard colors for 1970 and 1971 Models:

	Targa	Coupe
Light ivory	1110	1111
Signal orange	1410	1414
Irish green	1510	1515
Tangerine	2310	2323
Bahia red	1310	1313
Albert blue	1810	1818
Pastel blue	2010	2020
Burgundy red	2410	2424
Conda green	2610	2626

Optional Colors for 1970 and 1971 Models:

	Targa	Coupe
Black	1010	1010
Olive	3910	3939
Ivory	4610	4646
Light yellow	6210	6262
Turquoise	6410	6464
Turquoise green	6510	6565
Glaze blue	6610	6666
Signal yellow	7210	7272
Cristal blue	7310	7373
Sepia brown	7410	7474
Beige grey	7510	7575
Grey white	7610	7676
Bush green	7710	7777
Signal green	7810	7878
Light red	7910	7979
Metallic silver	8010	8080
Metallic red	8110	8181
Metallic green	8310	8383
Metallic blue	8410	8484
Metallic gemini	8610	8686
Metallic gold	8810	8888
Optional colors to order		9898

NOTE

Beginning with 1970 models, all metallic finishes are applied in the two-coat wet-on-wet process.

COLOR CODES FROM 1972

General

Beginning with 1972 models, a new numbering code is used in identifying paints on the paint nomenclature plate. The change was necessary to ensure right shipment of paint when ordered for given vehicle.

The new color code on the vehicle paint data plate is identical with the order numbers in the color catalogue.

Identification of the new 5-digit code numbers on the paint nomenclature plate:

Example: 131 9 2

1.	Three-digit paint number	<u>131</u> 9 2	light ivory
2.	Place of application	131 <u>9</u> 2	Porsche company
3.	Paint manufacturer	131 9 <u>2</u>	Glasurit company

Standard colors from 1972 model: Metallic colors:

131	light ivory				
117	light yellow	to Sep-1st	133		metallic gold
114	signal yellow	from Sep-2nd	140		VW-metallic gold
018	tangerine		224		metallic green
022	bahia red		324		metallic blue
025	aubergine		330		metallic gemini
225	viper green	to Sep-2nd	925		metallic silver
325	albert blue	from Sep-3rd	936		VW-metallic silver
415	sepia brown				

Optional colors from 1972 model:

019	gulf orange
024	fraise
116	signal orange
132	ivory
213	irish green
218	bush green
226	lind green
227	light green
326	icing blue
328	gulf blue
329	sea blue
341	lilac
414	olive
622	beige grey
700	black
999	optional colors to sample

9 Door hardware interchange

HARDWARE INTERCHANGE 1964 TO 1968

Replacement doors, to '68 models	901.531.005./006.21 for Coupe and Targa
As replacement for doors with Part #	901.531.003./004.20/21/22/23
Matching door handle	901.531.035.20 only

Interchangeability:

- ✛ = Standard installation
- ⊕ = No longer supplied
- ○ = Installation possible
- — = Installation not possible

		Window regulator			Regulator rail			Window with regulator rail			(brass)	(brass)	(aluminium)	(aluminium)	(aluminium)	Door window frame (brass)	(brass)		
		901.542.041./042.20	901.542.041./042.21	901.542.041./042.22	901.542.045./046.20	901.542.045./046.21	901.542.045./046.40	901.542.011./012.20/30	901.542.011./012.25/35	901.542.011./012.40/45	901.542.005./006.20/22	901.542.005./006.30/32	901.542.005./006.25/26	901.542.005./006.35/36	901.542.021./022.27	901.542.005./006.40/45	901.542.005./006.41/46	901.542.005./006.43/48	901.542.005./006.51/55
Window regulator	901.542.041./042.20	⊕			⊕	—	—	⊕	—	—	✛	✛	○	○	○	○	○	○	○
	901.542.041./042.21				—	✛	✛	✛	✛	✛	○	○	✛	✛	○	✛	✛	○	○
	901.542.041./042.22				—	○	✛	✛	✛	✛	○	○	○	○	—	○	○	○	○
Regulator rail	901.542.045./046.20	⊕	—	—				✛	✛	○	○	○	—	—	—	—	—
	901.542.045./046.21	—	✛	✛				○	○	✛	✛	○	—	—	—	—	—
	901.542.045./046.40	—	✛	✛				—	—	—	—	—	✛	✛	○	○
Window with regulator rail	901.542.011./012.20/30	⊕	—	—				✛	✛	—	—	—	—	—	—	—
	901.542.011./012.25/35	—	✛	✛				—	—	—	✛	✛	○	—	—
	901.542.011./012.40/45	—	✛	✛				—	—	—	—	—	✛	✛	○	○
Door window frame (brass)	901.542.005./006.20/22	✛	✛	○	✛	✛	—	✛	—	—									
	901.542.005./006.30/32	✛	✛	○	✛	✛	—	✛	—	—									
(aluminium)	901.542.005./006.25/26	○	✛	✛	✛	✛	—	○	✛	—									
	901.542.005./006.35/36	○	✛	✛	✛	✛	—	○	✛	—									
	901.542.021./022.27	○	○	✛	○	○	—	—	✛	—									
(brass)	901.542.005./006.40/45	○	✛	✛	—	—	✛	—	—	✛									
	901.542.005./006.41/46	○	✛	✛	—	—	✛	—	—	✛									
	901.542.005./006.43/48	○	○	○	—	—	○	—	—	○									
	901.542.005./006.51/55	○	○	○	—	—	○	—	—	○									

HARDWARE INTERCHANGE 1969 ONWARDS

Replacement doors, from '69 models   901.531.005./006.27 for Coupe and Targa

or   911.531.005./006.00 for Coupe with power windows

Matching door handle   901.531.037.00 only

Interchangeability:

- **+** = Standard installation
- **O** = Installation possible
- **−** = Installation not possible

		Window regulator				Regulator rail				Window with regulator rail					Door window frame								
		901.542.041./042.21	901.542.041./042.22	901.542.041./042.23	911.542.041./042.00	901.542.045./046.21	901.542.043./044.40	901.542.045./046.23	901.542.043./044.43	901.542.011./012.21/31	901.542.011./012.25/35	901.542.011./012.27/37	901.542.011./012.40/45	901.542.011./012.43/47	901.542.005./006.20/30	901.542.005./006.22/32	901.542.005./006.25/35	901.542.005./006.26/36	901.542.021./022.27	901.542.005./006.40/45	901.542.005./006.41/46	901.542.005./006.43/48	901.542.005./006.51/55
Window regulator From '69 models	901.542.041./042.21					O	O	−	−	O	O	−	O	−	O	O	O	O	O	O	O	O	O
	901.542.041./042.22					+	+	−	−	+	+	−	+	−	O	O	O	O	O	O	O	O	O
	901.542.041./042.23					−	−	+	+	−	−	+	−	+	O	O	O	O	+	O	O	+	+
	911.542.041./042.00					−	−	+	+	−	−	+	−	+	O	O	O	O	+	O	O	+	+
Regulator rail	901.542.045./046.21	O	+	−	−										+	+	+	O	−	−	−	−	−
	901.542.043./044.40	O	+	−	−										−	−	−	−	−	+	+	O	O
	901.542.045./046.23	−	−	+	+										O	O	O	+	−	−	−	−	−
	901.542.043./044.43	−	−	+	+										−	−	−	−	−	O	O	+	+
Window with regulator rail	901.542.011./012.21/31	O	+	−	−										+	+	−	−	O	−	−	−	−
	901.542.011./012.25/35	O	+	−	−										−	−	+	+	O	−	−	−	−
	901.542.011./012.27/37	−	−	+	+										O	O	O	+	−	−	−	−	−
	901.542.011./012.40/45	O	+	−	−										−	−	−	−	−	+	+	O	O
	901.542.011./012.43/47	−	−	+	+										−	−	−	−	−	O	O	+	+
Door window frame	901.542.005./006.20/30	O	O	O	O	+	−	O	−	+	−	O	−	−									
	901.542.005./006.22/32	O	O	O	O	+	−	O	−	+	−	O	−	−									
	901.542.005./006.25/35	O	O	O	O	+	−	O	−	−	+	O	−	−									
	901.542.005./006.26/36	O	O	O	O	+	−	O	−	−	+	O	−	−									
	901.542.021./022.27	O	O	+	+	O	−	+	−	O	O	+	−	−									
	901.542.005./006.40/45	O	O	O	O	−	+	−	O	−	−	−	O	O									
	901.542.005./006.41/46	O	O	O	O	−	+	−	O	−	−	−	+	O									
	901.542.005./006.43/48	O	O	+	+	−	O	−	+	−	−	−	O	+									
	901.542.005./006.51/55	O	O	+	+	−	O	−	+	−	−	−	O	+									

CHAPTER 13 - TECHNICAL DATA

1 Torque wrench settings
2 Technical specifications 2.0 Litre vehicles
3 Technical specifications 2.2 and 2.4 Litre vehicles
4 Lubrication chart

1 TORQUE WRENCH SETTINGS
Settings in mkg (lb ft in brackets)

Engine:
- Crankcase bolts ... 2.2 to 2.5 (16 to 18)
- Camshaft housing to cylinder head ... 2.2 (16)
- Crankcase through-bolts and nuts ... 3.5 (25.3)
- Flywheel bolts ... 15 (108.5)
- Connecting rod bolts ... 5 (36.2)
- Cylinder head nuts ... 3 to 3.3 (21.7 to 23.9)
- Camshaft sprocket nut ... 10 (72.3)
- Rocker arm shafts ... 1.8 (13)
- Pulley to crankshaft ... 8 (58)
- Pulley to generator ... 4 (29)

Transmission:
- Housing nuts ... 2.5 (18)
- Guide tube nuts ... 1.0 (7.2)
- Withdrawal fork screw ... 1.0 (7.2)
- Bolt for elbow drive ... 2.5 (18.1)
- Detent plug ... 2.5 (18.1)
- Filler and drain plugs ... 2.0 to 2.5 (14.5 to 18.1)
- Bolts for clamping plate (intermediate plate) ... 2.5 (18.1)
- Input shaft nut ... 10 to 12 (72.3 to 86.8)
- Castle nut on input shaft ... 6.0 to 6.5 (43.4 to 47)
- Reinforced castle nut on input shaft ... 9 to 11 (65.1 to 79.6)
- Pinion shaft bolt ... 11 to 12 (79.6 to 86.8)
- Selector fork bolts ... 2.5 (18.1)
- Crownwheel (ring gear) bolts ... 9.5 to 10 (68.7 to 72.3)
- Bolts for universal joint flanges ... 4.5 to 5 (32.5 to 36.2)
- Ballpin for clutch withdrawal fork ... 2.1 to 2.3 (15.2 to 16.6)

Extra for Sportomatic transmission:
- Housing nuts ... 2.1 to 2.3 (15.2 to 16.6)
- Screw for elbow drive ... 1.5 (10.8)
- Torque converter and servo unit nuts ... 2.1 to 2.3 (15 to 17)
- Torque converter and starter nuts ... 3.5 to 4 (25 to 29)
- Parking lock cap in front cover ... 3.5 to 4 (25 to 29)
- Clutch pressure plate bolts ... 1.4 (10)
- Freewheeling support bolts ... 1.4 (10)
- Torque converter to coupling plate bolts ... 2.4 to 2.6 (17.4 to 18.8)
- Bypass switch ... 4.5 to 5 (32.5 to 36.2)
- Reversing light switch ... 4.5 to 5 (32.5 to 36.2)

Rear axle:
- Control arm bolts ... 12 (86.8)
- Radius arm bolts ... 9 (65.1)
- Radius arm camber bolts ... 6 (43.4)
- Radius arm tracking bolts ... 5 (36.2)
- Damper bolt ... 7.5 (54.2)
- Castle nut for halfshaft ... 30 to 35 (217 to 253)
- Bolts for halfshaft flange (NADELLA) ... 4.7 (34)
- Bolts for halfshaft flange (LOBRO) ... 4.3 (31.1)
- Radius arm cover bolts ... 4.7 (34)
- Wheel nuts ... 13 (94)

Steering and front axle:

Castle nut for ball joint	4.5 (32.5)
Steering lever bolts	4.7 (34)
Damper nut	8 (57.9)
Castle nut for control arm	7.5 (54.2)
Castle nut for tie rod ball stud	4.5 (34)
Bolt for clamping nut (axle)	2.5 (18.1)
Bolt for Flanblock mounting	4.7 (34)
Bolts for bearing carrier	4.7 (34)
Crossmember bolt	9 (65.1)
Bolt for crossmember brace	4.7 (34)
Nut for crossmember brace	6.5 (47)
Bolts for bush support (stabilizer)	2.5 (18.1)
Bolts for stabilizer lever	2.5 (18.1)
Bolt for tie rod yoke	4.7 (34)
Bolts for steering housing	4.7 (34)
Lower shaft bearing cap bolts	2.5 (18.1)
Steering coupling bolts	2.5 (18.1)
Eyebolt locknut	6.5 (47)
Castle nut for pinion flange	2.5 (18.1)
Steering housing base plate bolts	2.2 (15.9)
Steering wheel nut	8 (57.9)
Bolts for switch assembly clamp	2.5 (18.1)
Bolts for steering post	2.5 (18.1)
Bolts for universal joint	3.5 (25.3)
Bolts for post extension	2.5 (18.1)
Wheel nuts	13 (94)
Bolts for splined universal joints	2.5 (18.1)

Brakes:

Master cylinder flange nut	2.5 (18.1)
Nut, bottom shield	6.5 (47)
Bolt, bottom shield	4.7 (34)
Nut, disc to hub	2.3 (16.6)
Brake carrier bolts	4.7 (34)
Disc shroud bolts	2.5 (18)
Bolt, front caliper	7 (50.6)
Bolt, rear caliper	6 (43.4)
Bolt, brake carrier plate	2.5 (18.1)
Castle nut, half-axle	30 to 35 (217 to 253)
Half-axle flange bolt	4.7 (34)
Socket-head bolt, front caliper	3.4 (24.6)
Socket-head bolt, rear caliper	1.8 (13)
Hollow bolt, hydraulic banjo	2 (14.5)

NOTES

2 TECHNICAL DATA 2.0 LITRE VEHICLES

Metric sizes are given first, followed by inch sizes in brackets. The word 'limit' indicates the maximum permissible wear or clearance

ENGINE

Capacity	1991 cc (121.5 cu in)
Bore and stroke	80 x 66 (3.15 x 2.60)
Compression ratio:	
911T	8.6:1
911, 911L	9:1
911E	9.1:1
911S	9.8:1
Firing order	1-6-2-4-3-5
Crankshaft:	
Main bearings 1 to 7	Split inserts, tri-metal
Main bearing 8	Sleeve, hard lead
Thrust taken	Main bearing 1
Main journal diameters:	
Bearings 1 to 7 (Standard)	56.990 to 56.971 (2.2437 to 2.2429)
Bearing 8 (standard)	30.993 to 30.980 (1.2202 to 1.2197)
Undersizes	−.25, −.50 and −.75 (−.01, −.02 and −.03)
Main bearing running clearance:	
Bearings 1 to 7	.030 to .088 (.0012 to .0034)
Bearing 8	.048 to .104 (.0019 to .004)
End float	.110 to .195 (.0043 to .0076, limit .30 (.011)
Interference fits:	
To timing and distributor gears	−.002 to −.038 (−.0001 to −.0014)
To flywheel	.000 to .049 (.000 to .0019)
To pulley	+.007 to +.073 (+.0003 to +.0028)
Runout (on V-blocks)	Maximum .03 (.0012)
Big-end journal diameters	As main bearings 1 to 7
Big-end undersizes	As main bearings
Connecting rods:	
Big-end running clearance	As main bearings 1 to 7
Gudgeon pin running clearance	.020 to .039 (.0008 to .0015), limit .055 (.002)
Small-end bush interference fit in rod	−.014 to −.055 (−.0005 to −.002)
Pistons:	
Type (except 911S)	Cast light alloy
Type, 911S	Forged light alloy
Clearance in cylinder:	
Up to and including 1967 models	.055 to .075 (.0022 to .0029) limit .180 (.007)
1968 models on (except 911S)	.035 to .055 (.0014 to .002)
1968 models on (911S)	.045 to .065 (.0018 to .0026)
Piston rings:	
Types	2 compression, 1 oil control
Gap	.30 to .45 (.012 to .018), limit 1.00 (.039)
Side clearance in groove:	
Top ring	.075 to .107 (.003 to .004)
Second ring	.060 to .072 (.0023 to .0028)
Oil control ring	.025 to .052 (.001 to .002)
Limit	.20 (.008)

Gudgeon (piston) pin:
   Colour code white ... ... Tolerance 0 to .003 (0 to .0001) on diameter of 22 (.866)
   Colour code black ... ... Tolerance of —.003 to —.006 (—.0001 to —.0002) on diameter of 22 (.866)

Cylinders:
   Type 911T ... ... Grey cast iron
   Type (all other models) ... ... Grey cast iron bores with light alloy cooling fins (Biral)
   Bore sizes ... ... See Chapter 1
   Height (group 5) ... ... 82.200 to 82.225 (3.236 to 3.237)
   Height (group 6) ... ... 82.225 to 82.250 (3.237 to 3.238)

Camshafts:
   Bearings:
     Type ... ... 3 plain, direct in housing
     Diameter ... ... 46.926 to 46.942 (1.8474 to 1.8481)
     Running clearance ... ... .025 to .066 (.001 to .0025), limit .10 (.004)
   Runout (at centre bearing) ... ... Maximum .02 (.0008)
   End float ... ... .15 to .20 (.006 to .008)
   Sprocket mounting diameter ... ... 29.979 to 30.000 (1.179 to 1.181)
   Sprocket fit on shaft ... ... 0 to .034 (.0013) clearance

Camshaft housings:
   Bores for camshaft ... ... 46.967 to 46.992 (1.849 to 1.850)
   Bores for rocker shafts ... ... 18.000 to 18.018 (.7086 to .7093)
   Rocker shaft diameter ... ... 17.992 to 18.000 (.7083 to .7086)
   Rocker clearance ... ... .016 to .035 (.0006 to .0013), limit .080 (.003)
   Rocker end float ... ... .100 to .350 (.004 to .014), limit .500 (.020)
   Clearances (timing case):
     Carrier shaft to tensioner housing ... ... .016 to .045 (.0006 to .0018)
     Carrier shaft to sprocket carrier ... ... .016 to .045 (.0006 to .0018)
     Sprocket carrier to sprocket shaft ... ... .000 to .029 (.000 to .0011)
     Sprocket to shaft ... ... .032 to .061 (.0012 to .0024)
     Shaft to chain guide rail ... ... .105 to .129 (.004 to .005)
     Shaft to chain housing ... ... —.014 to —.038 (—.0005 to —.0014)
   Sprocket alignment ... ... Maximum deviation .25 (.01)

Intermediate shaft:
   Bearing 1 diameter ... ... 29.767 to 29.780 (1.1719 to 1.1724)
   Bearing 2 diameter ... ... 23.967 to 23.980 (.9435 to .9440)
   Running clearance ... ... .020 to .054 (.0007 to .0021), limit .10 (.004)
   End float ... ... .080 to .150 (.003 to .006)
   Sprocket mounting diameter ... ... 36.026 to 36.037 (1.4183 to 1.4187)
   Sprocket interference fit ... ... —.010 to —.037 (—.0003 to —.0014)

Valves:
   Head diameter, inlet:
     Except 911S and 1968 911T onwards ... 39 ± .10 (1.535 ± .004)
     911S and 1968 911T onwards ... ... 42 ± .10 (1.654 ± .004)
   Head diameter, exhaust:
     Except 911S and 1968 911T onwards ... 35 ± .10 (1.378 ± .004)
     911S and 1968 911T onwards ... ... 38 ± .10 (1.496 ± .004)
   Stem diameter:
     Inlet ... ... 8.97 —.012 (.353 —.0005)
     Exhaust ... ... 8.95 —.012 (.352 —.0005)

Valve stem clearance:
- Inlet ... .03 to .057 (.001 to .002), limit .15 (.006)
- Exhaust ... .05 to .077 (.002 to .003), limit .20 (.008)

Overall length:
- Inlet (except 911S) ... 111.15 ± .05 (4.376 ± .002)
- 911S ... 114.0 ± .05 (4.488 ± .002)
- Exhaust (except 911S) ... 111.75 ± .05 (4.40 ± .002)
- 911S ... 113.5 ± .05 (4.47 ± .002)

Seat angle ... 45 deg.

Valve springs:

Installed length (inlet):
- Except 911S and 911T ... 36.0 ± .30 (1.42 ± .01) up to Engine No. 911.000
- Except 911S and 911T ... 35.0 ± .30 (1.38 ± .01) from Engine No. 911.001
- 911S ... 35.5 + .50 (1.40 + .02)
- 911T (dual springs) ... 35.0 ± .30 (1.38 ± .01)
- 911T (single spring) ... 41.0 − .50 (1.61 − .02)

Installed length (exhaust):
- 911 up to Engine No. 911.000 ... 36.0 ± .30 (1.42 ± .01)
- 911 From Engine No. 911.001 ... 35.0 ± .30 (1.38 ± .01)
- 911S and 911T (dual springs) ... 35.0 ± .30 (1.38 ± .01)
- 911T (single spring) ... 41.0 − .50 (1.61 − .02)

Spring-load at installed length with both end collars:
- 911 and 911S ... 20 kg (44 lb) at 42 to 42.5 (1.65 to 1.67)
- 911T ... 26 kg (57 lb) at 44.5 to 45 (1.75 to 1.77)

Load variation ... ± 5 per cent on used springs

Valve lift (inlet):
- 911S and 911 up to Engine No. 911.000 ... 11.5 (.453)
- 911 from Engine No. 911.001 ... 10.5 (.413)
- 911T ... 9.7 (.382)

Valve lift (exhaust):
- Except 911T ... 10.5 (.413)
- 911T ... 8.9 (.35)

Valve clearance:
- Inlet and exhaust (cold) ... .10 (.004)

Valve timing (clearance .10 or .004 inch):
- Inlet opens BTDC ... 29 deg. (911), 15 deg. (911T), 38 deg. (911S) and 20 deg. (911L)
- Inlet closes ABDC ... 39 deg. (911), 29 deg. (911T), 50 deg. (911S) and 34 deg. (911L)
- Exhaust opens BBDC ... 39 deg. (911), 41 deg. (911T), 40 deg. (911S) and 40 deg. (911L)
- Exhaust closes BTDC ... 5 deg. (911T)
- Exhaust closes ATDC ... 19 deg. (911), 20 deg. (911S) and 6 deg. (911L)

For timing of 911 from Engine No. 911.001 ... See 911L

Inlet valve lift at TDC with clearance of .10 (.004):
- 911 up to Engine No. 909.927 ... 4.2 to 4.6 (.165 to .181), desired value 4.3 (.169)
- 911T ... 2.3 to 2.7 (.091 to .106), desired value 2.5 (.098)
- 911S ... 5.0 to 5.4 (.197 to .213), desired value 5.2 (.205)
- 911L ... 3.0 to 3.3 (.118 to .130), desired value 3.15 (.124)

Valve guides:
- Diameter (standard) ... 13.06 to 13.049 (.514 to .5137)
- Diameter (first oversize) ... 13.260 to 13.249 (.522 to .5216)
- Diameter (second oversize) ... 13.460 to 13.449 (.530 to .5294)
- Bore in head (standard) ... 13.00 to 13.018 (.5118 to .5125)
- Bore in head (first oversize) ... 13.20 to 13.218 (.5196 to .5203)
- Bore in head (second oversize) ... 13.40 to 13.418 (.5275 to .5282)

Valve seats:
- Diameter (standard inlet) ... 42.180 to 42.164 (1.6606 to 1.6599)
- Diameter (standard exhaust) ... 38.20 to 38.184 (1.5039 to 1.5033)
- Diameter (oversize inlet) ... 42.50 to 42.484 (1.6732 to 1.6724)
- Diameter (oversize exhaust) ... 38.76 to 38.744 (1.5259 to 1.5253)
- Bore in head (standard inlet) ... 42.00 to 42.025 (1.6535 to 1.6545)
- Bore in head (standard exhaust) ... 38.00 to 38.025 (1.4960 to 1.4970)
- Bore in head (oversize inlet) ... 42.320 to 42.345 (1.6661 to 1.6670)
- Bore in head (oversize exhaust) ... 38.560 to 38.585 (1.5180 to 1.5190)

Flywheel:
- Bore for crankshaft ... 65.00 to 65.030 (2.559 to 2.560)
- Clearance in bore ... Up to .049 (.0019)
  - Lateral runout at clutch mounting ... Maximum .040 (.0015)
  - Lateral runout at clutch face ... Maximum .040 (.0015)
  - Vertical runout ... Maximum .200 (.0078)
- Bronze bush for rear end of transmission shaft ... Running clearance .075 to .229 (.003 to .009). Interference fit in steel bush —.001 to —.035 (—.000 to —.013)
- Steel bush ... Interference fit —.001 to —.035 (—.000 to —.0013)

Oil pump:
- Spring (pressure release and safety valve):
  - Free length ... 70 (2.75)
  - Compressed length ... 33.3 (1.31)
  - Pressure at length of 52 (2.04) ... 10.6 kg (76.7 lb ft)
  - Pressure at length of 46 (1.81) ... 14.1 kg (102 lb ft)

Crankcase:
- Bore for main bearings ... 62.00 to 62.019 (2.4409 to 2.4416)
- Bore for intermediate shaft:
  - Bearing 1 ... 29.80 to 29.821 (1.732 to 1.1740)
  - Bearing 2 ... 24.00 to 24.021 (.9448 to .9457)

FUEL SYSTEM

Solex carburetter 40.PI:
- Venturi ... 30
- Main jet ... 117.5 to Engine No. 900.323, 130 to Engine No. 903.359 and 125 to Engine No. 903.910
- Air correction jet ... 150 to Engine No. 900.323, 160 to Engine No. 903.359 and 180 to Engine No. 903.910
- Emulsion tube ... 25 to Engine No. 900.323, 8 (open bottom) to Engine No. 903.359 and 8 (open bottom) to Engine No. 903.910
- Idle jet ... 60 to Engine No. 903.359, 55 to Engine No. 903.910

Idle air bleed	1.0
Pump injector nozzle	.5 dia. to Engine No. 903.359 and .8 dia. to Engine No. 903.910
Pump jet	.5 dia.
Float needle valve	2.0
Float weight	7 g
Injection quantity	.45 to .50 cc (2 strokes, warm) and .55 to .60 cc (2 strokes, cold)

Weber carburetter:

Types	40.IDS.3C and 3C1 (911S), 40.IDAP.3C and 3C1 (911L with emission control), 40.IDAP.3C and 3C1 (911 with emission control), 40.IDA.3C and 3C1 (911L) and 40.IDT.3C and 3C1 (911T)
Venturi	32 (911S and 911T), 30 (all others)
Main jet	110 (911T), 125 (all others)
Air correction jet	185 (911S and 911T), 180 (all others)
Idle jet	50 (911T), 52 (911 and 911L with EEC), 55 (911L Sportomatic)
Idle air bleed	110 (all)
Pump jet	50 (all)
Emulsion tube	F2 (911T), F3 (911S), F26 (all others)
Float weight	25.5 g
Float needle valve	1.75
Enrichment jet	70 (911S)
Pump injection quantity	.8 ± .2 cc per stroke (911S and 911L with Sportomatic), .5 ± .1 per stroke (all others)
Float chamber vent	4.5 dia. (911S), 6.0 dia. (all others)

Fuel pump:

Mechanical:

Fuel delivery (each pump)	800 cc in 1 minute at 3000 rev/min
Fuel pressure	.18 to .22 atm (2½ to 3¼ lb/sq in)

Electric (Bendix):

Minimum delivery	900 cc per minute
Pressure with closed float needle valve	.28 to .33 atm (4 to 5 lb/sq in)
Maximum current	.65 amp

Electric (Hardi):

Minimum delivery	900 cc per minute
Pump pressure	.28 to .30 atm (4 to 4.4 lb/sq in)
Contact point gap	1.2 (.048)

IGNITION SYSTEM

Sparking plug type:

911	Bosch W.250.P21 or WG.265.T2SP, Beru 260/14/3S and Champion N6Y
911T	Bosch W.230.T30, Beru 240/14/3
911S	Bosch W.265.P21 or WG.265.T2SP, Beru 260/14/3S
Sparking plug gap	Bosch W (.35 or .012), Bosch WG (.40 or .014), Beru (.50 or .018), Champion (.55 or .019)
Firing order	1-6-2-4-3-5

Ignition timing (see **Chapter 3**):
  911 ... TDC basic, 30 deg. BTDC at 6000 rev/min (no load)
    Engines with EECS ... 3 deg. ATDC (idling), 30±2 deg. BTDC at 6000 rev/min
  911T ... TDC (basic), 35 deg. BTDC at 6000 rev/min (with or without load)
  911S ... 5 deg. BTDC (basic), 30 deg. BTDC at 6000 rev/min (with or without load)

Distributor type:
  911 ... Bosch JFR.6
  911L and 911S ... Bosch JFDR.6 (yellow label for 911S)
  911T ... Marelli S.112.AX

CLUTCH

Type ... Single dry plate with diaphragm spring
Pedal clearance ... 20 to 25 (¾ to 1)
Driven plate:
  Thickness uncompressed ... 10.1 — .40 (.397 — .015)
  Runout of linings ... Maximum .60 (.023)

TRANSMISSION

Type, manual gearchange ... Four or five forward speeds and one reverse. All synchromesh, all-indirect. Integral with final drive in one casing

Type, Sportomatic ... Four forward speeds and one reverse. Hydrodynamic torque converter and vacuum-controlled single dry plate clutch

Pinion to ring gear (crownwheel):
  Ratio:
    Manual gearbox ... 7:31
    Sportomatic ... 7:27

Gear ratios (standard):
  911 (5-speed):
    1st ... 12:34
    2nd ... 18:32
    3rd ... 23:28
    4th ... 26:25
    5th ... 28:23
  911 (5-speed from transmission No. 221.722):
    1st ... 11:34
    2nd ... 18:34
    3rd ... 22:29
    4th ... 25:26
    5th ... 28:24
  911 (4-speed):
    1st ... 11:34
    2nd ... 19:32
    3rd ... 24:27
    4th ... 28:24
  911S and 911T (4-speed):
    1st ... 11:34
    2nd ... 19:31
    3rd ... 25:26
    4th ... 29:23

911S (5-speed transmission type 901/02):
- 1st ... 11:34
- 2nd ... 18:34
- 3rd ... 22:29
- 4th ... 25:26
- 5th ... 29:23

911T from 1968 models (except USA):
- 1st ... 14:37
- 2nd ... 18:32
- 3rd ... 22:29
- 4th ... 26:26
- 5th ... 28:23

911 (1966-67 models), 911S (1967 model), 911S (from 1968 model except USA), 911L (from 1968 model) and 911 (from 1968 model, USA) ... See preceding figures

911 (from 1968 model, USA) and 911L with Sportomatic:
- 1st ... 15:36
- 2nd ... 19:31
- 3rd ... 23:28
- 4th ... 26:25

911S and 911T (from 1968 model except USA) with Sportomatic:
- 1st ... 15:36
- 2nd ... 19:31
- 3rd ... 23:28
- 4th ... 27:25

911 (from 1968 model, USA) 911L, 911S, and 911T (from 1968 model except USA) ... Any four or five-speed ratios on request

Tolerances:
- Backlash between gears ... .06 to .12 (.0023 to .0047) new, limit .22 (.0086)
- End float of free gears on either shaft:
  - 1st speed ... .30 to .40 (.011 to .015) new, limit .50 (.019)
  - 2nd, 3rd and 4th ... .20 to .30 (.007 to .011) new, limit .40 (.015)
- Selector shaft clearance ... .095 to .156 (.004 to .006) new, limit .40 (.015)
- Selector shaft runout ... .10 (.004) maximum
- Shift fork end float ... .10 to .30 (.004 to .011), limit .50 (.019)
- Synchronizing ring outside diameter, installed ... 76.12 to 76.48 (2.996 to 3.011), renew when any of molybdenum coating has worn off
- Pilot journal at rear of input shaft:
  - Runout ... .10 (.004) maximum
  - Clearance in flywheel bush ... .145 to .231 (.006 to .009), limit .30 (.011)

STEERING

- **Type** ... ZF rack and pinion
- **Steering ratio** ... 1:16.5 in centre
- **Steering turns** (stop to stop) ... 2.8 (approx.)
- **Turning circle** ... 10.3 m (33¾ ft)
- **Track:**
  - Original ... 1337 (52.6)
  - After Chassis No. 305.101 ... 1353 (53.3)
  - 1968 models onwards ... 1367 (53.8)
  - Cars with self-levelling suspension:
    - With steel wheels 5½J x 15 ... 1362 (53.6)
    - With light alloy wheels 6J x 15 ... 1374 (54.1)
    - With light alloy wheels 5½J x 14 ... 1364 (53.7)

Wheel alignment:
   Toe-in (total before 1968 models) ... 40' (wheels pressed with load of 15 kg (33 lb)
   Toe-in (total) 1968 models on ... 0' (wheels pressed with load of 15 kg (33 lb)
   Angle differential in 20 deg. turn (before 1968 models) ... 40' to 1 deg. 10'
   Angle differential in 20 deg. turn (1968 models on) ... 0' to 30'
   Camber angle (wheels straight-ahead) ... 0' ± 20' (max. deviation left to right 20')
   Castor angle ... 6 deg. 45' ± 45' (max. deviation left to right 30')

FRONT SUSPENSION

Type (not self-levelling) ... Independent torsion bar springing with control arms and damper struts

Type, self-levelling (911E and optional on 911T and 911S) ... Control arms and hydropneumatic suspension struts without springs

Dampers:
   BOGE ... 911T, 911L, Targa (standard)
   KONI ... 911S (standard), optional for all except Targa

Stabilizers (anti-roll bars): Not fitted to 911 or cars with self-levelling suspension)
   Diameter before 1968 models:
     911L ... 13 (.512) standard
     911S ... 14 (.55) standard
     Optional ... 11, 14 and 15 (.43, .55 and .59)
   Diameter from 1968 models on:
     911L (except USA) ... 11 (.43) standard
     911L (USA) and 911S ... 15 (.59) standard
     Optional ... 13, 14 and 15 (.512, .55 and .59)

Height adjustment:
   Difference between wheel centre height and rear centre of torsion bar ... 108 ± 5 (4.25 ± .20). Max. deviation left and right 5 (.20)

REAR SUSPENSION

Type ... Independent, with torsion bar springing. Triangulated control arm, telescopic dampers

Stabilizer (anti-roll bar):
   911S before 1968 models ... 16 (.63) diameter
   911S, 1968 models on ... 15 (.59) diameter
   Optional for all cars before 1968 models ... 15 (.59)
   Optional for all cars from 1968 models on ... 15 and 16 (.59 and .63)

Dampers:
   BOGE ... 911T, 911L and Targa (standard)
   KONI ... 911S (standard). Optional for all others except Targa

From 1968 models on, internal rubber buffers have 9 rings instead of original 8

Track:
   Original ... 1317 (51.8)
   After Chassis No. 305.101 ... 1321 (52.0)
   From 1968 models on with solid brake discs ... 1335 (52.5)
   Cars with ventilated brake discs ... 1339 (52.7)

Torsion bar diameter:
   Before 1968 models ... 23 (.905)
   1968 models on ... 22 (.866)

Torsion bar adjustment:
  All cars before 1968 models ... ... 36 deg. radius arm angle
  All cars from 1968 models on ... ... 39 deg. radius arm angle
Wheel alignment:
  Toe-in (per wheel) ... ... 0' ± 10'
  Camber angle (before 1968 models) ... ... —55' to —1 deg. 35'
  Camber angle (1968 models on) ... ... —30' to —1 deg. 10'
  Latest adjustment angles may be applied to earlier models)
Height adjustment:
  Centre of torsion bar carrier above wheel centre
    height ... ... 12 ± 5 (.47 ± .2). Maximum deviation between left and right 8 (.32)

BRAKES

Type ... ... Footbrake, disc front and rear, hydraulically operated. Handbrake, mechanical in rear drums. Dual-circuit hydraulic system from 1968 models on
Disc diameter:
  Solid ... ... 282 (11.1) front, 285 (11.22) rear
  Vented ... ... 282.5 (11.12) front, 286 (11.26) rear
Handbrake:
  Drum diameter 180 (7.09)
  Lining width 32 (1.26)
Disc thickness (new):
  Solid ... ... 12.7—.2 (.50—.008) front, 10.0—.2 (.394—.008) or 10.5—.20 (.413—.008) rear
  Vented ... ... 20.0—.20 (.787—.008) front and rear
Disc thickness (minimum when evenly worn):
  Solid ... ... 11.0 (.43) front and 8.5 (.33) rear
  Vented ... ... 18.0 (.71)
  Maximum deviation in thickness ... ... .03 (.001) solid and vented
Disc runout ... ... .05 (.002) solid and vented
Minimum pad thickness ... ... 2.0 (.08)
Master cylinder bore:
  Single and dual-circuit systems ... ... 19.05 (.75)
Wheel brake cylinder bores:
  911T (not Sportomatic) ... ... 48 (1.89) front, 35 (1.38) rear
  911T Sportomatic, 911L and 911S ... 48 (1.89) front, 38 (1.49) rear

ELECTRICAL EQUIPMENT

System ... ... 12-volt, negative earth (ground)
Battery ... ... 45 amp/hr
Generator (alternator) ... ... 12-volt, 500 watt, 35 to 40A at 14 volts, Bosch or Motorola (911T)
Alternator data (Bosch):
  Minimum brush length ... ... 14 (.55)
  Brush spring pressure ... ... 300 to 400 g (10½ to 14 oz)
  Resistance:
    Stationary windings ... ... .26 ohm + 10 per cent
    Rotor windings ... ... 4 ohm + 10 per cent (originally 3.5 ohm)
  Slip rings:
    Runout ... ... .03 (.001) maximum
    Minimum diameter 31.5 (1.24)
  Rotor runout ... ... .05 (.002) maximum

Alternator data (Motorola):
   Rotor coil resistance ... ... 4.5 to 6.5 ohm

Alternator test:
   Bosch ... ... Load current 28 to 30A. Voltage should be 13.5 to 14.5 at 3000 rev/min
   Motorola ... ... Load current 28 to 30A. Voltage should be 13.4 to 14.6 at 2500 ± 150 rev/min

Starter:
   Type ... ... Bosch EB 12-volt, .80 hp (0001.212.002)
   Speed test (free) ... ... 11.5V, 33 to 50A at 6400 to 7900 rev/min

Starter data:
   Brush spring pressure ... ... $1200 + 150 - 50$ g ($42.3 + 5.3 - 1.76$ oz)
   Armature end float ... ... .10 to .15 (.004 to .006)
   Commutator runout ... ... Maximum .05 (.002)
   Commutator minimum diameter 33.5 (1.32)

Bulbs (all 12V):
   Twin filament headlamp ... ... 45/40 watt
   Sealed-beam headlamp ... ... 50/40 watt
   Parking and number plate ... ... 4 watt
   Flashers (except USA) ... ... 18 watt
   Flashers and reversing lights (USA) ... 32 cp or 25 watt
   Stop and tail (except USA) ... ... 18/5 watt
   Stop and tail (USA) ... ... 32/4 cp or 25/3.2 watt
   Reversing lights ... ... 25 watt
   Interior lights ... ... 10 watt
   Luggage compartment light ... ... 5 watt
   Instrument and control lamps ... ... 2 watt
   Parking lights (USA) ... ... 2 cp or 2 watt

Fuses:
   Wipers and auxiliary heater ... ... 25/40 amp
   All others ... ... 8/15 amp

CAPACITIES

Fuel tank ... ... 62 litres (including 6 litre reserve) (16.4 US gallons or 13.6 Imp. gallons)
Engine (not Sportomatic) ... ... 9 litres (9.5 US qts. or 2 Imp. gallons)
Engine and Sportomatic unit ... ... 11.5 litres (12.1 US qts., 2.55 Imp. gallons)
Transmission ... ... 2.5 litres (2.6 US qts., 4.4 Imp. pints)
Brake fluid reservoir ... ... .20 litre (.16 US qt., .35 Imp. pint)
Windscreen washer reservoir ... ... 2 litres (1.6 US qts., 3.5 Imp. pints)

NOTES

3 TECHNICAL DATA 2.2 AND 2.4 LITRE VEHICLES

Metric sizes are given first, followed by inch sizes in brackets. 'Limit' indicates maximum wear

ENGINE

General:
- Bore and stroke, 1970 models .. .. .. 84 x 66 (3.307 x 2.60)
- 1972 models .. .. .. 84 x 70.4 (3.307 x 2.76)
- Capacity, 1970 models .. .. .. 2195 cc (134 cu in)
- 1972 models .. .. .. 2341 cc (142.9 cu in)
- Compression ratio (1970) 911TC .. .. 8.6:1 (2.2 litre)
- 911EC .. .. 9.1:1 (2.2 litre)
- 911SC .. .. 9.8:1 (2.2 litre)
- (1972) 911TV .. .. 7.5:1 (2.4 litre)
- 911T (USA) .. .. 7.5:1 (2.4 litre)
- 911E .. .. 8.0:1 (2.4 litre)
- 911S .. .. 8.5:1 (2.4 litre)

Crankshaft .. .. See 2.0 Litre technical data
- Crankpin, 2.4 models, diameter .. .. 51.990 (2.0468) to 51.971 (2.0461)
- width .. .. 24 (.945)
- stroke 70.4 (2.757)

Connecting rods .. .. See 2.0 Litre technical data and Chapter 1
- 2.4 models, weight variation .. .. Not exceeding 9 gr (less inserts)

Pistons .. .. See 2.0 Litre technical data and Chapter 1
- 2.4 model 911S, type .. .. Cast light alloy, slipper-type

Piston rings .. .. See 2.0 Litre technical data

Gudgeon pins .. .. See 2.0 Litre technical data

Cylinders .. .. See 2.0 Litre technical data and Chapter 1

Camshaft .. .. See 2.0 Litre technical data

Camshaft housing .. .. See 2.0 Litre technical data

Intermediate shaft .. .. See 2.0 Litre technical data

Valves:
- 2.2 and 2.4 litre:
  - Head diameter, inlet .. .. .. $46\pm.10$ ($1.811\pm.004$)
  - exhaust .. .. .. $40\pm.10$ ($1.575\pm.004$)
  - Stem diameter, inlet .. .. .. $8.97\pm.012$ ($.353\pm.0005$)
  - exhaust .. .. .. $8.95\pm.012$ ($.352\pm.0005$)
  - Complete length, inlet .. .. $114\pm.10$ ($4.488\pm.004$)
  - exhaust .. .. $113.5\pm.10$ ($4.469\pm.004$)
  - Seat angle .. .. 45°

Valve springs:
- 2.2 911T and 2.4 litre .. .. .. Two springs per valve
- Installed length, 2.2 and 2.4 litre .. See Chapter 1

Valve timing .. .. See 2.0 Litre technical data
- Inlet opens, 911T, 2.2/2.4 .. .. 15° BTDC
- 911EC, 2.2 .. .. 20° BTDC
- 911E, 2.4 .. .. 18° BTDC
- 911S, 2.2/2.4 .. .. 38° BTDC
- Inlet closes, 911T, 2.2/2.4 .. .. 29° ABDC
- 911EC, 2.2 .. .. 34° ABDC
- 911E, 2.4 .. .. 36° ABDC
- 911S, 2.2/2.4 .. .. 50° ABDC
- Exhaust opens, 911T, 2.2/2.4 .. .. 41° BBDC
- 911EC, 2.2 .. .. 40° BBDC
- 911E, 2.4 .. .. 38° BBDC
- 911S, 2.2/2.4 .. .. 40° BBDC

Exhaust closes, 911T, 2.2/2.4 .. .. .. 5° BTDC
       911EC, 2.2 .. .. .. 9° ATDC
       911E, 2.4 .. .. .. 8° ATDC
       911S, 2.2/2.4 .. .. .. 20° ATDC

Valve guides and seats .. .. See 2.0 Litre technical data
Flywheel .. .. See 2.0 Litre technical data

FUEL SYSTEM

Solex-Zenith 40 TIN .. .. Fitted to 911TC and T. 911TV

	911TV	1969 911T	1970
Venturi	K 28.5	K 27.5	
Main jet	Gg 120	Gg 115	Gg 110
Air correction jet	a 190	a 185	a 195
			a 170
Emulsion tube, diameter	4.3 (.169)	4 (.158)	4.3
Idle air jet	g 47.5	g 47.5	g 47.5p
Idle air bleed	u 160	u 140	u 155
			u 165
Float needle valve	P 1.5	P 1.5	P 1.5
Float weight	15.7 gr	15.7 gr	15.7 gr
Fuel jet	50	50	50
Air correction jet (submersion)	100	100	100
Idle speed	900±50 rev/min		

Fuel injection system:
Type, 911T (2.4), 911E and 911S (2.2 and 2.4) .. Bosch double row, six plunger injection pump
Fuel pump .. .. Electric roll-cell

IGNITION SYSTEM

Type, 2.2 and 2.4 litre .. .. Capacitive Discharge System
Distributor type:
  2.2 litre, 911T .. .. Marelli S112BX or Bosch JFDRG 0231159008
      911E .. .. Bosch JFDRG 0231159006
      911S .. .. Bosch JFDRG 0231159007
  2.4 litre, 911T .. .. Marelli 50.10.974.1 or Bosch JFRDR6 0231169003
      911E .. .. Marelli 50.10.974.2 or Bosch JFUDR6 0231169004
      911S .. .. Marelli 50.10.974.3 or Bosch JFRDR6 0231169005

Basic ignition timing:
  2.2 litre, at 6000 rev/min:
   911T .. .. 35° BTDC
   911E .. .. 30° BTDC
   911S .. .. 30° BTDC
  2.4 litre, at 900 rev/min .. .. .. 5° ATDC
Dwell angle:
  2.2 and 2.4 litre, Marelli .. .. .. 40°±3°
       Bosch .. .. 38°±3°
Points gap:
  2.2 and 2.4 litre, Marelli .. .. .. .40 (.016)
       Bosch .. .. .35 (.014)

Sparking plugs:

Type, 2.2 litre, 911T	Beru 240/14/3, 250/14/3P or Bosch W230/T30, W250/P21
911E, 911S	Beru 265/14/3P or Bosch W265/P21
2.4 litre, 911T	Beru 225/14/3 or Bosch W230/T30
911T (USA)	Beru 235/14/3 or Bosch W235/P21
911E, 911S	Beru 265/14/3P or Bosch W265/P21

Gap:
  All types .. .6 (.023)

Firing order:
  2.2 and 2.4 litre .. 1:6:2:4:3:5

STEERING

Type	See 2.0 Litre technical data
Ratio, 2.2 and 2.4 litre	17.78:1
Wheel turns, lock to lock	3.1 approx.
Turning circle	10.7 m (35 ft) approx.
Toe-in with 15 kg (33 lb) load on front):	
Front, 2.2 and 2.4 litre	0°
Rear, 2.2 litre	0°±10′ per wheel
2.4 litre	0°±20′ per wheel
Camber:	
Front, 2.2 litre	0°±20′ with max. deviation left to right of 20′
2.4 litre	0°±10′
Rear, 2.2 litre	−50′±20′
2.4 litre	−1°±10′
Caster:	
2.2 and 2.4 litre	6°5′±15′
Pivot inclination:	
2.2 and 2.4 litre	10° 55′

FRONT SUSPENSION

Type	See 2.0 Litre technical data
Springing:	
2.2 litre, 911T and 911S	One round longitudinal bar and SA struts or one suspension strut per wheel
911E	One hydro-pneumatic suspension strut per wheel
2.4 litre	One round longitudinal bar per wheel and DA hydraulic dampers
Stabilizer bar, 911S	Transversely mounted 2.4 has 15 mm (.59) diameter

REAR SUSPENSION

Type .. See 2.0 Litre technical data

BRAKES

Type .. See 2.0 Litre technical data

ELECTRICAL EQUIPMENT

Battery:
   2.2 and 2.4 litre .. .. 2 x 12v at 36 Ah each

Alternator rating:
   2.2 and 2.4 litre .. .. 770W AC

Starter type:
   2.2 litre .. .. Bosch 12v, .80 hp
   2.4 litre .. .. Bosch 12v, 1.50 hp
   Sportomatic .. .. As 2.2 litre

Bulbs (12v):
   2.4 litre:
      Halogen headlights, H1 .. .. .. 55W, 2 each lamp
      Halogen drive lights, H1 and H3 .. .. 55W
      Foglamps 55W (USA-35W)
      Stop and tail 21/5W
      Reverse lamps 15W
      Fog tail lamp 18W

CAPACITIES

See 2.0 Litre technical data
Engine, 2.4 litre .. .. 8 litres (1¾ Imp. galls), 8.5 US quarts

---

NOTES

4 LUBRICATION CHART

ITEM	APPLICATION		SHELL GRADE	REMARKS
Every 3,000 Miles				
A1	Engine (a)	above 90°F	X-100 30 or 20W/40)	Drain, flush; clean magnetic drain
		32°F to 90°F	X-100 30 or 20W/40)	plug, replace; refill (b)
		below 32°F	X-100 20W or 20W/40)	
A2	Gearbox and Differential	all temperatures	SPIRAX 90 E.P.	Top up if necessary
Every 6,000 Miles				
B1	Gearbox and Differential (a)	all temperatures	SPIRAX 90 E.P.	Drain, flush and refill
B2	Oil Filter (a)		—	Renew element
B3	Air Cleaner — dry type (c)		—	Remove, clean with low pressure air gun, replace (d)
	oil wetted (c)		AS FOR ENGINE	Remove, wash in gasoline, dry, dip in oil, drain, replace
B4	Distributor — Cam		RETINAX A	Smear lightly
B5	Carburetter Linkage		AS FOR ENGINE	Oil can — few drops
B6	Brake Fluid Supply Tank		DONAX B	Top up if necessary

(a) Initially after first 300 to 600 miles (b) Remove and clean oil strainer every 6,000 miles
(c) More often in dusty conditions (d) Renew element if necessary

CAPACITIES		TYRE SIZES AND PRESSURES (lbs. sq. in.)	ENGINE ADJUSTMENTS
Engine	911 — 15¾ Imp.pts.(19 U.S.pts.)	165 HR–15 Front 26	Valve clearances (cold)
	912 — 7 Imp.pts. (8½ U.S.pts.)	Rear 28	911 — Inlet & Exhaust .004"
Gearbox and Differential	4½ Imp.pts.(5¼ U.S.pts.)	Increase pressures by 3 lbs.sq.in.	912 — Inlet .004"
Fuel Tank	14 Imp.glns.(17 U.S.glns.)	for Autobahn driving with full load.	Exhaust .006"
ALL CAPACITIES ARE REFILL QUANTITIES			Spark Plug Gap .014"

VELOCEPRESS MANUALS - MOTORCYCLE

1930'S BRITISH MOTORCYCLE CARBS & ELEC COMPONENTS (BOOK OF)
1930'S BRITISH MOTORCYCLE ENGINES (OVERHAUL & MAINTENANCE)
1930'S BRITISH MOTORCYCLE GEARBOXES & CLUTCHES (BOOK OF)
AJS 1932-1948 SINGLES & TWINS 250cc THRU 1000cc (BOOK OF)
AJS 1945-1960 SINGLES 350cc & 500cc MODELS 16 & 18 (BOOK OF)
AJS 1955-1965 SINGLES 350cc & 500cc (BOOK OF)
ARIEL 1932-1939 PREWAR MODELS (BOOK OF)
ARIEL 1933-1951 (WORKSHOP MANUAL)
ARIEL 1939-1960 4 STROKE SINGLES (BOOK OF)
ARIEL 1958-1964 LEADER & ARROW (BOOK OF)
BMW R26 R27 (1956-1967) FACTORY WORKSHOP MANUAL
BMW R50 R50S R60 R69S (1955-1969) FACTORY WORKSHOP MANUAL
BRIDGESTONE 90 SERIES FACTORY WSM & PARTS CATALOGUE
BRIDGESTONE 175 SERIES FACTORY WSM & PARTS CATALOGUE
BSA BANTAM ALL MODELS FROM 1948 ONWARDS (BOOK OF)
BSA SINGLES & V-TWINS UP TO 1927 (BOOK OF)
BSA SINGLES & V-TWINS UP TO 1935 (BOOK OF)
BSA SINGLES & V-TWINS 1936-1939 (BOOK OF)
BSA SINGLES & V-TWINS 1936-1952 (BOOK OF)
BSA OHV & SV SINGLES 250-600cc 1945-1954 (BOOK OF)
BSA OHV & SV SINGLES 250cc 1954-1970 (BOOK OF)
BSA OHV SINGLES 350 & 500cc 1955-1967 (BOOK OF)
BSA TWINS 1948-1962 (BOOK OF)
BSA TWINS 1962-1969 (SECOND BOOK OF)
CYCLEMOTOR (BOOK OF)
DOUGLAS 1929-1939 PREWAR ALL MODELS (BOOK OF)
DOUGLAS 1948-1957 POSTWAR ALL MODELS FACTORY SHOP MANUAL
DUCATI 160cc, 250cc & 350cc OHC MODELS FACTORY SHOP MANUAL
HONDA 50 ALL MODELS UP TO 1970 INC MONKEY & TRAIL (BOOK OF)
HONDA 90 ALL MODELS UP TO 1966 (BOOK OF)
HONDA 125-150cc TWINS C/CS/CB/CA FACTORY WORKSHOP MANUAL
HONDA 250-305 TWINS C/CS/CB FACTORY WORKSHOP MANUAL
HONDA C100 SUPER CUB FACTORY WORKSHOP MANUAL
HONDA C110 SPORT CUB 1962-1969 FACTORY WORKSHOP MANUAL
HONDA TWINS & SINGLES 50cc THRU 305cc 1960-1966 (BOOK OF)
HONDA TWINS ALL MODELS 125cc THRU 450cc UP TO 1968 (BOOK OF)
J.A.P. ENGINES 1927-1952 & MOTORCYCLES 1934-1952 (BOOK OF)
LAMBRETTA 1947-1957 ALL 125 & 150cc MODELS (BOOK OF)
LAMBRETTA 1957-1970 LI & TV MODELS (SECOND BOOK OF)
MATCHLESS 1931-1939 ALL MODELS 250cc THRU 990cc (BOOK OF)
MATCHLESS 1945-1956 350 & 500cc SINGLES (BOOK OF)
MATCHLESS 1955-1966 350 & 500cc SINGLES (BOOK OF)
NEW IMPERIAL ALL SV & OHV FROM 1935 ONWARDS (BOOK OF)
NORTON 1932-1939 PREWAR MODELS (BOOK OF)
NORTON 1932-1947 (BOOK OF)
NORTON 1938-1956 (BOOK OF)
NORTON 1955-1963 MODELS 19, 50 & ES2 (BOOK OF)
NORTON 1955-1965 DOMINATOR TWINS (BOOK OF)
NORTON 1957-1970 TWINS FACTORY WORKSHOP MANUAL
NSU PRIMA 1956-1964 ALL MODELS (BOOK OF)
NSU QUICKLY 1953-1963 ALL MODELS (BOOK OF)
PANTHER 1932-1958 LIGHTWEIGHT MODELS 250 & 350cc (BOOK OF)
PANTHER 1938-1966 HEAVYWEIGHT MODELS 600 & 650cc (BOOK OF)
RALEIGH MOPEDS 1960-1969 (BOOK OF)
RALEIGH MOTORCYCLES 1919-1933 (BOOK OF)
ROYAL ENFIELD 1934-1946 SINGLES & V TWINS (BOOK OF)
ROYAL ENFIELD 1937-1953 SINGLES & V TWINS (BOOK OF)
ROYAL ENFIELD 1946-1962 SINGLES (BOOK OF)
ROYAL ENFIELD 1958-1966 250cc & 350cc SINGLES (SECOND BOOK OF)
ROYAL ENFIELD 736cc INTERCEPTOR FACTORY WORKSHOP MANUAL
RUDGE 1933-1939 (BOOK OF)
SUNBEAM 1928-1939 (BOOK OF)
SUNBEAM 1946-1957 S7 & S8 (BOOK OF)
SUZUKI 50cc & 80cc UP TO 1966 (BOOK OF)
SUZUKI T10 1963-1967 FACTORY WORKSHOP MANUAL
SUZUKI T20 & T200 1965-1969 FACTORY WORKSHOP MANUAL
TRIUMPH 1935-1939 PREWAR MODELS (BOOK OF)
TRIUMPH 1935-1949 (BOOK OF)
TRIUMPH 1937-1951 (WORKSHOP MANUAL)
TRIUMPH 1945-1955 FACTORY WORKSHOP MANUAL
TRIUMPH 1945-1958 TWINS (BOOK OF)
TRIUMPH 1956-1969 TWINS (BOOK OF)
VELOCETTE 1925-1970 ALL SINGLES & TWINS (BOOK OF)
VESPA 1951-1961 (BOOK OF)
VESPA 1955-1963 125 & 150cc & GS MODELS (SECOND BOOK OF)
VESPA 1955-1968 GS & SS (BOOK OF)
VESPA 1963-1972 90, 125 & 150cc (THIRD BOOK OF)
VILLIERS ENGINE UP TO 1959 INC. 3 WHEELERS (BOOK OF)
VILLIERS ENGINE UP TO 1969 (BOOK OF)
VINCENT 1935-1955 (WORKSHOP MANUAL)

VELOCEPRESS TECHNICAL BOOKS – MOTORCYCLE

CATALOG OF BRITISH MOTORCYCLES (1951 MODELS)
INDIAN PONYBIKE, BOY RACER & PAPOOSE ILL PARTS LIST & SALES LIT
MOTORCYCLE ENGINEERING (P.E. Irving)
SPEED AND HOW TO OBTAIN IT (Motor Cycle Magazine UK)
TUNING FOR SPEED (P.E. Irving)

VELOCEPRESS MANUALS – THREE WHEELER'S

BSA THREE WHEELER (BOOK OF)
VINTAGE MORGAN THREE WHEELER (BOOK OF)

VELOCEPRESS MANUALS – AUTOMOBILE

AUSTIN-HEALEY 6-CYLINDER WORKSHOP MANUAL
AUSTIN-HEALEY SPRITE & MG MIDGET WORKSHOP MANUAL 1958-1971
BMW 600 LIMOUSINE FACTORY WORKSHOP MANUAL
BMW 600 LIMOUSINE OWNERS HAND BOOK & SERVICE MANUAL
BMW 2000 & 2002 1966-1976 WORKSHOP MANUAL
BMW ISETTA FACTORY WORKSHOP MANUAL
CORVAIR 1960-1969 WORKSHOP MANUAL
CORVETTE V8 1955-1962 WORKSHOP MANUAL
FIAT 500 FACTORY WORKSHOP MANUAL 1957-1973
FIAT 600, 600D & MULTIPLA FACTORY WORKSHOP MANUAL 1955-1969
JAGUAR E-TYPE 3.8 & 4.2 SERIES 1 & 2 WORKSHOP MANUAL
JAGUAR MK 7, 8, 9 & XK120, 140, 150 WORKSHOP MANUAL 1948-1961
METROPOLITAN FACTORY WORKSHOP MANUAL
MGA & MGB OWNERS HANDBOOK & WORKSHOP MANUAL
MG MIDGET TC, TD, TF & TF1500 WORKSHOP MANUAL
PORSCHE 356 1948-1965 WORKSHOP MANUAL
PORSCHE 911 2.0, 2.2, 2.4 LITRE 1964-1973
PORSCHE 912 WORKSHOP MANUAL
TRIUMPH TR2, TR3, TR4 1953-1965 WORKSHOP MANUAL
VOLKSWAGEN TRANSPORTER, TRUCKS & WAGONS 1950-1979 WSM
VOLVO 1944-1968 ALL MODELS WORKSHOP MANUAL

VELOCEPRESS TECHNICAL BOOKS - AUTOMOBILE

FERRARI 250/GT SERVICE AND MAINTENANCE
FERRARI GUIDE TO PERFORMANCE
FERRARI OWNER'S HANDBOOK
FERRARI TUNING TIPS & MAINTENANCE TECHNIQUES
HOW TO BUILD A FIBERGLASS CAR
HOW TO BUILD A RACING CAR
HOW TO RESTORE THE MODEL 'A' FORD
MASERATI OWNER'S HANDBOOK
OBERT'S FIAT GUIDE
PERFORMANCE TUNING THE SUNBEAM TIGER
SOUPING THE VOLKSWAGEN
SOLEX CARBURETORS (EMPHASIS ON UK & EU AUTOMOBILES)
SU CARBURETORS (EMPHASIS ON UK AUTOMOBILES)
WEBER CARBURETORS (EMPHASIS ON ALFA & FIAT)

VELOCEPRESS BOOKS & GUIDES - AUTOMOBILE

ABARTH BUYERS GUIDE
COMPLETE CATALOG OF JAPANESE MOTOR VEHICLES
FERRARI 308 SERIES BUYER'S AND OWNER'S GUIDE
FERRARI BERLINETTA LUSSO
FERRARI BROCHURES AND SALES LITERATURE 1946-1967
FERRARI BROCHURES AND SALES LITERATURE 1968-1989
FERRARI OPP, MAINTENANCE & SERVICE H/BOOKS 1948-1963
FERRARI SERIAL NUMBERS PART I - ODD NUMBERS TO 21399
FERRARI SERIAL NUMBERS PART II - EVEN NUMBERS TO 1050
FERRARI SPYDER CALIFORNIA
HENRY'S FABULOUS MODEL "A" FORD
MASERATI BROCHURES AND SALES LITERATURE

VELOCEPRESS BOOKS – RACING

CARRERA PANAMERICANA - MEXICAN ROAD RACE (BOOK OF)
DIALED IN - THE JAN OPPERMAN STORY
IF HEMINGWAY HAD WRITTEN A RACING NOVEL
LE MANS 24 (THE BOOK THAT THE FILM WAS BASED ON)
VEDA ORR'S NEW REVISED HOT ROD PICTORIAL

AUTOBOOKS WORKSHOP MANUALS & BROOKLANDS ROAD TEST PORTFOLIOS

FOR A COMPLETE LISTING OF THE AUTOBOOKS & BROOKLANDS TITLES THAT WE CURRENTLY HAVE AVAILABLE, PLEASE VISIT OUR WEBSITE.

www.ingramcontent.com/pod-product-compliance
Lightning Source LLC
Chambersburg PA
CBHW060250240426
43673CB00047B/1902